The best of
Weaver's

28 innovative designers

36 uniquely beautiful
projects

15 in-depth articles on
new twill theory

from

11 years of

Weaver's magazine

TWILL
THRILLS

PUBLISHER
Alexis Yiorgos Xenakis

PUBLISHING DIRECTOR
David Xenakis

EDITOR
Madelyn van der Hoogt

COPY EDITOR
Holly Brunner

GRAPHIC DESIGNER
Bob Natz

PHOTOGRAPHER
Alexis Yiorgos Xenakis

PRODUCTION DIRECTOR
Denny Pearson

BOOK PRODUCTION MANAGER
Carol Skallerud

PRODUCTION ARTISTS
Ev Baker
Nancy Holzer
Jay Reeve

MIS
Jason Bittner

SECOND PRINTING, 2006; FIRST PUBLISHED IN USA IN 2004 BY XRX, INC.
PO BOX 1525, SIOUX FALLS, SD 57101-1525

ISBN 1-893762-19X

Produced in Sioux Falls, South Dakota, by XRX, Inc., 605.338.2450

Printed in USA

 BOOKS

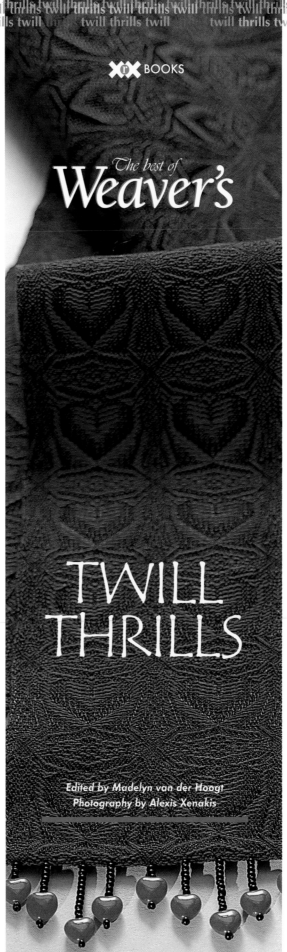

XRX BOOKS

The best of
Weaver's

TWILL
THRILLS

Edited by Madelyn van der Hoogt
Photography by Alexis Xenakis

twill thrills twill thrills twill thrills twill thrills twill thrills twill thrills twill thrills twill thrills twill thrills twill thrills twill thrills twill thrills twill thrills twill thrills twill
thrills twill thrills twill thrills twill thrills twill thrills twill thrills twill thrills twill thrills twill thrills twill thrills twill thrills twill thrills twill thrills twill thrills twill th
ills twill thrills twill thrills twill thrills twill thrills twill thrills twill thrills twill thrills twill thrills twill thrills twill thrills twill thrills twill thrills twill thrills twill thrill

Designers & Authors &

thrills twill thrills twill thrills twill thrills twill thrills twill thrills twill thrills twill thrills twill thrills twill thrills twill thrills twill
thrills twill thrills twill thrills twill thrills twill thrills twill thrills twill thrills twill thrills twill thrills twill thrills twill thrills twill
thrill twill thrill twill thrills twill thrills twill thrills twill thrills twill thrills twill thrills twill thrills twill thrills twill thrills twill th

Contents

introduction

Weaver's Editor Madelyn van der Hoogt has prepared for this volume more than thirty-five articles from *Weaver's* magazine and *Prairie Wool Companion* that focus on twill. Although each article has stand-alone value, in the order presented here they become a comprehensive text of twill theory available nowhere else. You'll find the concepts easy to understand and the ideas irresistible—they'll take you to your loom again and again as you use this book to design and weave the next generation of new twills.

Madelyn succeeded David Xenakis as Editor of *Prairie Wool Companion* in 1986, and was Editor of *Weaver's* from 1988 to 1999.

An age-old handweaver's maxim goes, "There is nothing new under the sun; whatever weave structure you think you've just invented has been woven before, sometime, somewhere." You'd think this maxim would apply especially to twill—next to plain weave the oldest and most common weave structure of all. But over the last fifteen years, something *very, very* new has been happening with twill.

Before 1988, for example, the terms "networked twill" and "advancing twill" did not even exist. Weaving literature included drafts of advancing twills (sometimes called progressive, intermittent, or skip twills), but there was no written theory about how they worked that would enable their principles to be explored and extended in new ways. If you wanted to weave one of these twills, you just went to a book or magazine, found a draft, and wove it more or less "as is."

In fact, that's what most of us used to do to weave most fabrics —start with a draft. Experimentation came only with our selection of specific fibers, colors, and setts. *Weaver's* magazine (and *Prairie Wool Companion* before it) changed all that.

In the late 1980s, Alice Schlein began her ground-breaking series of articles in *Weaver's* on network drafting, and Bonnie Inouye and Ingrid Boesel their exploration of advancing twills. As these articles appeared, readers recognized immediately the potential of the two drafting concepts and used them as springboards for further theory and new applications. Their articles (and the use of the computer to quickly generate weaving drafts) led to even more ideas, more applications, and more glorious fabrics—all included here.

In this fourth volume of the *Best of Weaver's* series, you'll find everything you need to know to weave and design twills: old twills and new twills, simple twills and fancy twills, twills on four shafts and twills on more. If you'd rather weave than read, however, you can use the easy-to-follow directions to make the glorious fabrics shown here and leave the theory to us.

Madelyn

thrills twill thrills twill thrills twill thrills twill thrills twill thrills twill thrills twill thrills twill thrills twill thrills twill thrills twill
thrills twill thrills twill thrills twill thrills twill thrills twill thrills twill thrills twill thrills twill thrills twill thrills twill thrills twill
thrill twill thrill twill thrills twill thrills twill thrills twill thrills twill thrills twill thrills twill thrills twill thrills twill thrills twill th

plain and fancy twills

twill basics

Madelyn van der Hoogt Madelyn van der Hoogt Madelyn van der Hoogt **Madelyn van der Hoogt** *Mad*

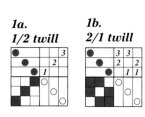

1a.
1/2 twill

1b.
2/1 twill

2a.
2/2 twill

2b.
1/3 twill

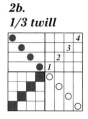

2c.
3/1 twill

3a. Drawdowm

3b. Drawup

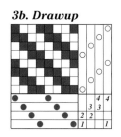

4a. 3/2/1/2 twill (ratio moves up one shaft on each treadle)

4b. 3/2/1/2 twill (ratio moves down one shaft on each treadle)

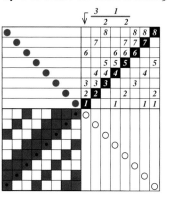

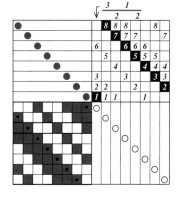

5a. 4-shaft M and W twill

5b. 8-shaft M and W twill

Of all the weave structures, twill is the most versatile. It can produce more designs, blend colors and fibers in more ways, and produce more types of fabrics—from gossamer scarves to sturdy rugs—than any other interlacement!

TWILL CHARACTERISTICS

Twill is characterized by warp and weft floats: warp and weft threads pass over and/or under more than one thread in the interlacement. For this to happen, a minimum of three weft threads and three warp threads are required (see *1a–1b*). In *1a*, one warp thread is up and two down for each pick, creating 2-thread weft floats (2-thread warp floats occur on the back of the cloth). In *1b*, two warp threads are up and one down for each pick, creating 2-thread warp floats (2-thread weft floats occur on the back of the cloth).

Note that the ratio of warp threads up to warp threads down (1:2 in *1a* and 2:1 in *1b*) moves to the left by one warp thread in each succeeding pick, creating a diagonal line—the second characteristic of twill. If this order were to move to the right instead of to the left, the diagonal would develop in the opposite direction. When four warp and four weft threads are used, there are three possible ratios of warp threads up to warp threads down; see *2a–2c*.

TWILL DIRECTIONS

Sometimes it is desirable to produce a twill fabric with one diagonal direction rather than the other. Z-twist yarns, for example, tend to show the twill lines more distinctly if woven in a left twill, S-twist yarns in a right twill. (We usually identify a left twill as one that moves upward toward the left as you are weaving and a right twill as one that moves upward toward the right.)

This brings up an interesting drafting dilemma. Most weavers are accustomed to creating drafts with draw*downs*; that is, we draw each weft beginning at the top and working downward. On the loom, however, the first pick is placed at the bottom of the weaving and the subsequent weft threads are inserted moving upward. Compare *3a* and *3b*. The actual cloth looks like the draw*up* in *3b*.

Most of us don't worry about this difference and continue to make drawdowns rather than drawups, since it feels more comfortable beginning at the top of a page and working downward. If we want the direction of the twill to change during weaving from left to right or right to left, we simply reverse the direction in which the treadles are used.

TWILL RATIOS ON EIGHT SHAFTS

On eight shafts there are many possible ratios of warp threads up to warp threads down. In *4a*, an 8-shaft twill is woven with a ratio of 3 (up), 2 (down), 1 (up), 2 (down). You can find the ratio of a twill by reading any treadle in the tie-up. On treadle 1 in *4a*, for example, shafts 1-2-3 are up (3 up), 4-5 down (2 down), 6 up (1 up) and 7-8 down (2 down). Each successive treadle shows the same ratio, beginning one shaft above the shaft that begins the ratio on the previous treadle. This shift from treadle to treadle can also go down one shaft; see *4b*.

The ratio used in *4a* and *4b* can be written as 3:2:1:2 or 3/2/1/2 or a line can be drawn representing a weft thread with the numbers of warp threads up written above it and numbers down written below it (as shown in *4a* and *4b*).

The advantage to weaving twills on more than four shafts (besides gaining even more possible variations in threading and treadling orders) is that 1-, 2-, and 3-thread (or longer) floats can occur within the same interlacement. This allows greater contrast between warp and weft colors and shading between them; compare ***5a*** and ***5b***. Using different tie-up ratios will produce different effects.

TWILL TYPES

Most twills fall into one of four categories: straight, point, extended point, or broken. In straight twills, the shafts are threaded in succession from first to last and the treadles are used in succession from first to last. In a point twill, the shafts are threaded in succession, but the threading reverses on the last and first shafts. If the treadling also reverses on the last and first treadles, diamond motifs are created as in ***6a***. In extended point-twill threadings, the direction changes after more than one threading sequence of all the shafts and/or more than one treadling sequence of all the treadles. Extended point-twill threading and treadling orders produce concentric diamonds; see ***6b***. The more sequences that are threaded before the twill reverses, the larger the diamond becomes.

In broken twills, a shaft or shafts are skipped at reversal points; see ***6c***.

FANCY TWILLS

Twills are considered 'regular' when the tie-up can be expressed by a twill ratio. Notice, however, that the tie-ups in ***6d*** and ***6e*** cannot be expressed as twill ratios; successive treadles lift different combinations of shafts. These drafts are often called 'fancy' or 'irregular' twills. Note that the drawdown in ***6d*** looks like a twill, but the drawdown in ***6e*** looks more like a block design. In fact, you can think of twill as a block weave in which each thread (i.e., each shaft) represents one block. (When you are designing fancy twills you must always consider practical float length.)

ADVANCING AND NETWORKED TWILLS

Advancing twills have been a part of our weaving repertoire for more than a century, but the recent use of the computer has led to an explosion of new designs since it allows long threading and treadling repeats to be evaluated without time-consuming loom setup. Advancing twill threadings are characterized by "runs" of three, four, or more threads (see Ingrid Boesel, pp. 38–41). Each run begins one or more shafts higher (or lower) than the starting shaft of the previous run. In ***7a*** pairs of 3-thread runs (1-2-3, 1-2-3; 2-3-4, 2-3-4, etc.) each begin one shaft higher than the previous pair. ***7b*** shows the drawdown for an 8-shaft advancing twill with a 4-thread run. Advancing twills tend to expand the scale of characteristic twill designs (diagonals, zigzags, x's, plaits, diamonds, etc.).

Networked twills (see Alice Schlein, pp. 62–82) are derived using twill threading and treadling networks to produce large-scale shaded and curvy images.

TWILL BLOCKS

In the drafts in ***1–7***, designs are created by individual warp and weft threads. Twill can also be used for block weaves in which designs are formed by *groups* of warp and weft threads. In ***8***, groups (units) of four warp and weft threads produce either 3/1 twill (pattern) or 1/3 twill (background) for a 3-block design on 12 shafts. Two-block profile drafts can be used with 4-thread twill units on eight shafts; 16 shafts can produce 4-block designs with 4-thread twill units (see pp. 92–98).

Not only are there unlimited possible variations in threading, tie-up ratios, and treadling orders with twill, but varying fiber type, color, and texture adds even further design dimension. ✂

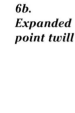

6a. Point twill

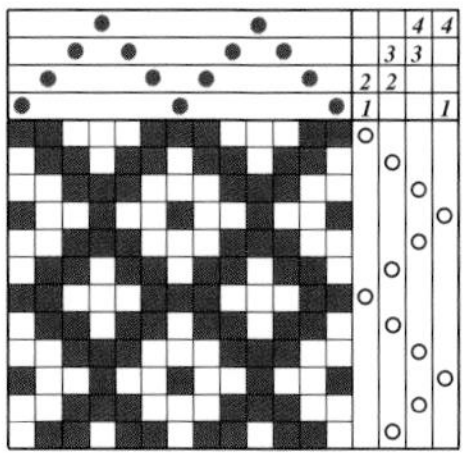

6b. Expanded point twill

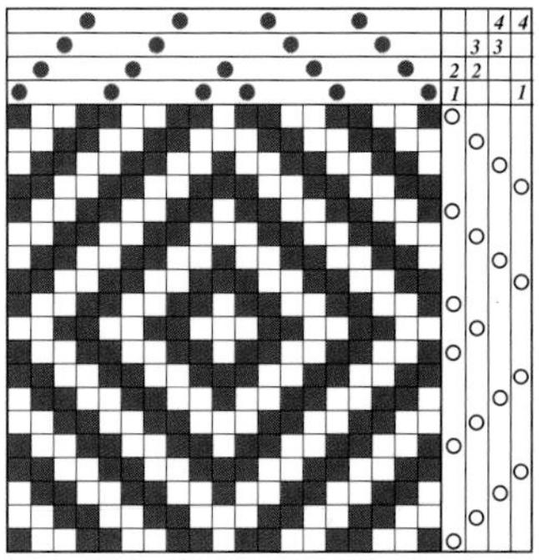

6c. Broken twill

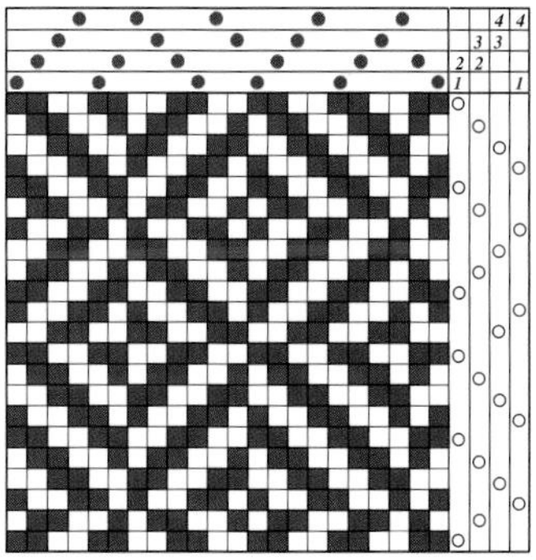

6d. 4-shaft fancy twill

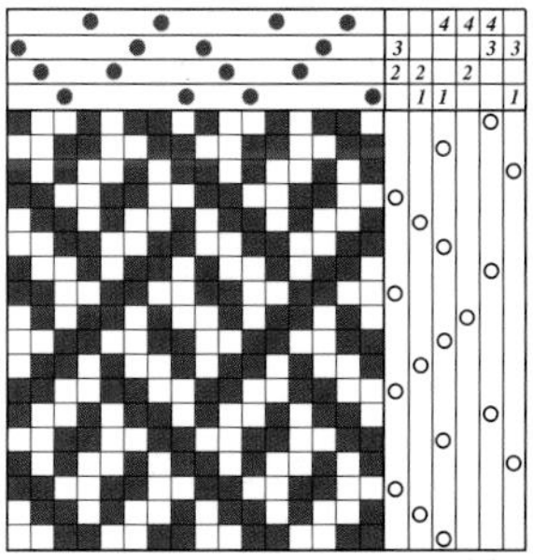

6e. 8-shaft fancy twill

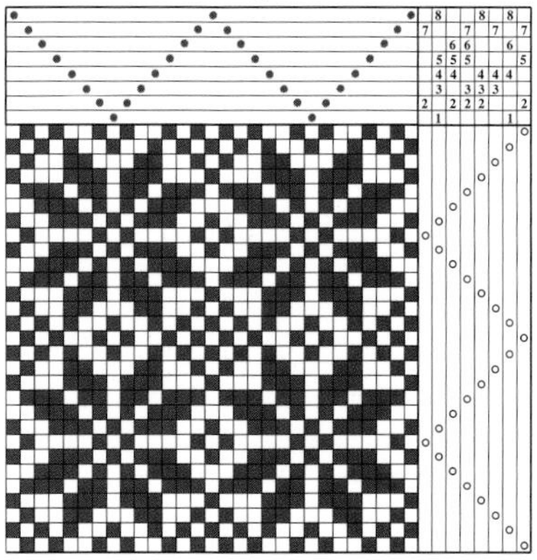

7a. 4-shaft advancing twill

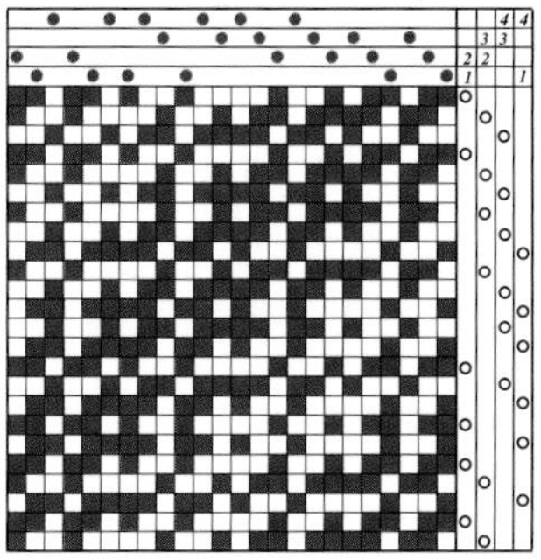

7b. 8-shaft advancing twill

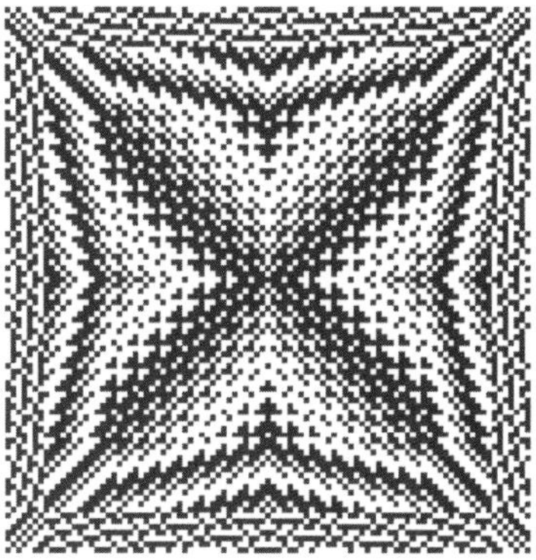

8. 12-shaft, 3-block twill

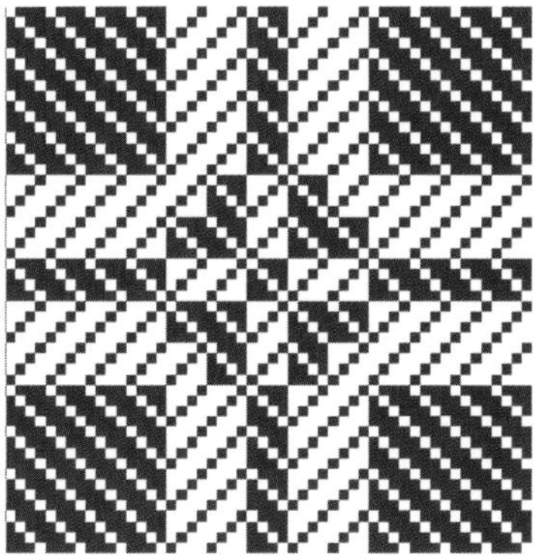

blue tick hound

Mattress ticking has historically had a lowly reputation, most often hidden under more colorful or more ornamental pillowcases and sheets. Now and then contemporary designers 'discover' it and lavish it on custom-made sofas, touting its sturdy character and homely origins that go so well with a fake moosehead over the fireplace. Its use here as the fabric for Diane's blue tick hound seems somehow 'weaverly correct.' Add this very laid-back dog in twill ticking stripes to your household. Its embroidered facial features and softly stuffed body make it a huggable, washable toy for a small child*—or a decorative addition to any area of the house.

BLUE TICK HOUND

❑ Equipment. 4-shaft loom, 16" weaving width; 12-dent reed; 1 boat shuttle; straight edge; pins; needle.

❑ Materials. Warp: 8/2 unmercerized cotton (3360 yds/lb), natural 5 oz, blue 2 oz. Weft: 10/2 pearl cotton (4200 yds/lb), natural 3 oz; commercial fabric or large sheets of paper for pattern drafting; ivory sewing thread; blue embroidery thread; red balloon (if not intended for an infant); polyester fiberfill pillow stuffing, ½ bag; commercial twill cotton fabric for underbody and ear lining, ivory, ½ yd.

❑ Wind a warp of 366 total ends (90 ends blue and 276 ends natural) in the following order: 12 natural, [24 natural, 2 blue, 2 natural, 6 blue, 2 natural, 2 blue]x9, 12 natural.

❑ Sley 2/dent in a 12-dent reed, 24 epi; center for 15¼" weaving width.

❑ Thread in straight order (1-2-3-4) on four shafts. Weave as 2/2 twill (raise 1-2, 2-3, 3-4, 4-1, etc.).

❑ Finish by removing the fabric from the loom. Machine wash and dry both handwoven and commercial twill fabrics.

❑ Cut and assemble the hound by first enlarging the pattern pieces (shown here at 21%; enlarge using a photocopier at 476%) according to indicated measurements. Cut 2 ears, 2 sides, and 1 tail from the handwoven fabric. Cut 2 ears and 1 underbody from the commercial twill fabric. Plan the layout so that the stripes converge at the nose. Carefully pin and sew sides from nose to tail. Leaving a 4"

opening on one side between legs, pin and sew underbody to sides. Clip seam allowances and turn. Lightly stuff the body, leaving unstuffed the 'hip' joints so that the legs can move and spread out when the hound sleeps on his belly.

The mouth area is formed by pushing in the point and placing the balloon so it lolls out one side. Handsew to close the opening. Sew one handwoven ear piece to one commercial fabric

piece, leaving open the narrow edge where it will be attached to the head. Turn right side out. Leave unstuffed. Tuck the raw edges inside and handsew on the head. Fold the tail piece lengthwise and sew, leaving the straight end open for turning. Stitch carefully in the middle of the folded tail, and the seam allowance becomes the stuffing when you turn it. Embroider the features to suit your hound's special personality! ✄

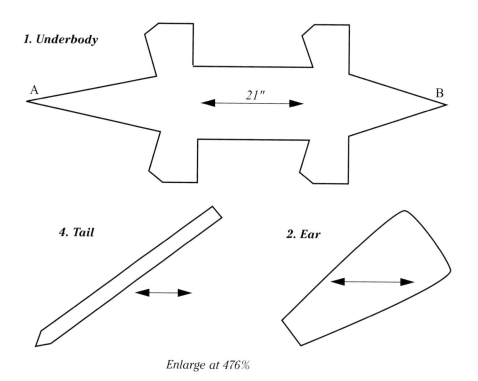

1. Underbody

A   21"   B

4. Tail

2. Ear

Enlarge at 476%

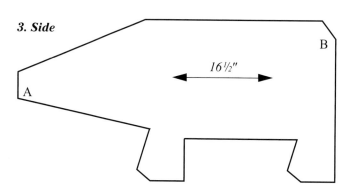

3. Side

B

16½"

A

*Omit the balloon tongue for children so young that the balloon might present a danger. Blue Tick Hound © 1992 Diane Ferguson. For personal use only, not for commercial reproduction without permission of the artist.

thrills twill thrills twill thrills twill thrills twill thrills twill thrills twill thrills twill thrills twill thrills twill thrills twill thrills twill thrills twill thrills twill thrills twill thrills twill thrills twill thrills twill thrills twill thrill twill thrill twill thrills twill thrills twill thrills twill thrills twill thrills twill thrills twill thrills twill thrills

Diane Ferguson Diane Ferguson Diane Ferguson Diane Ferguson Diane Ferguson Diane Ferguson Diane

Use a soft unmercerized cotton and this simple twill to weave a fabric designed from old-fashioned mattress ticking. The fabric is slightly warp-dominant, causing the 2/2 twill blue warp stripes to stand out on the natural background. Lay out the pattern pieces, and then cut, sew, and stuff to turn this traditional fabric into Diane's Blue Tick Hound. Embroider facial features and add a colorful comic touch with a red balloon for a tongue.

feathered friends

Berent with Rebecca Winter Mary Berent with Rebecca Winter **Mary Berent with Rebecca Winter** M

Fancy point-twill patterns with their chevron-like designs can suggest the patterns in bird feathers. This connection led to a series of fabrics for a flock of stuffed chickens. Color differences between warp and weft emphasize the feather-like designs. Finer yarns would make the small pattern pieces slightly easier to work with, but it would also reduce the scale of the feather designs. This project doubles as a great twill sampler. Before you know it you'll have an egg-straordinary flock!

FIRST FOUR CHICKENS
by Mary Berent

❑ Equipment. 8-shaft loom, 10" weaving width; 12-dent reed; 1 shuttle.

❑ Materials. Warp: 8/2 unmercerized cotton (3360 yds/lb), Tan, 750 yds. Weft: 8/2 unmercerized cotton: Chicken 1, Red, 180 yds; Chicken 2, Black, 180 yds; Chicken 3, Turquoise, 180 yds; and Chicken 4, Wine, 180 yds; rooster pattern in *Miniature Barnyard Fowl Collection* (Raspberry Hill Patchwork) or use a photocopier to enlarge the drawings in *3* by 200%.

❑ Wind a warp of 240 ends 2¾ yds long. Add 2 ends for floating selvedges if desired (smooth edges aren't essential since the pieces will be cut from the fabric and the selvedges discarded).

❑ Sley 2/dent in a 12-dent reed, 24 epi; center for 10" weaving width.

❑ Thread following the draft in *1*.

❑ Weave 20" for each chicken following the treadling sequence in *1*.

❑ Finish by securing ends of fabric with machine straight stitching to prevent raveling. Machine wash in cold water, gentle cycle; hang or dry flat; steam press before cutting. Use *Fray Check* on all cut edges. Follow pattern directions.

SECOND FOUR CHICKENS
by Rebecca Winter

❑ Equipment. 8-shaft loom, 10" weaving width; 12-dent reed; 1 shuttle.

❑ Materials. Warp: 8/2 unmercerized cotton (3360 yds/lb), 750 yds natural. Weft: Chicken 5, 8/2 unmercerized cotton, Pink, 180 yds; Chicken 6, 16/2 unmercerized cotton (6720 yds/lb), Dark Red, 550 yds; Chickens 7 and 8, 16/2 unmercer-

1. Draft for Chickens 1–4

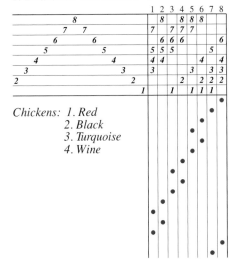

Chickens: 1. Red
2. Black
3. Turquoise
4. Wine

ized cotton, Khaki, 550 yds ea; rooster pattern from *Miniature Barnyard Fowl Collection* (or enlarge the drawings in *3* by 200%).

❑ Wind a warp and prepare the loom as for Chickens 1–4; thread following the draft in *2*.

❑ Weave 20" for each chicken following the designated treadling sequence in *2*. When you are using 16/2 cotton as weft, triple the yarn on the bobbin.

❑ Finish as for Chickens 1–4.

Note: The *Miniature Barnyard Fowl Collection* of patterns is not available as of this writing. For fabulous patterns for animals and directions for cutting

2. Draft for Chickens 5–8

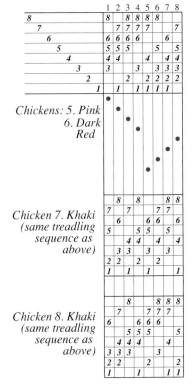

Chickens: 5. Pink
6. Dark Red

Chicken 7. Khaki
(same treadling sequence as above)

Chicken 8. Khaki
(same treadling sequence as above)

and sewing animal skins made of small handwoven fabric pieces, see Amy Preckshot, *Weaving a Zoo*, available from Carol Leigh's Hillcreek Fiber Studio, 573-874-2233. ✂

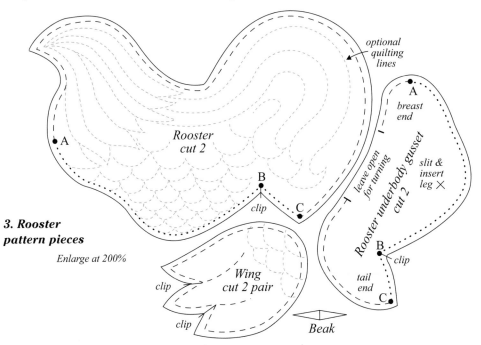

optional quilting lines

A

breast end

Rooster
cut 2

*Rooster underbody gusset
cut 2*

slit & insert leg ✕

leave open for turning

B

C

clip

B

clip

tail end

C

3. Rooster pattern pieces

Enlarge at 200%

clip

Wing
cut 2 pair

clip

clip

Beak

ll thrills twill thrill twill thrill twill thrills twill thrills twill thrills twill thrills twill thrills twill thrills twill thrills twill thrills twill thrills twill th

with Rebecca Winter Mary Berent with Rebecca Winter Mary Berent with Rebecca Winter Mary Be

"There are as many reasons to weave as there are weavers. If you spend the time and money to weave fabric by hand, it should be perfect for its intended use. To me, fancy twills seem to say 'feathers.' It's only a small step from thinking 'feathers' to dreaming up a flock of handwoven chickens!"

11

redeeming the dinos

Dinosaurs are the dragons of secular humanism. They are symbols of mystery— something big and powerful that is no longer around. It's this very mystery and power that has made them so appealing, not only to children, but also to many adults! My interest in making soft-sculpture dinosaurs grew out of a confluence of events. I had finished weaving a room-sized denim rag rug and was pondering the disposition of the leftover 75 pairs of old jeans. Independently, I had begun playing with soft sculpture for using up small scraps of handwoven fabric. (As we all know, even the tiniest bits are very precious!)

Then, my husband began dickering with his publisher about the cover art for his book on dinosaurs, *Extinction: Bad Genes or Bad Luck?*. It all came together. How could anyone with a closetful of grungy denim and a penchant for puns resist playing with his title? A line of stuffed animals with denim skins was born.

Sadly, the publisher wasn't interested, even though the first dinosaur was accompanied by a pair of denim dice. It turned out that a lot of other people were interested, however, and amused and entertained as well. "Dinosaurs are box office," as a friend put it—and this was before *Jurassic Park*! Sure enough, they sold immediately.

Encouraged, I began recycling other fabric scraps to make more skins. Delilah (they all have names) was a svelte brontosaurus, constructed of black velvet and gold lamé. Triceratops Darth had a bright green cotton jungle-print body with a brooding black face mask.

Dorothy, a rather sweet brontosaurus of handwoven fabric in peach cotton, pointed me in a new direction. Up to then I'd considered most of my handwovens inappropriate for dinosaur skins—too fuzzy, too loosely woven, wrong pattern, etc. But why not weave fabric designed especially for dinosaurs?

Creating patterns to emulate scaly, armored dinosaur hide was fun and challenging (with the help of a good computer weaving program and my AVL Compu-Dobby). After considerable experimentation, I found that plaited twills are ideal for imitating dinosaur scales, and my fun with jeans led to using zippers for teeth!

1. Draft for Dunc's and Blu's fabric

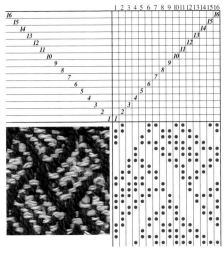

2. Draft for Merk's fabric

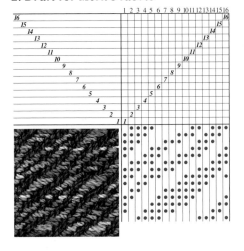

THE DINOSAURS

The fabrics for Dunc, Blu, and Merk are the results of varying the weft colors and treadling orders on a blue unmercerized cotton warp threaded in a 16-shaft straight draw.

Dunc and Blu (the brontosaurus and the tyrannosaurus, respectively) are woven using the same plaited twill treadling (see the draft in *1*), but different wefts disguise their similarity. Blu's belly markings are created with a light brushing of chlorine bleach; the insides of his legs are handpainted cotton broadcloth. A natural 2-ply rayon/silk is used as weft for Blu's body, part of his tail, and the insides of his legs; a variegated blue 20/2 rayon for his face, tail stripe, and the outsides of his legs.

Merk's fabric is an irregular undulating twill (see the draft in *2*) with a variegated 16/2 rayon weft. Denim fabric is used for the insides of his legs.

❑ Equipment. 16-shaft loom, 30" weaving width; 10-dent reed; 1 shuttle; serger (optional). (You can simulate these fabrics with plaited twills or undulating twills on four or eight shafts.) The fabric in *1* requires 21 treadles if it is converted to be woven on a treadle loom; reduce the treadling sequence to fewer treadles if no dobby is available.

❑ Materials. Warp for all three dinos: 16/2 unmercerized cotton (6720 yds/lb, Webs), denim blue, ½ lb. Weft: for Dunc a thick and thin cotton/linen knitting yarn with bits of metallic (Lustrino, 1750 yds/lb, Webs), blue-green, 4 oz; for Blu 2-ply rayon/silk (6000 yds/lb, Webs), natural, 3 oz, and 20/2 rayon variegated from light blue to navy (8400 yds/lb, Webs), 2 oz; for Merk 16/2 rayon (6720 yds/lb) variegated

from blue to lavender to pink, 4 oz; small bits of contrasting fabric for the insides of Merk's and Dunc's legs; Pellon fusible interfacing (3 yds), polyester fiberfill (3 lb), sewing thread, jeans zipper (trimmed to fit) for Blu's mouth.

❑ Wind a warp of 800 ends (add 2 ends if floating selvedges are desired—selvedges will be discarded after cutting pattern pieces) 4 yds long (wind 5 yds if sampling is desired). Each dino requires approximately 1 yd of 26" fabric.

❑ Sley 3/dent in a 10-dent reed, 30 epi; center for 26⅔" weaving width.

❑ Thread following the draft in *1*. Weave 1 yd fabric for Dunc using the Lustrino weft. For Blu, weave ¾ yd with natural weft and ¼ yd with blue weft (lay out pattern pieces to determine the exact fabric amounts for the different-colored pieces). Change the tie-up or the dobby peg plan as in *2* and weave 1 yd for Merk's fabric.

❑ Remove the fabric from the loom. Secure raw edges with machine straight stitching. Machine wash, gentle cycle; hang to dry. Press well.

❑ Lay out and cut out the pattern pieces (shown at 43%, pp. 14–15; use a photocopier to enlarge pieces 233%) from fusible interfacing. Lay the pieces of fusible interfacing on the handwoven fabric and fuse before cutting to prevent fraying and stretching. If a serger is available, serge raw edges. Serged edges are easier to piece (as in Blu's tail strips) or to turn when very small (Merk's horns and Blu's claws).

SUGGESTED READING

Raup, David M. *Extinction: Bad Genes or Bad Luck?* New York: W. W. Norton, 1991. ✄

thrills twill thrills twill thrills twill thrills twill thrills twill thrills twill thrills twill thrills twill thrills twill thrills twill thrills twill t
twill thrills twill thrills twill thrills twill thrills twill thrills twill thrills twill thrills twill thrills twill thrills twi
ll thrill twill thrill twill thrills twill thrills twill thrills twill thrills twill thrills twill thrills twill thrills twill th

to Judie Yamamoto Judie Yamamoto Judie Yamamoto Judie Yamamoto Judie Yamamoto Judie Yamamoto Judie Yamal

'Bad' jeans bring Judie Yamamoto good luck by inspiring her line of soft-sculpture dinosaurs. She goes beyond jeans to design handwoven scaly skins using twill and cotton yarns to create a fanciful world of prehistoric creatures. They can enchant a child (or adult!) or decorate any room.

will thrills twill thrills twill thrills twill thrills twill thrills twill thrills twill **thrills** twill thrills twill thrills twill thrills twill **thrills** twill thrills twill **thrill** thrills twill thrills twill thrills twill thrills twill thrills twill **thrills** twill thrills twill **thrill** thrills twill thrills twill **thrill** thrills twill thrills twill **thrills** twill thrills twill thrills twill **thrills** twill thrills twill thrills twill thrills twill thrillss twill thrills twill **thrills** twill thrills **twill thrills** twill thrills **twill** thrills twill thril

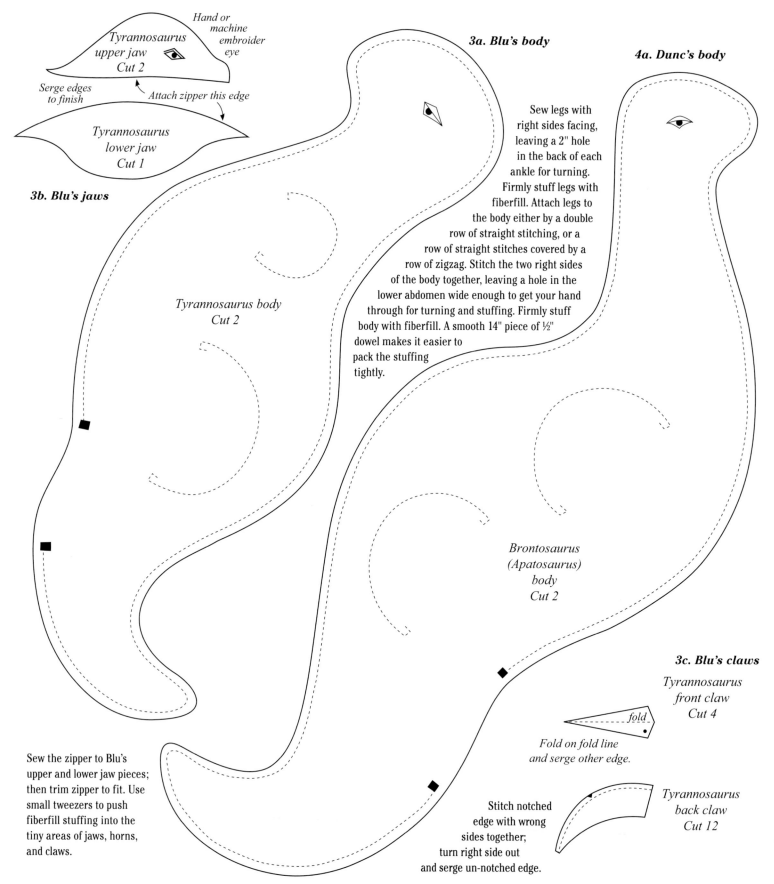

Tyrannosaurus upper jaw Cut 2

Hand or machine embroider eye

Serge edges to finish

← *Attach zipper this edge*

Tyrannosaurus lower jaw Cut 1

3b. Blu's jaws

3a. Blu's body

4a. Dunc's body

Tyrannosaurus body Cut 2

Sew legs with right sides facing, leaving a 2" hole in the back of each ankle for turning. Firmly stuff legs with fiberfill. Attach legs to the body either by a double row of straight stitching, or a row of straight stitches covered by a row of zigzag. Stitch the two right sides of the body together, leaving a hole in the lower abdomen wide enough to get your hand through for turning and stuffing. Firmly stuff body with fiberfill. A smooth 14" piece of ½" dowel makes it easier to pack the stuffing tightly.

Brontosaurus (Apatosaurus) body Cut 2

3c. Blu's claws

Tyrannosaurus front claw Cut 4

fold

Fold on fold line and serge other edge.

Tyrannosaurus back claw Cut 12

Sew the zipper to Blu's upper and lower jaw pieces; then trim zipper to fit. Use small tweezers to push fiberfill stuffing into the tiny areas of jaws, horns, and claws.

Stitch notched edge with wrong sides together; turn right side out and serge un-notched edge.

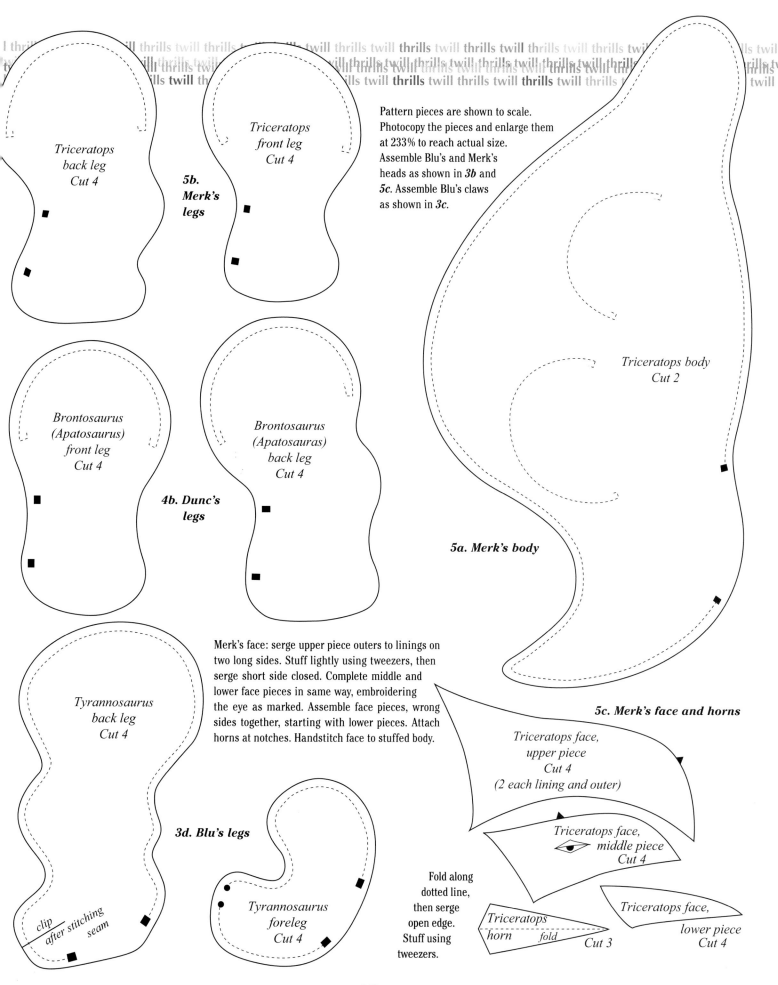

Triceratops
back leg
Cut 4

Triceratops
front leg
Cut 4

5b. Merk's legs

Pattern pieces are shown to scale.
Photocopy the pieces and enlarge them
at 233% to reach actual size.
Assemble Blu's and Merk's
heads as shown in *3b* and
5c. Assemble Blu's claws
as shown in *3c*.

Triceratops body
Cut 2

Brontosaurus
(Apatosaurus)
front leg
Cut 4

Brontosaurus
(Apatosauras)
back leg
Cut 4

4b. Dunc's legs

5a. Merk's body

Tyrannosaurus
back leg
Cut 4

Merk's face: serge upper piece outers to linings on
two long sides. Stuff lightly using tweezers, then
serge short side closed. Complete middle and
lower face pieces in same way, embroidering
the eye as marked. Assemble face pieces, wrong
sides together, starting with lower pieces. Attach
horns at notches. Handstitch face to stuffed body.

5c. Merk's face and horns

Triceratops face,
upper piece
Cut 4
(2 each lining and outer)

3d. Blu's legs

Triceratops face,
middle piece
Cut 4

clip
after stitching
seam

Tyrannosaurus
foreleg
Cut 4

Fold along
dotted line,
then serge
open edge.
Stuff using
tweezers.

Triceratops
horn   *fold*
Cut 3

Triceratops face,
lower piece
Cut 4

will thrills twill thrills twill thrills twill thrills twill thrills twill thrills twill thrills twill thrills twill thrills twill thrills twill thrills twill thrills twill thrills twill
thrills twill thrills twill thrills twill thrills twill thrills twill thrills twill thrills twill thrills twill thrills twill thrills twill thrills twill thrills twill thrills th
ills twill thrills twill thrills twill thrills twill thrills twill thrills twill thrills twill thrills twill thrills twill thrills twill thrills twill thrills twill thrills twill thrills twi

extraordinary stripes

"How many shafts does that take?" Even experienced weavers ask, dismayed, when they see these striped fabrics. They're surprised when I tell them it takes only four shafts and one shuttle! The secret is in varying the color and the structure of each warp stripe.

These complex-looking fabrics are nothing more than a combination of rosepath, straight-twill, point-twill, broken-twill, and basket-weave stripes in varying colors in the warp. A rosepath treadling gives the basket-weave stripe a beautiful asymmetrical look. Discover the design possibilities of this technique by weaving the vest, p. 17, or throw, p. 19—or create your own striped fabric design.

A MIX OF STRUCTURES

The idea comes from Michelle Fillios, a member of the Contemporary Handweavers of Houston. Inspired by the weft-way stripes in a Navajo rug, she designed a fabric alternating warp-way stripes of rosepath and basket weave. I fell in love with the idea and have been weaving variations of it ever since.

Besides Michelle's rosepath and basket weave, I use stripes of straight, broken, and 3-thread twill (see *1a–f*), in ten or more colors, with no discernible repeat. My favorite yarns are 5/2 pearl cotton and cotton/rayon blends of similar size sett at 20 ends per inch. I usually throw in a bouclé or silk noil yarn for added texture.

Plan the warp

Start with six or more colors, picking one main color to use for the narrow basket-weave stripes that set off the other sections. Using different dye lots or yarns in the same colors but different textures adds to the richness of the finished cloth.

Next consider the pattern possibilities for the stripes. How many twills? Vary their width? Change colors within a stripe? I usually choose colors and proportions based on a photograph I like. I go for variety and balance rather than perfect repeats or mirror images. One no-fail design plan is to rotate three value families—dark, medium, light—while alternating the two structural categories: basket weave, twill variation, basket weave, twill variation, etc.

Design as you go by winding the striped warp and writing down the plan for each stripe as it's wound: i.e., 7 ends blue, point twill; 4 ends black, basket weave. Beam, then thread directly from your notes.

1. Drafts for stripes: a. basket weave threading; b–f. twill threadings; rosepath treadli

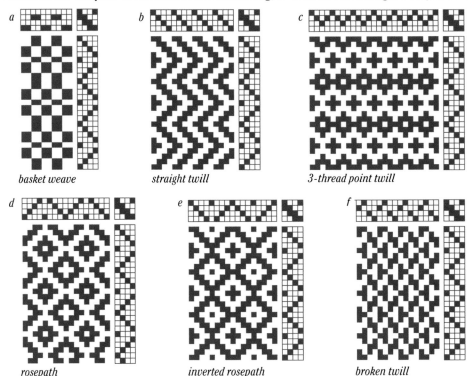

basket weave   *straight twill*   *3-thread point twill*

rosepath   *inverted rosepath*   *broken twill*

A STRIPED VEST (page 17)

❏ Equipment. 4-shaft loom, 22" weaving width; 10-dent reed; 1 boat shuttle.

❏ Materials. Warp and weft: 8/2 unmercerized cotton (3360 yds/lb, Webs), Navy (N) 9 oz; Plum (Pl) 4 oz; Teal (T), Light Blue (LB), Rose (R), and Black (B), 1 oz each; natural silk noil fleck (3290 yds/lb, The Silk Tree), (S) 1 oz; Cotton Knot (3200 yds/lb, Robin and Russ Handweavers), White (W) 1 oz; Cajun Cotton (900 yds/lb, Bernat), Pink (P) 1 oz; Spighetta cotton ribbon (776 yds/lb), Fuchsia (F) 1 oz; vest pattern (such as McCall's 7173), lining fabric, sewing notions.

Vest front

❏ Wind a warp of 278 ends of 8/2 cotton and assorted yarns 2½ yds long in the following order: 6B, 6N, 2P, 4B, 2LB, 4R, 8T, 4LB, 1Pl, 4LB, 2S, 2W, 2S, 4LB, 1Pl, 4LB, 8T, 4S, 4R, 1P, 4R, 4S, 4B, 4W, 12LB, 4S, 7R, 2P, 4LB, 4N, 1B, 4N, 4LB, 2P, 7R, 2B, 6N, 6T, 6Pl, 1F (counts as 2 basket-weave ends), 7P, 2R, 8LB, 1F (counts as 2 basket-weave ends), 12N, 4S, 4R, 1P, 4R, 4S, 10T, 4LB, 1T, 4 LB, 2S, 2W, 2S, 4LB, 1T, 4LB, 6T, 8R, 2LB, 4B, 4P, 6N, 6B. Total ends each color: 27 Black, 38 Navy, 19 Pink, 64

Light Blue, 44 Rose, 40 Teal, 8 Plum, 28 silk fleck, 8 White, 2 Fuchsia ribbon. Two yds produces one vest back and 1 yd loom waste.

❏ Beam the warp; center for 14".

❏ Thread following draft in *2a*, p. 18. Add a floating selvedge to each side.

❏ Sley 2/dent in 10-dent reed (except 1/dent for the Fuchsia ribbon), 20 epi, 14.2" wide.

❏ Weave following draft in *2a*, 50" with Plum for two vest fronts 22" long after shrinkage.

Vest back

The fabric for the vest back is woven mostly in basket weave, with only a few stripes.

❏ Wind a warp of 437 ends of 8/2 cotton and assorted yarns 2 yds long in the following order: 70N, 9R, 60N, 9B, 42N, 8T, 48N, 6LB, 60N, 1F (counts as 2 basket-weave ends), 6N, 1F (counts as 2 basket-weave ends), 48N, 9B, 60N. Total ends of each are: 394 Navy, 9 Rose, 18 Black, 8 Teal, 6 Light Blue, 2 Fuchsia ribbon. Two yds produces one vest back and 1 yd loom waste.

❏ Beam, centered for 22" weaving width.

❏ Thread following the draft in *2b*, p. 18. Add a floating selvedge to each side.

thrills twill thrills twill

Lanning Gwen Lanning Gwen Lanning Gwen Lanning Gwen Lanning Gwen Lanning Gwen Lanning Gwen Lanning Gwen Lanning G

The warp stripes in Gwen's vest produce a fabric that looks far more complicated than its combination of simple 4-shaft weaves. Even better, the weaving is easy with one shuttle and a simple rosepath treadling. Once you see how it works, you'll add your own ideas to these juxtapositions of structure and color.

twill thrills twill th
ills twill thrills twill thrills twill thrills twill thrills twill thrillss twill thrills twill thrills twill thrills twill thrills twill thrills twill thrills twill thrills twill thrills twill thrill

2a. Draft for front of vest, page 17

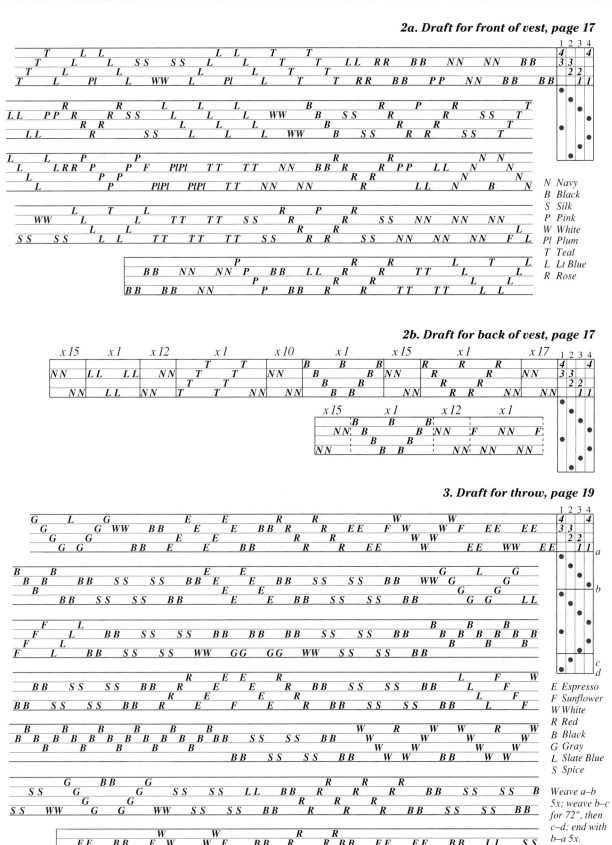

N Navy
B Black
S Silk
P Pink
W White
Pl Plum
T Teal
L Lt Blue
R Rose

2b. Draft for back of vest, page 17

3. Draft for throw, page 19

E Espresso
F Sunflower
W White
R Red
B Black
G Gray
L Slate Blue
S Spice

Weave a–b
5x; weave b–c
for 72", then
c–d; end with
b–a 5x.

thrills twill thrills twill thrills twill thrills twill thrills twill thrills twill thrills twill thrills twill thrills twill thrills twill thrills twill thrills twill thrills twill thrills twill thrills twill thrills twill thrills twill thrills twill thrill twill thrill twill thrills twill thrills twill thrills twill thrills twill thrills twill thrills twill thrills twill thrills twill thrills twill thrills twill thrills twill thrills twill th

- Sley 2/dent in a 10-dent reed (except 1/dent for Fuchsia ribbon), 20 epi; center for 22" width.
- Weave with Navy following *2b* for 1 yd.
- Finish fabric by machine washing and drying, regular permanent-press cycle. Steam press. Shrinkage is 14%.
- Cut and assemble by first laying out the pattern pieces on the handwoven cloth, taking advantage of the slightly different looks of front and back fabrics. Sew according to pattern directions.

A STRIPED THROW (photo above)

- Equipment. 4-shaft loom, 50" weaving width; 8-dent reed; 1 shuttle.
- Materials. Warp: Hampshire Brights 6/2/2 cabled mercerized cotton (1260 yds/lb, Webs) used double (or substitute 3/2 pearl cotton used double), Spice (S) 7 oz, Black (B) 10 oz, Red (R) 4 oz, Gray (G) 3 oz; Camden Cotton (cabled mercerized cotton, 700 yds/lb, Classic Elite Yarns), Sunflower (F) 39 yds, Slate Blue (L) 48 yds, Bleach (W) 141 yds; Rockland Cotton (cabled mercerized cotton, 625 yds/lb, Classic Elite Yarns) Espresso (E) 150 yds. Weft: Hampshire Brights used double, Spice (S) 1 lb, 9 oz. Amounts provide a 2-yd throw plus 1 yd loom waste; use loom waste for fringe.
- Wind a warp of 402 ends, 3 yds long in the following order: 4E, 2W, 4E, 1F, 7W, 1F, 4E, 8R, 4B, 8E, 4B, 2W, 4G, 1L, 4G, 2L, 4G, 1L, 4G, 2W, 4B, 8S, 4B, 8E, 4B, 8S, 25B, 8S, 2W, 2B, 2G, 2B, 2G, 2B, 2W, 8S, 4B, 4L, 4F, 1W, 4F, 4L, 4B, 8S, 4B, 4R, 4E, 1F, 4E, 4R, 4B, 8S, 4B, 4W, 1R, 4W, 2B, 4W, 1R, 4W, 4B, 8S, 29B, 8S, 4B, 12R, 4B, 2L, 8S, 2W, 4G, 2B, 4G, 2W, 8S, 2L, 4B, 8E, 4B, 8R, 4B, 1F, 7W, 1F, 4B, 2W, 4E. Total number of each color: 48 Espresso, 47 White, 13 Sunflower, 16 Slate Blue, 132 doubled Black, 28 doubled Gray, 80 doubled Spice, 38 doubled Red.
- Beam; center for 50" weaving width.
- Thread following the draft in *3*, p. 18. Add 1 floating selvedge to each side.
- Sley 1/dent in an 8-dent reed.
- Weave for 72" following the draft in *3* with Spice.
- Finish by making a twisted fringe; machine wash, gentle cycle for 3 minutes; rinse and spin; hang to dry. ✄

Tracy Kaestner

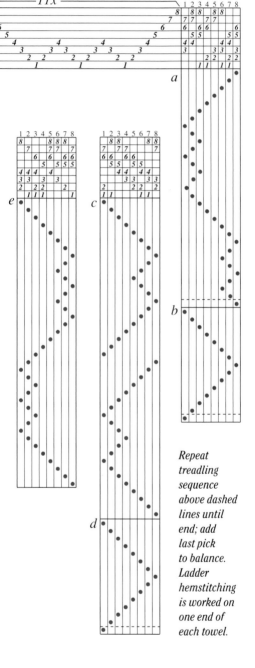

The discovery of a sample notebook in the Calgary guild library led me to seek a copy of How to Weave Linens *by Edward Worst, published in 1926. The notebook samples include many different twill patterns in very fine linen—all on the same threading, and Worst's now out-of-print book is listed as the source. The draft for these towels, page 124 in Worst, produces an amazing number of designs with different tie-ups and treadling sequences: diamonds, zigzags, lattices, rectangles, squares, etc. Here are five of my favorites. Put on a long warp and discover more!*

How to Weave Linens is a wonderful source for twill patterns as well as for information about the special warping, weaving, and finishing techniques suitable for working with linen. Handweavers are fortunate to have many fine linens available. In fact, the firmly spun, 2-ply line linens recommended for the warp and weft in these towels are almost as easy to use as pearl cotton. You'll only need to remember that linen lacks elasticity so it must be beamed under even tension. Also, make sure to leave sufficient weft in the shed for each pick. Linen's lack of elasticity does not accommodate draw-in. If you draw in too much, the reed will abrade the selvedge threads.

SIX FINGERTIP TOWELS

❑ Equipment. 8-shaft loom, 13" weaving width; 8-dent reed; 1 shuttle.

❑ Materials. Warp: 30/2 boiled line linen (4500 yds/lb, Webs), natural, one 250-gram tube. Weft: 30/2 line linen (4500 yds/lb, Talisman Fibre), bleached white, one 250-gram tube.

❑ Wind a warp of 420 ends 5 yds long (enough for six towels; includes 2 ends for floating selvedges).

❑ Sley 4/dent in an 8-dent reed, 32 epi; center for 13" weaving width.

❑ Thread following the draft.

❑ For each towel, weave 2½" plain weave; work ladder hemstitching; weave ½" plain weave, weave 17" pattern (plus the amount necessary to finish a treadling repeat); end with 2½" plain weave. Repeat treadling sequence a for first towel, b for second towel, etc. Select your favorite treadling to repeat for the sixth towel. The total length of each towel on the loom is 22½". For ladder hemstitching instructions see *Finishing Touches for the Handweaver.*

❑ Remove fabric from loom; serge between towels or sew two lines of straight stitching. Cut towels apart. Wash in warm water, delicate cycle. Line dry, press while still damp with a hot iron.

❑ For hems, fold up ¾" of plain weave and then fold again to the hemstitching on one end and to the beginning of the pattern on the other end. Sew hems by hand. Press again. Finished size is 11" x 18" each towel.

Repeat treadling sequence above dashed lines until end; add last pick to balance. Ladder hemstitching is worked on one end of each towel.

BIBLIOGRAPHY

West, Virginia M. *Finishing Touches for the Handweaver.* Revised Edition. Loveland, Colorado: Interweave Press, 1988, pp. 16–17.

Worst, Edward F. *How to Weave Linens.* Milwaukee, Wisconsin: Bruce Publishing Company, 1926. ✄

ll thrills **twill** thrills **twill** thrills twill thrills twill thrills **twill** thrills twill thrills twill thrills twill thrills twill thrills **twill** thrills twill thrills twill t
twill **thrills** twill thrills twill thrills twill thrills twill thrills twill thrills twill thrills twill thrills twill thrills twill thrills twill thrills twill thrills
ll thrill twill thrill twill **thrills twill** thrills twill thrills twill thrills twill **thrills** twill thrills twill **thrills** twill thrills twill thrills twill thrills twill th

The M and W twill threading for these towels proves very versatile. Many different designs can be woven using it. When a bleached linen is used in the weft and a natural linen in the warp, the twill weft floats are as prominent as the pattern weft in overshot—but this is a quick one-shuttle weave!

happy families: a video game for weavers

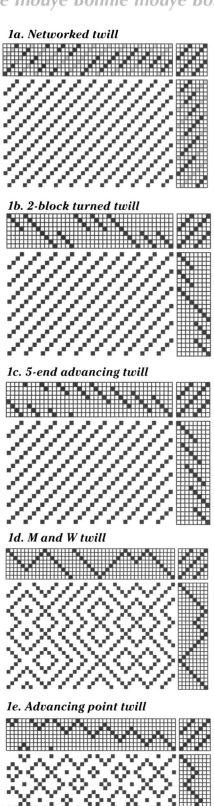

1a. Networked twill

1b. 2-block turned twill

1c. 5-end advancing twill

1d. M and W twill

1e. Advancing point twill

When I was a child, we loved to play a card game called 'Happy Families'—or 'Go Fish'! Today, kids play games on video screens instead, and I find myself playing a kind of Happy Families for weavers on my computer. Like any game, it has its own rules. Not every combination is a winner. If you don't have a computer, you can try it with graph paper, or you can play it directly on your loom!

How do I play this game? *I* get to be both the dealer *and* the player, and *I* determine the value of each of the tricks—no brothers or sisters are necessary! The parts of the drawdown are the suits of cards, and to make a 'trick' I need a threading, a tie-up, and a treadling order that can work together.

RULES OF THE GAME

Usually, I start with a threading that I have been considering. I could randomly use it with the tie-ups and treadling orders that I have saved on my computer, but I already know that many of them won't work. I need to establish 'families' of weaves, as my 'deck' of choices is very large and rapidly growing.

Four-shaft families

When I design for my 4-shaft loom, I can recognize the families by their threadings—4-shaft overshot, for example. Any 4-shaft overshot threading can be combined with any 4-shaft overshot tie-up and treadling order. The same can be said for 4-shaft twills; twill-based threadings can be combined with any twill tie-ups and any twill treadling orders. The results are usually very successful.

If I try a cross *between* these two families—overshot and twill—I must be very careful: an overshot threading draft *can* be treadled as a twill, but the resulting drawdown may show overlong floats, and the resulting fabric will not have the same drape as an overshot fabric.

With four shafts, tie-up choices are very limited, but the treadling sequences can vary considerably. The game gets much more complicated and rewarding, however, when eight or more shafts are used.

Multishaft families: twill threading rules

The most fun comes with mixing twill threading drafts, tie-ups, and treadling orders (or peg plans) on eight or more shafts. Random combinations of these components, however, can produce long floats

or an uneven fabric. To avoid overlong floats, observe an important rule of the game: keep the twills within the same family. To qualify as a member of my favorite twill family, for example, an 8-shaft threading must produce a flawless 1/3 twill when woven with a 1/3/1/3 twill tie-up and treadled as drawn in (a 12-shaft threading must produce 1/3 twill with a 1/3/1/3/1/3 twill tie-up treadled as drawn in; a 16-shaft threading with a 1/3/1/3/1/3/1/3 tie-up, etc.).

A computer can quickly verify if this rule is met. Examine the drawdowns in *1a–e*. Each 8-shaft threading produces 1/3 twill with a 1/3/1/3 tie-up when treadled as drawn in, even though each is a different member of this twill family. The threading draft in *1a* is plotted on a network composed of 4-end straight initials. The threading in *1b* produces two blocks of turned twill (A = 1-2-3-4; B = 5-6-7-8). The threading in *1c* is a 5-end advancing twill.

A further restriction is that point-twill threading drafts must contain at least four threads in the ascending or descending run, including the thread at the point (i.e., 5-6-7-8-7-6-5 or 2-3-4-5-6-7-6-5-4-3-4-5-6-7-8, etc.). The threading in *1d* is a variation of an M and W twill, and the threading in *1e* is an advancing point twill; both threadings follow this rule.

The twill treadling rules

It follows that the game rules for threading orders also apply to treadling orders: a treadling order must produce 1/3 twill when used with a threading of the same order and a 1/3/1/3, etc., tie-up. Point-twill threading drafts must contain at least four threads in the ascending or descending run including the thread at the point to prevent overlong floats—no float spans more than five threads.

The twill tie-up rule

The most important rule for playing with the members of this family is the tie-up rule: no more than three consecutive squares in any vertical or horizontal row in the tie-up can be filled in or left blank. This guarantees that no shaft remains up or down for more than three consecutive picks to produce a warp float of more than three threads (or five consecutive picks where the treadling order reverses, as in point-twill treadling orders); and no more than three adjacent threads can be up or down for a single pick to produce a weft float of more than three threads (or five threads for point-twill threading orders).

thrills twill thrills twill thrills twill thrills twill thrills twill thrills twill thrills twill thrills twill thrills twill thrills twill thrills twill thrills twill thrills twill thrills twill thrills twill thrills twill thrills twill thrills twill thrills twill

twill thrills twill thrills twill thrills twill thrills twill thrills twill thrills twill thrills twill thrills twill thrills twill thrills twill thrills twi

thrill twill thrill twill thrills twill thrills twill thrills twill thrills twill thrills twill thrills twill thrills twill thrills twill thrills twill thrills twill th

Inouye Bonnie Inouye Bonnie Inouye Bonnie Inouye Bonnie Inouye Bonnie Inouye Bonnie Inouye Bonnie Inouye

A winning 'trick' is one you like and a useful threading is one that produces lots of winners! Two of Bonnie's Happy Families winners are the project gamp on eight shafts (see inset above) and the Sunset Strip shawl, woven with the threading from a 16-shaft gamp with a descending point-twill treadling order.

ill thrills twill th lls twill thrills twill thrills twill thrills twill thrills twill thrilss twill thrills twill thrills twill thrills twill thrills twill thrills twill thrills twill thrill

2. 8-shaft computer gamp

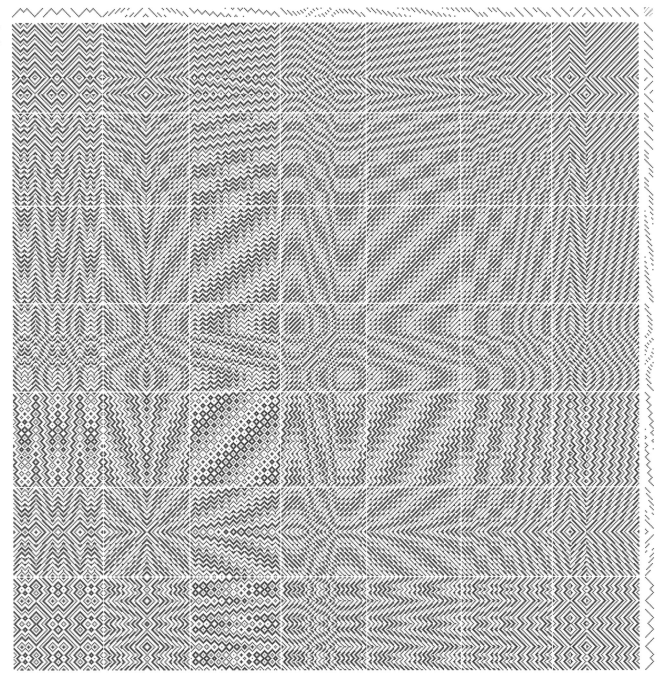

Who's in this family?

Twills that are included in this family are straight-draw twills on 8, 12, 16 or any number of shafts divisible by 4; point twills on 8, 12, 16, or any number divisible by 4; M and W twills if the shortest twill run is at least 4 threads long; 4-thread twill blocks; some advancing twills such as those with a run of 5 and an advance of 1 and related expanded advancing twills on eight or more shafts; network-drafted twills using a 4-thread straight initial; and some 'snowflake' or 'frost crystal' twills (skip twill runs that reverse in the center of the repeat; see *3f*).

To play, start with any threading draft from this family. Enter it in your weaving software program. Choose a twill tie-up that shows no more than three consecutive rising or sinking shafts (to produce no floats longer than three threads). Tie-ups that work best combine two or more 4-shaft twills (for example, 3/1/1/3 or 3/1/2/2 for an 8-shaft loom, 3/1/2/2/1/3 for 12 shafts). For clear designs with maxi-mum contrast between dark and light areas, include 3/1 and 1/3 in the tie-up. Then select 'as drawn in' and look at the result. Save this draft, using a name you will recognize later!

You can now try this threading with any tie-up and any treadling order from another draft of the same family (or any peg plan with no more than three filled-in or blank squares in any direction). A winning 'trick' is one you like, and a useful threading is one that produces lots of winners! With threading

ll thrills **twill** thrills **twill** thrills twill thrills twill thrills **twill** thrills twill **thrills** twill thrills **twill** thrills twill **thrills** twill thrills twill thrills **twill** thrills twill thrills twill th
twill **thrills** twill **thrills** twill thrills twill thrills twill thrills twill **thrills** twill thrills twill thrills twill **thrills** twill thrills twill thrills twill **thrills** twill thrills twi
ill thrill twill thrill twill **thrills** **twill** thrills twill thrills twill thrills twill **thrills** twill thrills twill **thrills** twill thrills twill thrills twill **thrills** twill thrills twill th

3. Draft for 8-shaft gamp

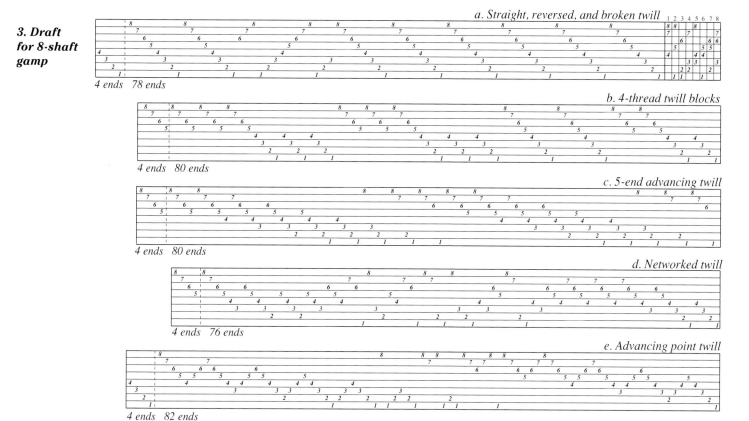

a. Straight, reversed, and broken twill

4 ends 78 ends

b. 4-thread twill blocks

4 ends 80 ends

c. 5-end advancing twill

4 ends 80 ends

d. Networked twill

4 ends 76 ends

e. Advancing point twill

4 ends 82 ends

f. Snowflake twill

4 ends 77 ends

g. M and W twill

81 ends

and treadling orders that maintain a constant direction, the longest float spans three threads; point-twill orders allow floats of five threads. All twills in this family produce fabrics that drape like a twill, wear like a twill, and require a sett as for twill.

The twill gamp game

Another way to play the game is by making a computer 'gamp,' so that several drafts can be compared side by side as in *2*. Type in at least one repeat of a threading, leave one space blank, and then enter the next threading. Use as many different sections as you like, load a tie-up, and treadle as drawn in. Next, try a variety of tie-ups.

Once you have made a pile of 'tricks,' take a good look at your choices. Some may be too large or too

small for a specific project but might be worth saving for future use. Often I like one part of a design and return to that draft for further work. Selected areas can be used and the rest changed or eliminated. Sometimes I combine favorite parts of two different treadling orders and then try them with several different tie-ups. When I come across a new draft that includes a threading, treadling, or tie-up that belongs to the same family, I give it a chance to play with other family members on my computer.

The prize? You pick the winners!

For a Happy Families first prize, combine your favorite threading and treadling systems and weave a gamp. To weave the 8-shaft gamp in *2* and *3* (see the photo inset, p. 23), wind a warp of 582 total ends

of any fiber appropriate for twill. To create separations between sections of the gamp, thread the four ends separated by dashed lines in a different color. Use the tie-up in *3*; treadle as drawn in. Then try another tie-up and add some treadling sequences of your own!

For further information on networked and advancing twills, see pp. 38–41, 62–92, 114–121, and the bibliography.

BIBLIOGRAPHY

Inouye, Bonnie. *Exploring Multishaft Design.* Hyattsville, Maryland: Weavingdance Press, 2000.

Schlein, Alice. *Network Drafting: An Introduction.* Greenville, South Carolina: Bridgwewater Press, 1994. ✂

twill thrills twill

samplemania! for a vest, jacket, and shirt

Flavian Geis Flavian Geis Flavian Geis Flavian Geis Flavian Geis Flavian Geis Flavian Geis Flavian Geis **Flavian Geis** Flavian Geis

I have been weaving for a good number of years and have heard over and over that you should do samples prior to weaving an actual project. Although I truly understand the merits of doing a sample, I hate weaving them!

A 10" sample does not always give an accurate idea of what a final piece 30" or 40" wide will look like. Why not add a few yards to the warp length for a project and do the creating and testing prior to weaving the final project?

CHOOSE A POINT-TWILL THREADING

By choosing a versatile threading such as a point twill you can easily create your own designs by simply changing the tie-up or treadling sequence for an infinite number of pattern possibilities. Weave ½" of plain weave between each 1" design to isolate the effects and create a beautiful patterned fabric instead of a useless sample. Not only can these fabrics become ends in themselves as vests, shawls, table runners, etc., but favorite designs emerge to be used for other projects. Think of a point-twill warp as a drawing board ready for design!

USE FOUR, EIGHT, OR SIXTEEN SHAFTS

The process works as well for four shafts as it does for eight or sixteen. An advantage to a 4-shaft warp, in fact, is that no tie-up changes need to be made between designs—only changes in the treadling order. For 8-shaft and 16-shaft threadings, tie-up changes produce the greatest variety of designs. Therefore a computer-aided dobby is a great advantage for designing. Table looms can provide much designing fun, however, for smaller fabrics. Whatever the number of shafts on your loom, thread a point twill and begin your experiments!

TAILORED ROSE VEST

❏ Equipment. 4 shaft loom, 32" weaving width; 10-dent reed; 1 shuttle.
❏ Materials. Warp: 18/2 pearl cotton (7560 yds/lb, Robin and Russ Handweavers), red-violet, 9¼ oz (or substitute 20/2 pearl cotton). Weft: 20/2 pearl cotton (8400 yds/lb, Cotton Clouds), Deep Lilac #90, 7 oz; commercial vest pattern; polyester charmeuse for lining, 1¾ yds x 45" wide; twill tape, 3 yds x ¼"; sewing notions.
❏ Wind a warp of 1280 ends 3⅓ yds long (yields 2⅗ yds x 30" of finished fabric and allows 20" loom waste and take-up); this is enough fabric for a size 10–12 vest; adjust amounts for a larger size.
❏ Sley 4/dent in a 10-dent reed, 40 epi; center for 32".
❏ Thread following the draft in *1*.
❏ Weave a header with rags or thick cotton to spread warp evenly. Weave 1" of each design following the treadling in *1*; separate designs with ½" of plain weave.
❏ Finish by removing the fabric from the loom; allow to soak in cold water and fabric softener in washing machine with no agitation. After 1 hour advance to final spin cycle to spin out water. Press both sides of cloth with a warm iron while still damp. Drape the fabric so that it can hang freely until completely dry. Cut pattern pieces on the bias. Serge all pieces to secure edges.

1a. 4-shaft draft

1b. 4-shaft twill designs

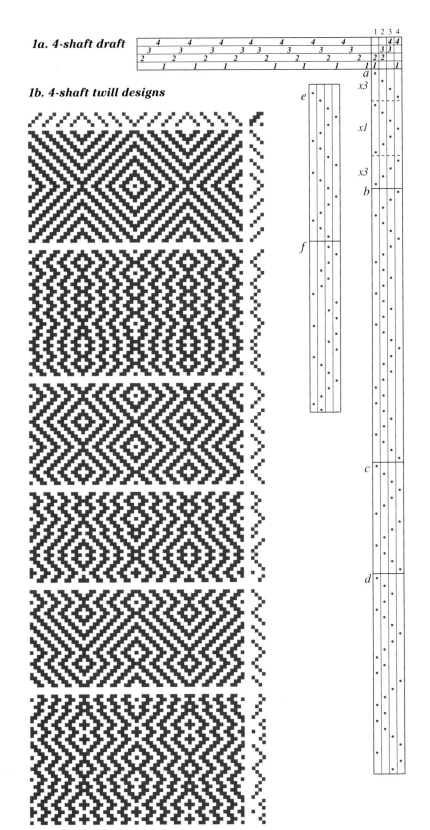

ll thrills **twill** thrills **twill** thrills twill thrills **twill** thrills twill thrills twill **thrills** twill **thrills** twill thrills twill thrills twill **thrills** twill thrills twill t
twill **thrills** twill thrills twill thrills twill thrills twill **thrills** twill thrills twill thrills twill thrills twill thrills twill thrills twill! thrills twill thrills twill
ll thrill twill thrills twill **thrills** **twill** thrills twill thrills twill thrills twill **thrills** twill thrills twill **thrills** twill thrills twill thrills twill **thrills** twill th

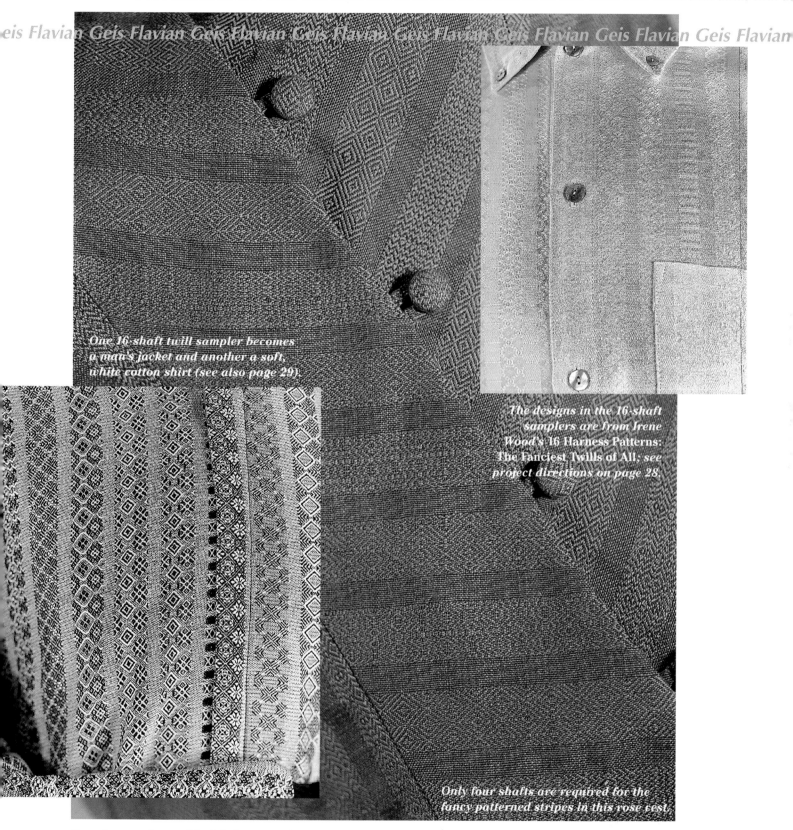

eis Flavian **Geis Flavian** Geis Flavian Geis Flavian Geis Flavian Geis Flavian Geis Flavian Geis Flavian Geis Flavian

One 16-shaft twill sampler becomes a man's jacket and another a soft, white cotton shirt (see also page 29).

The designs in the 16-shaft samplers are from Irene Wood's 16 Harness Patterns: The Fanciest Twills of All; see project directions on page 28.

Only four shafts are required for the fancy patterned stripes in this rose vest.

Samples can be usable fabrics as well as instructive design tools. Use a point-twill threading to design a variety of twill weft-way stripes by changing the tie-up and treadling sequences. The stripes will look like patterned ribbons in the cloth. Place them vertically or construct garments on the bias for added interest.

vill thrills twill thrills twill thrills twill thrills twill thrills twill thrills twill thrills twill thrills twill thrills twill thrills twill thrills twill thrills twill thrills twill thrills twill
thrills twill thrills twill thrills twill thrills twill thrills twill thrills twill thrills twill thrills twill thrills twill thrills twill thrills twill thrills twill thrills twill
ills twill thrills twill thrills twill thrills twill thrills twill thrillss twill thrills twill thrills twill thrills twill thrills twill thrills twill

2. 8-shaft draft

3. 16-shaft draft

□ Assemble and sew vest following pattern directions. For this vest, seamstress Gwen Dunham uses a commercial pattern modified by Gail Jones. Adapt a commercial vest pattern with princess seams for bias cut by reshaping the hem and cutting the front and back pieces diagonally; cut fronts and backs with 1" extra seam allowances and hang them from shoulders for a day to allow fabric to stretch. (This helps avoid puckering seams and droopy hems.)

Additionally, mark and cut according to commercial pattern instructions and stitch twill tape into center front and back seams, to keep them from stretching further. Mark fabric where princess seams split into curved hem. Stitch princess seams stopping at these marks (knot by hand instead of back-stitching here). Then stitch curved hem one piece at a time, starting exactly where the princess seam stops. Complete construction of the garment following commercial pattern instructions.

BLACK AND WHITE JACKET

□ Equipment. 4-, 8-, or 16-shaft loom, 28" weaving width; 10-dent reed; 1 shuttle.

□ Materials. Warp: 30/2 silk (7500 yds/lb, Treenway Silks) natural, 12 oz. Weft: 30/2 silk (7500 yds/lb, Treenway Silks) black, 11 oz; 4⅓ yds china silk for lining, black; standard bomber jacket pattern; zipper; 14" x 35" stretchy ribbing material for collar, bottom band, sleeves; 2 buttons; sewing notions as required by pattern. Amounts provide approx 4¼ yds finished fabric for medium-size jacket.

□ Wind a warp of 1120 ends 5 yds long.

□ Sley 4/dent in a 10-dent reed, 40 epi; center for 28" weaving width.

□ Thread following the draft in *1* (p. 26), *2*, or *3* (used for this jacket). To weave the 8-shaft and 16-shaft designs without a dobby, turn the treadling diagrams 90° and use the peg plans as tie-ups and/or choose other treadling sequences.

□ Weave header with thick cotton. Weave 1" of each design; separate designs with ½" of plain weave.

□ Finish by removing the fabric from the loom; allow to soak in cold water and fabric softener in washing machine with no agitation. After 1 hour spin out water. Press both sides of the fabric with a warm iron while still damp; drape so fabric hangs free until dry.

□ Cut fabric and lining using pattern pieces; serge to secure edges. Double the ribbing material for collar, sleeve, and bottom band ribbing. Assemble jacket according to pattern instructions.

SHIRT

□ Equipment. 4-, 8-, or 16-shaft loom, 40" weaving width; 10-dent reed; 1 shuttle.

□ Materials. Warp and weft: 60/2 silk (14,880 yds/lb, Webs), natural, 20 oz; Kwik Sew shirt pattern #2160; 8 small and 2 smaller buttons for collar; other sewing notions required by pattern.

□ Wind a warp of 2280 ends 5⅓ yds long with 1/1 threading cross.

□ Sley 6/dent in a 10-dent reed, 60 epi; center for 38"; leave lease sticks in cross.

□ Transfer lease sticks to heddle side of reed and thread following selected draft; beam.

□ Weave header with thick cotton. Weave ¾" of each design following selected draft, separated by ½" of straight twill.

□ Finish as for jacket; cut, assemble, and sew following pattern directions. ✄

thrills twill thrills twill thrills twill thrills twill thrills twill thrills twill thrills twill thrills twill thrills twill thrills twill t
thrills twill thrills twill thrills twill thrills twill thrills twill thrills twill thrills twill thrills twill thrills tw
thrill twill thrill twill thrills twill thrills twill thrills twill thrills twill thrills twill thrills twill thrills twill th

Flavian's soft, fine silk shirt and bomber jacket (sewn by Gwen Dunham) show vertical stripes in a variety of designs. The different twill treadling sequences that create the stripes are separated by rows of plain weave or straight twill. Use Flavian's designs or create your own—on four, eight, or sixteen shafts!

will thrills twill thrills twill thrills twill thrills twill thrills twill thrills twill thrills twill thrills twill thrills twill thrills twill thrills twill thrills twill thrills twill thrills twill
thrills twill thrills twill thrills twill thrills twill thrills twill thrills twill thrills twill thrills twill thrills twill thrills twill
ills twill thrills twill thrills twill thrills twill thrills twill thrills twill thrills twill thrills twill thrills twill thrills twill thrills twill

Angstadt twills: solving a weaving puzzle

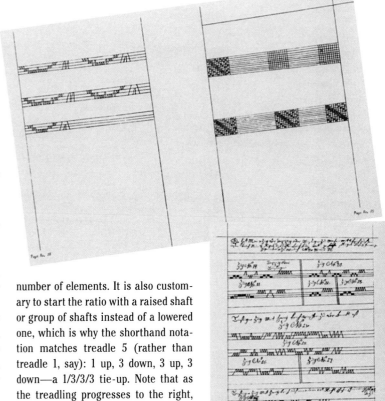

Old weaving books are fascinating. We can look into the past and see what the masters of our craft were weaving dozens or even hundreds of years ago. Old books can also be frustrating—often showing drafts or parts of drafts that don't seem to make sense when we try to duplicate them. I first encountered this problem in Jacob Angstadt His Weavers Patron Book. What appear to be 12-shaft twills are accompanied by 10-shaft tie-ups—how can this be?

Jacob Angstadt His Weavers Patron Book, an 18th-century manuscript reproduced for publication in 1976 by Ruth Holroyd and Ulrike Beck, provides a wealth of material for the contemporary weaver with eight or more (up to 32!) shafts. The original manuscript is photocopied in one volume. A companion volume, *Jacob Angstadt Designs Drawn from His Weavers Patron Book*, contains drawdowns—carefully prepared by Holroyd and Beck—of the original drafts, a translation of the original manuscript from German to English, and information about the Angstadt family and its weavers. Errors that appeared in some of the original manuscript's drafts and tie-ups are corrected with explanations in the *Designs* book. In some cases, however, the original intent is difficult to determine. Differences in past and present nomenclature and draft notation are one source of confusion. Drafts in old weaving books and manuscripts are often written on lines analogous to music staffs, and a variety of condensed notations are used to shorten lengthy threadings. Deciphering these abbreviated drafts becomes even more difficult in manuscripts such as Angstadt's, written with brief notes for personal use rather than with full explanations.

THE ANGSTADT MYSTERY

A mysterious discrepancy appears on pages 18 and 19 of the 12-shaft section of the *Patron Book* (see top photo at right). Five drafts for point twills are written in a zigzag notation seldom used by modern weavers. Although they appear in the 12-shaft section, the corresponding tie-ups are written for ten shafts. There is no text at all to provide a clue as to what was intended, and the pages appear to have been left incomplete.

The zigzag threading notation was a common and very graphic shorthand for twill threadings in the 17th and 18th centuries. The drafts on page 18 show twill threadings divided into three parts. In the larger motif, points are threaded within the thirds, and in the smaller motifs the point threadings extend over all the shafts as an 'M' or an inverted 'V.' Since the drafts appear in the 12-shaft section, one could assume that these drafts are for twills on 12 shafts, with three divisions of four shafts each. A portion of the first draft written for 12 shafts (using modern notation) with a regular 12-shaft twill tie-up is shown in *1*. Any of the drafts in the section can be woven as threaded on 12 shafts, but the corresponding 10-shaft tie-ups cannot be used with them.

The first three of the 10-shaft Angstadt tie-ups show two additional treadles tied for tabby, which suggests that a supplementary weft is used to produce pattern in twill on a plain-weave ground. All of the tie-ups are symmetrical along the diagonal. Only the first tie-up in the second row (shown here in *2a*, p. 31) is a regular twill tie-up, however, in which the ratio of shafts tied to go up and those tied to go down is the same for all treadles (except for the two tabby treadles). To determine the ratio, if the first and last shafts on a single treadle are both tied to go either up or down, they must be combined: the ratio always contains an even

number of elements. It is also customary to start the ratio with a raised shaft or group of shafts instead of a lowered one, which is why the shorthand notation matches treadle 5 (rather than treadle 1, say): 1 up, 3 down, 3 up, 3 down—a 1/3/3/3 tie-up. Note that as the treadling progresses to the right, the same ratio moves down one shaft on each successive treadle.

In the other Angstadt tie-ups on p. 19, however, the twill notation is *not* the same for each treadle—they are therefore not regular twill tie-ups. The second Angstadt tie-up in the same row is shown in *2b*. The twill notation for the second treadle (with first and last rising ties combined) is 4/2/1/3, but for the tenth treadle it is 2/3/1/2/1/1.

12-SHAFT DRAFTS ON 10 SHAFTS

I found the first clue to solving the mystery of these threading drafts and tie-ups in an article titled 'Huguenot coverlets,' by Carol Strickler (see the Bibliography, p. 33). She describes two coverlets woven on point-twill drafts with three divisions. The end points in each of the divisions *are common* to those of the adjacent set. Shaft 4 forms the top point of the first set but also the bottom point of the second, and shaft 7 the top of the second but also the bottom of the third (see *3*). Each division contains a group of four shafts, but because of the shared shafts, only ten shafts are needed. The tie-up is a 3/3/3/1 twill, an exact inversion of the Angstadt tie-up in *2a*. Similar drafts are used for a coverlet in the Helen Allen collection and also for one described as 'overshot' in *Heirlooms from Old Loom* (see the Bibliography).

Research done by Patricia Hilts on early German weaving books confirms the use of overlapping point-twill blocks in the 17th and 18th centuries. In *Neu Eingerichtetes Weber Kunst und Bild Buch* by Marx Ziegler, published in 1708, a rule is given for dividing (or 'breaking') 16 shafts into three divisions of six shafts each for block-effect twills: "When you take 16 shafts instead of 12 shafts

thrills twill thrill twill thrill twill thrills twill thrills twill thrills twill thrills twill thrills twill thrills twill thrills twill thrills twill thrills twill th

Jacquie Kelly Jacquie Kelly Jacquie Kelly Jacquie Kelly Jacquie Kelly Jacquie Kelly Jacquie Kelly Jacquie Kelly Jacquie

and proceed into the break, go through to the 6th shaft, then proceed into the 11th shaft, thereafter into the last of 16th, and again so in the return . . . ." Several examples of three-division point-twill drafts with 16-shaft tie-ups from Ziegler's earlier book (published in 1677) are included in Patricia Hilts's research.

The practice was not limited to German weavers. John Murphy mentions "diversifying the draughts of lined work patterns . . . by dividing the leaves [shafts] into two equal portions, and drawing a few sets of the diamond draught on each portion, alternately" . . . and introducing "a leaf into these mountings, immediately between the two divisions, which serves as a point leaf to both sets" (see the Bibliography, p. 33).

3. Huguenot coverlet

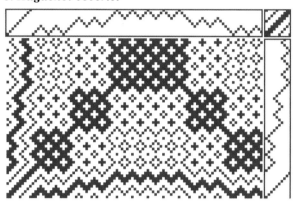

1. Angstadt 12-shaft draft with 12-shaft tie-up

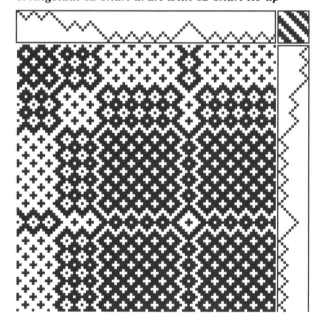

4. Angstadt: three overlapping blocks

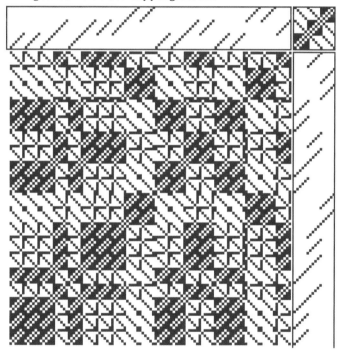

2. Angstadt 10-shaft tie-ups

a. Regular twill tie-up

1	2	3	4	5	6	7	8	9	10
10	10				10				10
9	9	9				9			9
	8	8	8				8		
		7	7	7				7	
			6	6	6				6
5				5	5	5			
	4				4	4	4		
		3				3	3	3	
			2				2	2	2
1				1					1

b. Irregular twill tie-up

1	2	3	4	5	6	7	8	9	10
10	10				10				10
9	9	9				9			9
	8	8	8				8		
		7	7	7				7	
			6	6	6				6
5				5	5	5			
	4				4	4	4		
		3				3	3	3	
2				2				2	2
	1				1				

c. Placemat tie-up

1	2	3	4	5	6	7	8	9	10	11	12
10	10				10				10	10	10
9	9	9				9				9	9
	8	8	8				8				8
		7	7	7				7			7
			6	6	6				6	6	
5				5	5	5					5
	4				4	4	4				4
		3				3	3	3			3
2			2				2	2	2		
1	1				1				1	1	

5. Angstadt overlapping block tie-up (p. 32, No. 60, in the Patron Book)

1	2	3	4	5	6	7	8	9	10	11	12	13	14	15	16
16					16					16	16	16	16		16
	15					15				15	15	15		15	
		14					14			14	14		14		14
			13					13		13		13		13	13
				12					12	12		12		12	12
11					11	11	11	11		11		11	11	11	
	10					10	10	10		10	10				
		9					9	9	9	9					
			8					8	8	8	8		8		
				7		7	7	7			7				
6	6	6	6			6	6	6	6						6
5	5	5		5		5				5					
4	4		4		4		4				4				
3		3		3	3		3				3				
	2		2	2	2			2				2			
1		1	1	1	1				1				1		

will thrills twill th thrills twill thrillss twill thrills twill thrills twill thrills twill thrills twill thrills twill thrills twill thrills twill thrills twill thrills twill

This method of designing point-twill threadings also clarifies another Angstadt mystery. On page 31 of the *Patron Book*, a 16-shaft tie-up, No. 60, looks at first glance like a tie-up for damask or twill blocks (shown here in *5*, p. 31). Above the tie-up is written (translated by Ulrike Beck), "To this one takes the drafts which are on the first page of the 12-shaft work," which at first glance seems impossible. A closer look shows that the 16-shaft tie-up contains three overlapping blocks of six shafts each. With overlapping threadings it is possible to use the 3-block profile drafts normally used with 12-shaft tie-ups (three blocks of 4-shaft twill) for 16 shafts (three overlapping blocks of 6-shaft twill). A portion of Angstadt's 3-block profile No. 4, p. 12, is shown in *4* using 6-shaft overlapping 'units' for each square in the profile draft with the tie-up in *5*.

Point-twill threading and treadling 'units' can also be used with 3-block profile drafts and overlapping tie-ups. Symmetrical twill tie-ups like those in *2a–c* can be expanded to use with overlapping threading units on 16 shafts. Additional possible variations include combining common block motifs with point threadings, as in drafts 19–23 and 28–30, p. 36, in the *Patron Book* (see the two top drafts in the lower photo, p. 30). These are 3-block profiles drafted on 16 shafts in which 2-block motifs alternate with point-twill groups. A drawdown of draft No. 19, with translation and comments for pp. 36 and 37, is given in the Angstadt *Designs* book.

THE PROOF IS IN THE WEAVING

The final test of any weaving draft is, of course, to weave it! Placemats are an ideal form for experimentation: different tie-ups and treadling orders can be designed for each placemat and the results used, compared, and enjoyed over and over again.

I chose the last draft on p. 18 of Angstadt's *Patron Book* and used the middle tie-up on the second row of p. 19 (given here in *2c* and *7*). The first placemat is woven as drawn in (*Photo a*). The second placemat (*Photo b*) is woven as drawn in but with the treadling inverted; as a result, the corners have a cross instead of a diamond, and star rather than rose figures in the center panel. In the third placemat the as drawn in order begins on treadle 7 (instead of 1 or 10), which restores the diamonds in the corners, but greatly changes the appearance of the center panel (*Photo c*). The fourth placemat (*Photo d*) is woven in shadow weave as a response to an editor's challenge in Carol Strickler's article on Huguenot coverlets. Light and dark wefts of equal thickness alternate throughout. One solid-color block appears in each of the two colors in addition to two blocks that blend the two colors differently. (For even more interesting shadow-weave effects, alternate dark and light threads in the warp as well as in the weft.)

The success of the shadow-weave adaptation, which is certainly not in the 18th-century tradition, encourages using other ways to explore overlapping twill/point-twill threading blocks. Fancy twill tie-ups that contain stars and/or roses and those with twill lines in opposite directions on either side of the diagonal (see the *Patron Book*, p. 23) produce interesting variations. Lace weaves using overlapping point-twill threadings can be adapted to weave blocks of lace, texture, and plain weave in varying combinations. The number of shafts per block doesn't have to be the same throughout the weave, nor do all blocks have to overlap. Experiment with this old draft idea, and weave something new!

6a. Angstadt, bottom draft, page 18; woven as drawn in (Photo a)

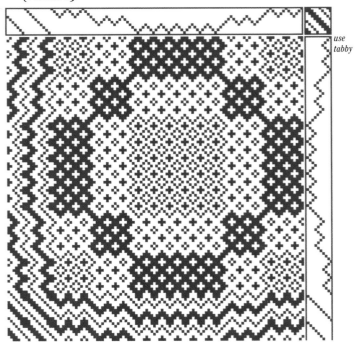

use tabby

6b. Treadling starts on treadle no. 1, as drawn in but in inverted order (Photo b)

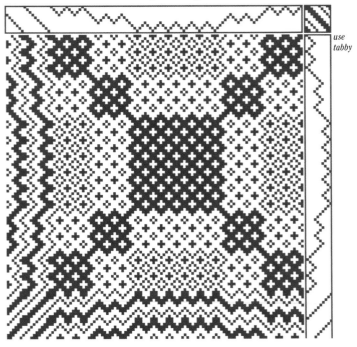

use tabby

thrills twill thrill twill thrills twill thrills twill thrills twill thrills twill thrills twill thrills twill thrills twill thrills twill thrills twill thrills twill

BIBLIOGRAPHY

Hilts, Patricia. 'Seventeenth and Eighteenth Century Twills, the German Linen Tradition.' *Ars Textrina*, Vol. III. Winnepeg: University of Manitoba, May 1985, p. 139.

Holroyd, Ruth, and Ulrike Beck. *Jacob Angstadt Designs Drawn From His Weavers Patron Book.* Pittsford, NY: Ruth Holroyd, 1972.

Murphy, John. *A Treatise on the Art of Weaving*, Glasgow: Blackie, Fullarton, & Co. 1827, p. 62.

Strickler, Carol. 'Huguenot Coverlets.' *The Weaver's Journal* 1:2, October 1976, pp. 8–10.

___ *American Coverlets of the Nineteenth Century.* Madison, Wisconsin, 1974, p. 32.

___ *Heirlooms from Old Looms: A Catalogue of Coverlets Owned by the Colonial Coverlet Guild of America and Its Members.* Chicago, 1940, p. 46.

THE PLACEMATS

- ❏ Equipment. 10-shaft loom, 14" weaving width; 8-dent reed; 2 shuttles.
- ❏ Materials. Warp and tabby weft: 20/2 pearl cotton (8400 yds/lb), 5 oz; pattern weft: 8/2 pearl cotton (3360 yds/lb), 4 oz. For the shadow-weave placemat, two colors of 10/2 pearl cotton (4200 yds/lb) are used alternately, 4 oz each.
- ❏ Wind a warp of 437 ends 4 yds long (includes 2 floating selvedges) for six placemats.
- ❏ Sley 4/dent in an 8-dent reed, 32 epi; center for 13½" weaving width.
- ❏ Thread following the draft in *7*. (Note that the threading reverses in sections c/d–e/f.)
- ❏ Weave using the tie-up in *2c* or other 10-shaft twill tie-up. Use tabby (alternate tabby and pattern wefts). Experiment with different treadling orders—see the as-drawn-in and inverted orders on page 32. Shadow-weave effects are achieved by alternating light and dark wefts. For this draft, one weft begins the as-drawn-in treadling order on treadle 4 and the other weft follows the same order but begins on treadle 8. ✂

Use Angstadt's overlapping threading blocks and mix and match 3-block profile drafts and 10-shaft tie-ups for twills, twill blocks, laces and more. Enjoy experimenting with this rediscovered idea.

a. Treadled as drawn in (with tabby)

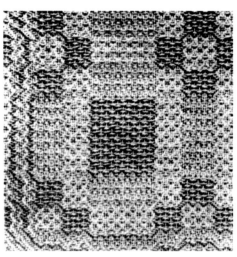

c. Treadled as drawn in, beginning sequence with treadle 7 (with tabby)

b. Treadled as drawn in, inverted order (with tabby)

d. Alternating light and dark wefts for a shadow-weave effect

7. Placemat threading draft

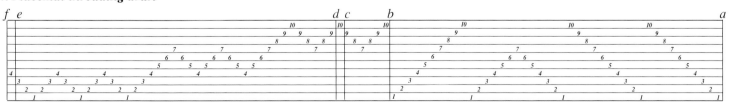

Thread a–b (43 ends); b–c (6 ends); [c–f, e–d]4x (336 ends); d–b (7 ends); b–a (43 ends) = 435 ends + 2 floating selvedges = 437 ends

twill thrills twill thrills twill thrills twill thrills twill thrills twill thrills twill thrills twill thrills twill thrills twill thrills twill thrills twill
thrills twill thrills twill thrills twill thrills twill thrills twill thrills twill thrills twill thrills twill thrills twill thrills twill thrills twill
ills twill thrills twill thrills twill thrills twill thrills twill thriss twill thrills twill thrills twill thrills twill thrills twill thrills twill thrill

the earl's canvas

Gebrochene twills, even on four shafts, look very complex. Use the drafts on page 36 to weave the project scarves or runner, or design an original gebrochene that fits the number of shafts on your loom. You'll enjoy the intricate points and delicate lacy shapes that are the magical result of this drafting technique.

In 1626, John Erskine, the second Earl of Mar in Scotland, had his portrait painted by Adam de Colone. The portrait, which now rests high on a storage rack in the National Portrait Gallery in Edinburgh, depicts an Elizabethan gentleman with a lace ruff and badge of office. What makes this portrait of interest to the handweaver is the 'canvas' on which it is painted, a 14-shaft gebrochene twill that was probably originally a tablecloth. (Martin Norgate, curator of the Dunfermline District Museum, analyzed the earl's canvas in the early 1970s.)

GEBROCHENE TWILLS

Gebrochene is the German term for the structure sometimes called an M and W twill by contemporary weavers. It is a twill interlacement with extensive threading and treadling repeats, usually including many points, woven with a twill tie-up. Usually both warp and weft are the same yarn, historically linen. Gebrochene tablecloths are pictured in medieval art, and gebrochene drafts are found in manuscripts and published books from the early 17th century. Patterns can be quite elaborate; one design by Jacob Angstadt shows over 900 ends in one repeat.

EARLY NOTATION SYSTEM

Early drafts show a compact notation, like scribbles on music paper (see the Angstadt drafts in Jacquie Kelly, 'Angstadt Twills: Solving a Weaving Puzzle,' pp. 30–33). The designs are broken into divisions, giving a visual clue to the origin of the contemporary labels of M's and W's; see *1a–b*. Horizontal lines represent turning points in the threading.

The same designs can be used on different numbers of shafts. On eight, the horizontal line in *1a* falls between shafts 4 and 5; on 16, between 8 and 9. More shafts allow for more complex patterning.

A gebrochene of three divisions as in *1b* can be woven on eight shafts using overlapping turning points 1-4, 3-6, 5-8 (again, see pp. 30–33). On 12 shafts, turning points with three divisions (and four shafts within each division) need not overlap 1-4,

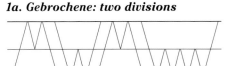

1a. Gebrochene: two divisions

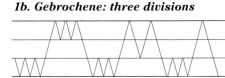

1b. Gebrochene: three divisions

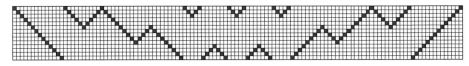

2a. The 'earl's canvas' draft on 14 shafts

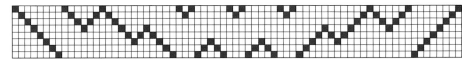

2b. The 'earl's canvas' draft reduced to eight shafts

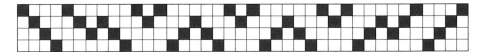

2c. The 'earl's canvas' draft reduced to four shafts

5-8, 9-12. On 16, three divisions do overlap (if six shafts are used in each division) 1–6, 6–11, 11–16.

Gebrochene tie-ups are regular twill tie-ups, usually slanting from lower left to upper right. The more twill lines there are in a tie-up, the more complex the pattern is.

The treadling order usually follows the threading order 'tromp as writ,' i.e., 'as-drawn-in,' so a 900-end threading repeat has a 900-pick treadling repeat. The pattern is 'squared' in the weaving.

DESIGNING GEBROCHENE TWILLS

Designing new gebrochenes is a simple matter of putting zigzags on paper and adding a twill tie-up. This is probably how early weavers designed them, although they had to weave the cloth to see the success of the design while we can use a computer to do the work and accept or reject the results quickly.

Any gebrochene draft can be reduced to fewer shafts, though the fewer the shafts the more obscure the divisions become. The original 14-shaft earl's canvas draft is shown in *2a*. (Horizontal divisions are not obvious in this draft because of the center ends on shafts 12–14. If two shafts are added at the bottom of the draft to make sixteen total shafts and these ends are transposed to shafts 1–2, the divisions would be 1–7, 7–11, 11–16. Perhaps this draft was once reduced to fourteen from sixteen!) To reduce

the draft in *2a* to eight shafts, the turns are maintained but condensed, as in *2b*. Even a 4-shaft version is possible; see *2c*. With each reduction the pattern becomes less elaborate but still very interesting.

To learn more about these drafts, weave a project on four, eight, or fourteen shafts. When you see the designs grow on the loom, you'll want to start designing other gebrochene twills.

4-SHAFT WOOL SCARF, page 35

❑ Equipment. 4-shaft loom, 10" weaving width; 12-dent reed; 1 shuttle.
❑ Materials. Warp: 24/2 worsted wool (5960 yds/lb, Super Lamb, JaggerSpun), Lead (gray), 2½ oz. Weft: 24/2 worsted wool, Mallard (teal), 2 oz.
❑ Wind a warp of 275 ends (includes 2 ends for floating selvedges) 3 yds long.
❑ Sley 2-2-3 in a 12-dent reed, 28 epi; center for 9¾".
❑ Thread following the draft in *3*.
❑ Weave 60" as-drawn-in (use the treadle that corresponds to the shaft number in the threading); leave 8" at each end for fringe.
❑ Finish by preparing a twisted fringe; handwash; lay flat to dry.

8-SHAFT SILK SCARF, page 35

❑ Equipment. 8-shaft loom, 10" weaving width; 12-dent reed; 1 shuttle.

thrills **twill** thrills **twill** thrills twill thrills twill thrills **twill** thrills twill thrills twill thrills twill thrills twill thrills twill thrills twill thrills **thrills** twill thrills twill thrills twill t
twill thrills twill thrills twill thrills twill thrills twill thrills twill thrills twill thrills twill thrills twill thrills twill thrills twill thrills twill thrills twi
ll thrill twill thrill twill **thrills** **twill** thrills twill thrills twill thrills twill **thrills** twill thrills twill **thrills** twill thrills twill thrills twill **thrills** twill th

Marjie Thompson Marjie Thompson Marjie Thompson Marjie Thompson Marjie Thompson Marjie Thompson Marjie Thom

Marjie's gebrochenes are also studies in fine threads. Weave a man's scarf in fine wool (24/2 worsted at 28 epi), a lady's scarf in fine silk (60/2 silk at 60 epi), or a table runner in fine linen (40/2 at 36 epi; see page 36)—or mix and match to select the draft that fits your loom and the fiber that fits your yarn shelf.

will thrills twill thrills twill thrills twill thrills twill thrills twill thrills twill thrills twill thrills twill thrills twill thrills twill thrills twill
thrills twill thrills twill thrills twill thrills twill thrills twill thrills twill thrills twill thrills twill thrills twill thrills twill thrills twill thrills twill th
ills twill thrills twill thrills twill thrills twill thrills twill thrills twill thrillss twill thrills twill thrills twill thrills twill thrills twill thrills twill

The 14-shaft draft for the earl's portrait canvas fabric produces this tablecloth in fine linen. You can substitute the 4-shaft draft in 3 or the 8-shaft draft in 4.

❑ Materials. Warp and weft: 60/2 silk (14,880 yds/lb, Webs), natural, 2½–3 oz.

❑ Wind a warp of 453 ends (includes 2 ends floating selvedges) 3 yds long.

❑ Sley 5/dent in a 12-dent reed, 60 epi; center for 7½" weaving width.

❑ Thread following the draft in *4*.

❑ Weave as for wool scarf using the draft in *4*.

❑ Finish by preparing a twisted fringe; soak in warm water, Ivory liquid; hang over rod to dry; press while still damp.

14-SHAFT LINEN RUNNER (at right)

❑ Equipment. 14-shaft loom, 17" weaving width; 12-dent reed; 1 shuttle.

❑ Materials. Warp and weft: 40/2 linen (6000 yds/lb, Webs), bleached, 7–8 oz.

❑ Wind a warp of 593 ends (includes 2 ends floating selvedges) 2½ yds long.

❑ Sley 3/dent in a 12-dent reed, 36 epi; center for 16½" weaving width.

❑ Thread following the draft in *5*.

❑ Weave for 1¼ yd as-drawn-in. Hemstitch ends or add plain-weave treadles for plain-weave hems.

❑ Finish by machine washing, then alternate ice water/hot water rinse three times; press while still damp. ✀

Thread a-b 2x, [a-e, d-c] 5x, c-a 1x, b-a 2x.

3. 4-shaft draft for wool scarf

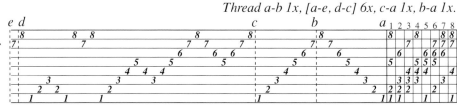

Thread a-b 1x, [a-e, d-c] 6x, c-a 1x, b-a 1x.

4. 8-shaft draft for silk scarf

Thread a-b 3x; [a-e, d-c] x4; c-a 1x; b-a 3x.

5. 14-shaft draft for linen runner

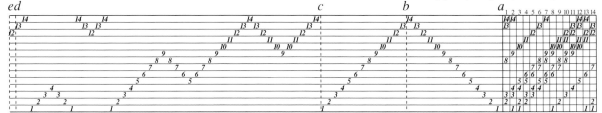

thrills twill thrills twill thrills twill thrills twill thrills twill thrills twill thrills twill thrills twill thrills twill thrills twill thrills twill thrills twill thrills twill thrills twill t
twill thrills twill thrills twill thrills twill thrills twill thrills twill thrills twill thrills twill thrills twill thrills twill thrills twill thrills twill thrills twi
ill thrill twill thrill twill thrills twill thrills twill thrills twill thrills twill thrills twill thrills twill thrills twill thrills twill thrills twill thrills twill th

advancing twills

advancing twills

1a. 5-end block, right twill, advance 1

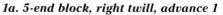

1b. 5-end block, left twill, advance 1

1c. 5-end block, left twill, advance 1, blocks reversed

2a. 5-end block, advance 2

An advance of two fewer than the number of ends in the twill run does not produce an advancing twill.

2b. 5-end block, advance 3

3a. 5-end block, advance 4   3b. 5-end block, advance 8

3c. 5-end block, advance 5

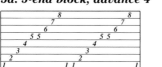

4a. 3-end block, advance 7, produces plain weave

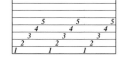

4b. 3-end block, advance 7, does not produce plain weave

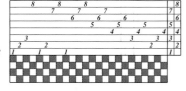

'Advancing' or 'skip' twills offer unique design opportunities for the multishaft loom. Jaquard-like, large-scale images create the illusion of three dimensions in weave structures that are suitable for all fabric uses.

In 'advancing' twills, a small section of twill is followed by another section of twill that begins on one shaft or more above the starting point of the previous section. These sections can be thought of as blocks, the blocks can be any size, and the 'advances' can be one of several possible numbers. The twill sections can be straight or point or other twill orders and there can be 3, 4, 5, or more ends in the each section.

SIMPLE ADVANCING TWILLS

Examine the threading draft in *1a* (the drafts in these examples are read from left to right). A section, or block, of 5 ends begins on shaft 1 and a second block on shaft 2; the advance is 1. Note that each twill section in *1a* progresses in the same direction, to the right. Compare the threading drafts in *1a* and *1b*. In *1a*, the ends within each block progress in the same direction as the blocks progress (1-5, 2-6, etc., and A–H). In *1b*, the ends within each block progress in the opposite direction as the blocks progress (5-1, 6-2, etc., A–H), which produces a different twill from the twill in *1a*.

The draft in *1c* shows 5-end right-twill blocks with an advance of 7. The twills and the blocks both progress in the same direction (8-4, 7-3, H-A). Note that *1b* and *1c* are mirror images of each other; they therefore produce essentially the same interlacement.

The advance: some restrictions

Not all numbers used as the advance produce advancing twills. An advance of 2 fewer than the total number of ends in the twill section does not result in an advancing twill: in *2a*, for example, an advance of 2 (3 fewer than 5) produces an advancing twill for a 5-end block, but an advance of 3 (2 fewer than 5) produces zigzags without breaks, as in *2b*.

The advance cannot be 1 fewer than the number of ends in the block, or ends are doubled, as in *3a*. The advance cannot be equal to the number of shafts being used, or the twill returns to the starting point as in *3b*. The advance cannot be equal to the number of ends in the twill run, or a straight twill is produced as in *3c*. The advance for a 5-end block, therefore, can be 1, 2, 6, or 7 but not 3, 4, 5, or 8. For 4-end blocks the advance can be 1, 5, 6, or 7.

Deriving plain weave

Plain weave can be produced on some advancing twill drafts but not on others. If the advance and the size of the block add up to an even number, plain weave can be woven, but if they add up to an odd number, the draft cannot produce plain weave. Note that a 3-end twill with an advance of 7 produces plain weave (*4a*), but a 4-end twill with an advance of 1 does not (*4b*).

Tie-up and treadling orders

Advancing twill drafts can be woven successfully with straight twill tie-ups and 'as-drawn-in' treadling orders. The tie-up should show float lengths of no more than 1 thread fewer than the number of threads in the twill run, 4 for a 5-end advancing twill, for example. See a sample tie-up and drawdown for a 5-end twill in *5a–b*.

5a. 16-shaft tie-up

twill thrills twill th

Ingrid Boesel Ingrid Boesel Ingrid Boesel Ingrid Boesel Ingrid Boesel Ingrid Boesel

A 13-thread expanded advancing twill threading and treadling produce all three of these silk scarves —the difference is in their tie-ups. Use advancing and expanded advancing twills to create large-scale motifs with subtle shading between pattern and background areas, especially effective in fine silk threads.

5b. *The twill tie-up in 5a is treadled as drawn in and in straight twill order*

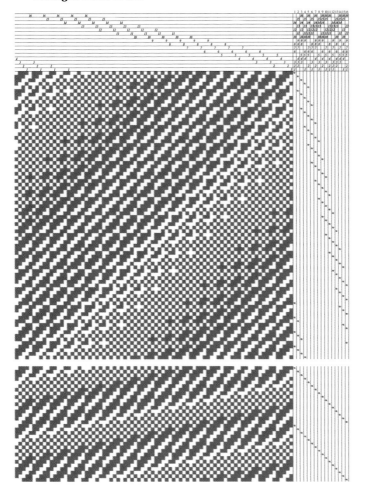

EXPANDED ADVANCING TWILLS

Advancing twills can be expanded to produce large figures with diffuse edges. The complexity of the design contrasts with a certain tranquil order produced by the regular sequence of the blocks; see the drawdowns in *8a–b*.

Expanded advancing twills

In the draft in *1*, p. 38, eight 5-end blocks (A–H) are threaded for a repeat of 40 total ends. The size of each block can be expanded by repeating the twill run in each block one or more times. In *6a*, for example, the 5-end run is threaded twice in each block. Notice that plain weave cannot be woven on this threading. Similarly, if a 4-end block is expanded, plain weave is interrupted in the transition from one block to the next, as shown in *6b*. To make plain weave possible, an incidental thread on the next highest shaft can be added between the blocks; see the circled ends in *6c*. The block need not be limited to 9 ends (two repeats plus the incidental), but can be 13 ends (three repeats), 17 ends (four repeats), or more. A 6-end block can be expanded to 13, 19, or more ends per block. When expanding blocks of odd numbers of ends, plain weave is not possible.

Designing tie-ups

Tie-ups for expanded advancing twills must be designed carefully to avoid over-long floats. With an expanded advancing twill threading based on a 4-thread run (see *6b–6d*), no more than three ties can appear together in any direction in the tie-up (1 thread fewer than the number of threads in the twill run). If this rule is followed, twill tie-ups can produce small blocks of 3/1 twill and 1/3 twill surrounded by various other twills and/or plain weave. With a black warp and a white weft, shaded gray blocks outline predominantly black (3/1 twill) or white (1/3 twill) blocks in the project scarves; see p. 38. The steep twill tie-up in *7b* produces the interlacement in *8a* and the scarf at top right. A second type of tie-up shows opposing diagonal float sequences in a background of plain weave (see *7c*, *8b*, and the scarf at bottom left). The edges of the twill figures, where they show a mix of twill and plain weave, appear almost lacy.

Another method for creating tie-ups is to draw an image directly in the tie-up, fill it with 3/1 twill, and then fill the rest with 1/3 twill. These tie-ups

6a. *5-end twill threaded twice in each block*

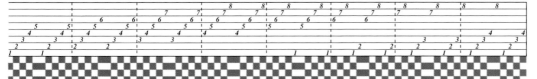

6d. *13-end blocks*

6b. *4-end twill threaded twice in each block*

Transition threads are added in **6c** *and* **6d** *so that plain weave can be produced on the expanded advancing twill threadings. A full repeat of the 13-end threading used in* **6d** *is 104 ends; only the first two blocks are shown in* **6d**.

6c. *Transition thread added to two 5-end twills for 9-end blocks*

7a. *Tie-up for triangle motifs*

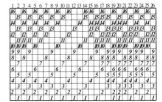

40

Il thrills **twill** thrills **twill** thrills twill thrills **twill thrills twill** thrills twill **thrills** twill thrills twill thrills twill thrills twill **thrills twill** thrills twill
twill **thrills twill thrills twill** thrills twill thrills **thrills twill thrills twill** thrills twill thrills twill thrills twill thrills twill thrills twill thrills twill thrills tw
ill thrill twill thrill twill **thrills twill** thrills twill thrills twill **thrills** twill thrills twill **thrills** twill thrills twill thrills **twill thrills** twill th

produce motifs of 3/1 twill and a background of 1/3 twill; the two twills are separated with fuzzy areas of intermediate weave structures. (See Bonnie Inouye, 'Imagery in Advancing Twills,' pp. 106–109, for further design techniques to use with advancing twills.)

Treadling orders

Treadling sequences that use the same expanded advancing twill order as in the threading are always successful. Any number of treadles can be used, but when they are converted to lift plans for dobby looms they tend to be very long. If a 16-treadle tie-up is used for 13-end blocks (as in *6d*), the treadling repeat is 208 picks! A regular treadle loom is preferable to a mechanical dobby for short fabrics (since pegging is so time-consuming and chains of more than 100–150 bars are unwieldy).

For tie-ups with more treadles than are available on a treadle loom, the treadling sequences can be converted to peg plans in a computer weaving program for use with computer-assisted dobby looms or for table looms. The draft in *8a* requires 624 picks or dobby bars. The same draft with 64 treadles would require 832 picks or bars for one repeat!

SILK SCARF

Fine threads, advancing twills, and silk scarves make perfect companions. Use a computer weaving program to design an original tie-up. Computer printouts give an accurate picture of the results; compare the scarves on page 39 with the drawdowns in 8a *and* 8b.

- ❑ Equipment. 16-shaft treadle, dobby, or table loom, 10" weaving width; 10-dent reed; 1 shuttle.
- ❑ Materials. Warp: 60/2 silk (14,880 yds/lb), black, 1½ oz. Weft: 60/2 silk, white, 1 oz.
- ❑ Wind a warp of 520 ends 3 yds long.
- ❑ Sley 6-5-6-5, etc., in a 10-dent reed for 55 epi; center for 9½".
- ❑ Thread following the advancing twill sequence in *6d*. There are 104 ends/repeat. Five repeats produce a scarf 9½" wide.
- ❑ Weave as drawn in using the tie-up in *5b* (for treadle looms) or *7a*, *7b*, or *7c* (for dobby or table looms; convert tie-ups and treadling orders to peg plans for dobby looms).
- ❑ Remove the scarf from the loom. Prepare a twisted fringe by twisting two bouts of 5 ends each in one direction, then twist them together in the opposite direction. Tie the ends in an overhand knot. Handwash the scarf gently in lukewarm water with Ivory liquid. Lay flat to dry. ✄

7b. Tie-up for steep twill steps

7c. Tie-up for floats, plain weave

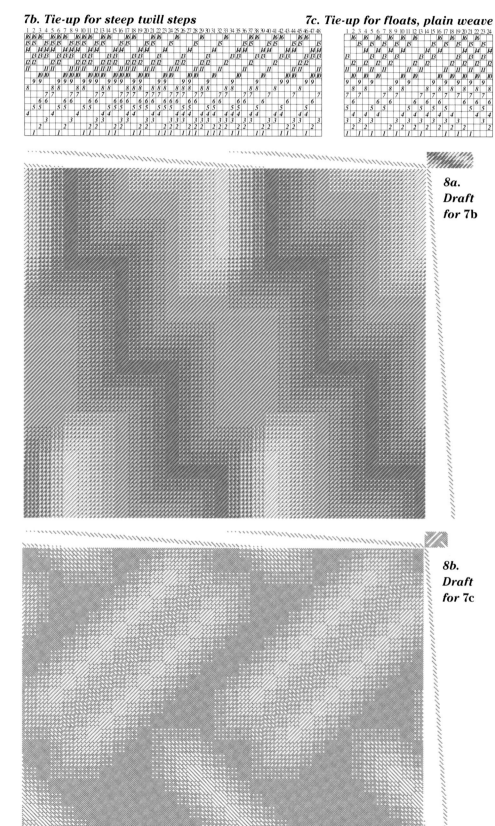

8a. Draft for 7b

8b. Draft for 7c

composing snowflakes

Placing several different interlacements in succession within a weaving draft is like joining parts of an alphabet to build words. For instance, different twill segments can be combined for the delightful patterns of the so-called 'snowflake' twill designs.

Apparently, the first one of these 8-shaft drafts to inspire North American weavers was introduced in 1945 by Mary Meigs Atwater in a *Shuttle-Craft Guild Bulletin* article on twills; see the Bibliography, p. 45. Since the draft came from a Swedish fabric, someone dubbed the pattern 'Swedish Snowflake.' One of the very few other versions offered to North American weavers since then is shown in 'Silk Snow-flakes and Stars,' pp. 55–57.

SNOWFLAKE PATTERNS

Surprisingly, these designs are rare in Scandinavian weaving books. I gained that knowledge along with the 'alphabet' analogy for creating these designs when I sought snowflake drafts from a Swedish-trained weaver. I did not expect the dearth of Swedish patterns I discovered, since while I was doing research for *A Joy Forever, Latvian Weaving*, I found a number of attractive variations in Latvian weaving literature.

The draft for the project runner (shown in *2*) is adapted from a draft for a blanket appearing in the Latvian weaving book, *Latvian Folk Art*, by Redigejis M. Stepermanis. Similar designs were popularized in the 1930s by Anna Antens; the drafts in *1* and *3* both appear in her book, *Handbook for Weavers*; see the Bibliography, p. 45.

Start with an advancing twill

The major component of the snowflake design is a large X formed by a long advancing twill that reverses in its center, see *1*. Twill runs of 4 ends progress up (or down) the threading rows (for more information about advancing twills, see Ingrid Boesel, pp. 38–41). Each run begins 1 shaft up (or down) from the previous run. The draft in *1* has eleven 4-end runs between reversing points, while the Atwater snowflake draft has eight. The treadling order is the same as the threading, i.e., 'as-drawn-in.' The customary 3/3/1/1 twill tie-up (allowing 3/1 and 1/3 twill and plain weave interlacements) gives intricate, graceful patterns with warp and weft floats up to 6 threads long.

1. A large X design is formed by an advancing twill that reverses in the center

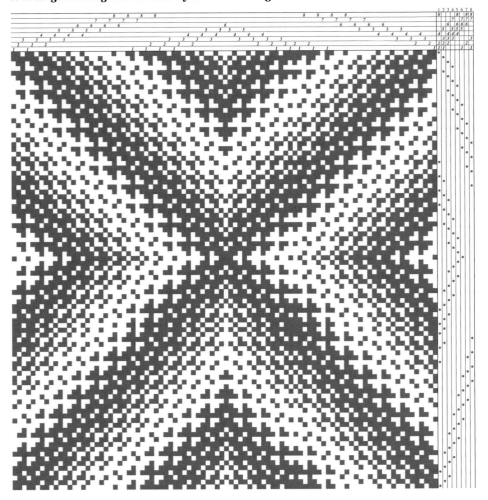

Add point twills

A second alphabet 'letter,' a point twill, is added to the advancing twill in the draft in *2*. The resulting design emphasizes the point-twill figures as much as the X's of the skip twill.

Photo a, p. 44 shows a tablecloth woven with a cotton warp and a linen weft. Its 'alphabet' creates a lengthy 'word,' on which the draft in *3* is based. First is the usual advancing twill. A point twill is added, its slopes following the neighboring angles of the first and then a second X. A straight-twill run, more point twills (on the same shafts as the single point between X's), and a final straight-twill run give nine lozenge figures before its word is finished—nearly a spelling bee! Note that this tablecloth design is not treadled as drawn in.

The draft in *3*, from a 1936 Latvian book by Anna

Skuja-Antene, shows threading and treadling orders identical to Mary Atwater's snowflake. The tie-up begins on a different treadle from the Atwater tie-up; thus slight differences result in the design. In *3*, the alphabet gains a new letter, a satin-based point. The final word contains: a basic advancing-twill X, a downward straight-twill run, 15 ends threaded down and then up in 8-shaft satin order, and finally an upward straight-twill run.

In most of the drafts, borders are formed by repeats of 8-end straight-twills, and more rarely, by point twills.

Designing with snowflake twills is very rewarding since they are open to variations in treadling as well as in threading. The wonderfully elegant twills are suitable for table pieces or towels of cotton and/or linen, wool blankets, and garment fabrics.

thrills **twill** thrills **twill** thrills twill thrills **twill** thrills twill **thrills** twill thrills twill **thrills** twill thrills twill thrills twill **thrills** twill thrills twill t
twill **thrills** twill thrills twill thrills twill thrills twill **thrills** twill thrills twill thrills twill thrills twill thrills twill thrills twill thrills tw
thrill twill thrill twill **thrills** **twill** thrills twill thrills twill thrills twill **thrills** twill thrills twill **thrills** twill thrills twill thrills twill thrills twill th

Reversing point twills separate the snowflake design in this runner. The point twills add diamonds and lozenge shapes and increase design complexity. Woven in a cotton warp and a linen weft with one shuttle on only eight shafts, this runner is easy to weave and makes an elegant addition to any table.

will thrills twill thrills twill thrills twill thrills twill thrills twill thrills twill thrills twill thrills twill thrills twill thrills twill thrills twill thrills twill thrills twill thrills twill thrills twill thrills twill
thrills twill thrills twill thrills twill thrills twill thrills twill thrills twill thrills twill thrills twill thrills twill thrills twill thrills twill thrills twill th
ills twill thrills twill thrills twill thrills twill thrills twill thrilss twill thrills twill thrills twill thrills twill thrills twill thrills twill thrills twill

2. Point twills are added to a 4-end advancing twill

3. Satin is threaded next to the advancing twill

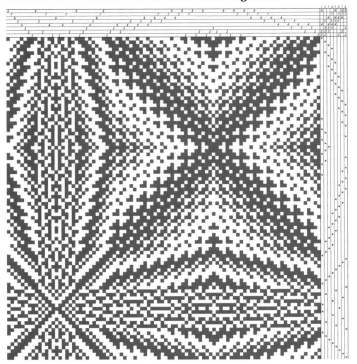

Use a variety of 'alphabet letters' to design your own snowflake twill drafts. Try varying treadling orders for surprising effects—these drafts are especially conducive to designing spontaneously at the loom. The designs appear far more complex than are usually produced on eight shafts, and the weaving is quick with one shuttle—but you'll need concentration or a computer to keep track of your place in the treadling draft.

a. Woven in Latvia in the 1930s of cotton warp and linen weft, this tablecloth is the gift of Mrs. Lonija Brivkalns to the Royal Ontario Museum. The portion represented by the draft in 4 is framed. (Royal Ontario Museum catalogue number 971.315.4, photo by Jane Evans)

4. Advancing, point, and straight twills are combined

5. Threading draft for Jane's Snowflake runner

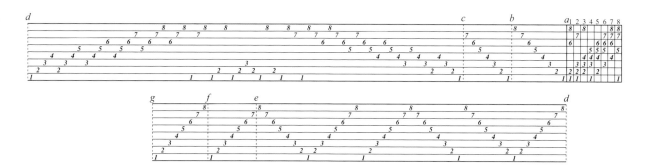

You'll be amazed by the complexity of the design in this twill runner, combining advancing, straight, point, and reversing-point twills. If you have a computer hook-up for your 8-shaft loom, you'll love not having to keep track of the treadling sequence. Using treadles, however, allows designing at the loom. Put on a long warp and do some experimenting with different treadling orders. Use this draft for table linens, blankets and afghans, fine silk scarves, fabric for clothing, curtains, and even wall hangings with shaded color arrangements in warp and weft.

JANE'S SNOWFLAKE RUNNER

❏ Equipment. 8-shaft loom, 20" weaving width; 15-dent reed; 1 shuttle.

❏ Materials. Warp: 16/2 unmercerized cotton (6,720 yds/lb, Bockens, Nordic Studio), bleached white, 10 oz. Weft: 8/1 linen (2400 yds/lb, Nordic Studio), natural, 14 oz.

❏ Wind a warp of 571 ends, 9½ ft long (allows 2 ft for tie-on and loom waste). Add to warp length for sampling and/or additional runners.

❏ Sley 2/dent in a 15-dent reed for 30 epi; center for 19".

❏ Thread following the draft in *5*:
  a to *b* 5x, *b* to *c* 1x (border);
  d to *e* 1x; *c* to *e* 4x (field);
  e to *f* 1x, *f* to *g* 5x (border).

❏ Weave as drawn in for about 85". (Read the threading diagram as though it is the treadling diagram, using the corresponding treadle number for each number in the threading draft. Treadle the straight-twill borders only at the beginning and end of the runner, repeating *c* to *e* for the field of snowflakes and reversing point twills.)

❏ Finish by removing the fabric from the loom and machine straight-stitching across cut ends. Fold ends under twice; sew hems by hand. Machine wash in hot water, Ivory liquid; lay flat to partly dry; hard press while still damp with a hot iron. Finished size: 16¼" wide x 78" long.

BIBLIOGRAPHY

Antens, Anna. *Rokas gramata audejam (Handbook for Weavers)*. Dusseldorf, Germany: Apgads J. Alksnis, 1949. This book was originally published as *Ausana (Weaving)* in 1931.

Atwater, Mary Meigs. *The Shuttle-Craft Guild Bulletin*. Basin, Montana: August 1945, pp. 4–5.

Evans, Jane A. *A Joy Forever, Latvian Weaving —Traditional and Modified Uses*. St. Paul, Minnesota: Dos Tejedoras Fiber Arts, 1991.

Morrison, Ruth, Madelyn van der Hoogt, and David Xenakis. 'Silk Snowflakes and Stars.' *Weaver's* Issue 13, Spring 1991, pp. 34–36.

Skuja-Antene, Anna. *Macies aust: rokas gramata skolatajam, instruktorem un audejam (Learn to Weave: Handbook for Teachers and Instructors and Weavers)*. Riga, Latvia: Latvju Sieviesu Nacionalas Ligas Izdevums, 1936.

Stepermanis, Redigejis M. *Latviesu tautas maksla (Latvian Folk Art)*; vols. 1–3. Riga, Latvia, 1961–1967. ✂

The 320-end draft in **4** *(shown across both pages 44 and 45) is derived from the tablecloth in* **Photo a**. *Nine point twills form the large section on the left of the draft. The treadling order is not as drawn in. The treadling repeat is 118 picks in length.*

twill thrills twill thrills twill thrills twill thrills twill thrills twill thrills twill thrills twill thrills twill thrills twill thrills twill thrills twill thrills twi
thrills twill thrills twill thrills twill thrills twill thrills twill thrills twill thrills twill thrills twill thrills twill thrills twill thrills twill thrills twill
ills twill thrills twill thrills twill thrills twill thrillss twill thrills twill thrills twill thrills twill thrills twill thrills twill thrills twill thri

frost crystals in twill

1a-c. Snowflake designs with bilateral symmetry

1d-f. Snowflake designs with radial symmetry

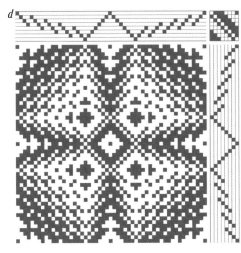

Fern-like crystal patterns spreading on a frosty windowpane have a special aesthetic appeal. Not only are they rare in temperate climates, occurring when temperature and moisture conditions are exactly right, but their innate fragility defies preservation.

How fortunate that twill can mimic the intricate branching and exquisite shading of ephemeral frost crystals in a more lasting form!

Relatives of snowflake twills, 'frost' patterns develop from an interrupted twill threading known variously as offset, skip, or advancing twill. Typical threading and treadling orders for snowflakes are based on short segments of straight twill, each starting consistently one or more steps higher than the beginning of the previous segment (see pp. 42–45). An example is shown in *1a*. A regular twill tie-up is usually treadled as drawn in to create wonderfully shaded and intricate snowflakes or starbursts (several variations are shown in this book, pp. 49–60). The drawdowns in *1b–1f* show the variations made possible by changing only the tie-up. Further modifications can transform a snowflake draft into the freer forms suggestive of crystals that I've nicknamed 'frost.'

SNOWFLAKES: A CLOSER LOOK

My exploration began with observing how changes in the tie-up affect the appearance of snowflake twills. Comparing different tie-ups is illuminating, but even a single tie-up offers plenty of variety depending on how the treadles are arranged.

Study the snowflake drafts in *1a-f*. All six drafts use a 1/3/3/1 tie-up, which balances warp and weft effects by raising exactly half of the shafts for every shed, produces reasonable float lengths in both warp and weft (maximum float over 6 threads), and provides good contrast with gentle shading. Notice that the order of the treadles in each of the tie-ups in *1a-c* is different, so that even though the treadling for all three is as-drawn-in, the resulting drawdowns look quite different.

Bilateral symmetry

The two-color (black-and-white) drawdowns in *1a-c* show bilateral symmetry. If we wish for the radial symmetry of a snowflake, we must look closely at the weave structure rather than the two different colors of warp and weft. Imagine these same designs woven with warp and weft of the same color. Ray-like ridges

thrills twill thrills twill thrills twill thrills twill thrills twill thrills twill thrills twill thrills twill thrills twill thrills twill thrills twill th
twill thrills twill thrills twill thrills twill thrills twill thrills twill thrills twill thrills twill thrills twill thrills twill thrills twill thrills twill thrills tw
thrill twill thrill twill thrills twill thrills twill thrills twill thrills twill thrills twill thrills twill thrills twill thrills twill thrills twill th

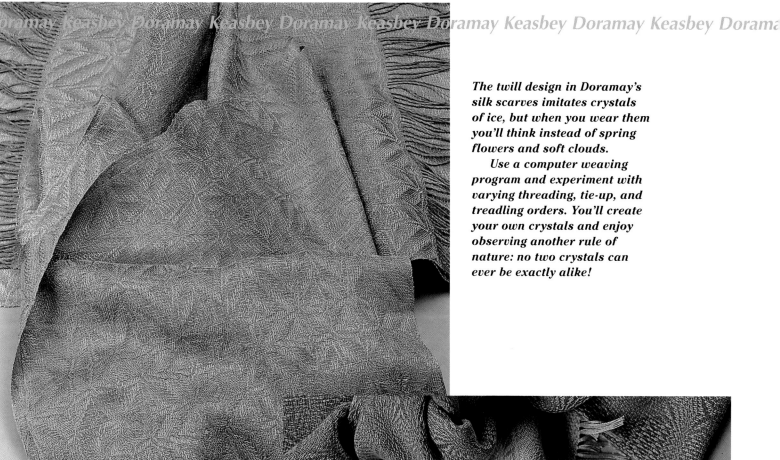

The twill design in Doramay's silk scarves imitates crystals of ice, but when you wear them you'll think instead of spring flowers and soft clouds.

Use a computer weaving program and experiment with varying threading, tie-up, and treadling orders. You'll create your own crystals and enjoy observing another rule of nature: no two crystals can ever be exactly alike!

Four-shaft weavers—don't be left out of the snowflake twill explosion! Use Laura Fry's design tips on page 49 and design frost and snowflake twills for your 4-shaft loom. Let your computer weaving program help you quickly discover how intricate and varied the patterns can be. Laura's 2/2 advancing twill fabrics (at right) are soft but sturdy, as suitable for silk scarves as for long-wearing table linens or yardage for clothing.

will thrills twill thrills twill thrills twill thrills twill thrills twill thrills twill thrills twill thrills twill thrills twill thrills twill thrills twill thrills twill thrills twill thrills twill thrills twill
thrills twill thrills twill thrills twill thrills twill thrills twill thrills twill thrills twill thrills twill thrills twill thrills twill thrills twill thrills twill thrills twill thrills twill
rills twill thrills twill thrills twill thrills twill thrills twill thrills twill thrillss twill thrills twill thrills twill thrills twill thrills twill thrills twill thrills twill thrills twill thrills twill thrill

are formed along the diagonals by long warp floats on one side of the diagonal offset by long weft floats on the other side. The three tie-ups in *1a-c* come very close to balancing the long warp floats (black areas) with contrasting weft floats (white areas) along the diagonals, but a sharp break along the diagonal does not occur because of the broken, or interrupted, nature of the threading and treadling.

Radial symmetry

True radial symmetry is achieved in *1d-f* by reversing the tie-ups while retaining the same as-drawn-in treadling arrangement. These designs are symmetrical vertically, horizontally, *and* diagonally because the tie-ups themselves are symmetrical with respect to an imaginary diagonal line running from the lower left corner of the design through the upper right corner of the tie-up. This diagonal bisects the design and tie-up so the triangles on either side of it mirror each other.

FROM SNOWFLAKE TO FROST

Artistic license allows any of these designs to qualify loosely as a snowflake although the actual hexagonal shape of snowflake crystals can only be simulated but not achieved in weaving since 60° angles are unnatural to the normal vertical and horizontal alignment of warp and weft.

Imitating frost patterns allows a designer to break away from the symmetry typical of snowflakes. Introducing occasional breaks in threading and treadling and varying the number of threads between breaks can mimic the fractured rhythm of frost patterns. Balance can be achieved by controlling the length of advancing twill runs. In *3*, for example, the typical symmetrical snowflake threading is modified: the threading shows an ascending stepped twill, a break, a descending stepped twill, a break, a narrower ascending twill, and a wider descending twill. Varying the sizes of the areas between breaks provides unexpected optical effects.

A newsletter article by Verda Elliott sharing the ideas for creating elaborate designs for 10 to 16 shafts found in *Textile Designing Pure and Applied* by E. B. Berry points out that a skip near the point at the center of a symmetrical threading can overcome static symmetry to produce the illusion of a more elaborate jacquard-like design. Although her article applies this principle to more than eight shafts, you might find it interesting to apply it to other pointed drafts for an 8-shaft loom. My wish to retain the rhythmic character of the design but break away from exact symmetry and easily recognized repeats took me just one step further to vary the proportions by lengthening or shortening sections of advancing twill between what used to be points.

Use a computer program to experiment with skipping and reversing directions or follow the draft in *2* to weave a frosty fantasy on only eight shafts—or try breaking the symmetry of other twills! ✂

2. Threading draft for Frost Crystals scarves

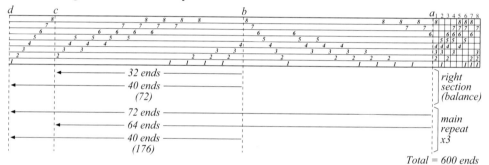

32 ends
40 ends
(72)

72 ends
64 ends
40 ends
(176)

right section (balance)

main repeat x3

Total = 600 ends

'FROST CRYSTALS' SCARVES

Soft colors, the sheen of silk, and the subtle shading of crystal patterns in these luxurious scarves will chase away the last of winter's chill. Put on extra warp and experiment with different tie-ups and treadling orders.

- ❑ Equipment. 8-shaft loom, 13" weaving width; 12-dent reed; 1 shuttle.
- ❑ Materials. Warp and weft: 60/2 spun silk (14,880 yds/lb, Treenway Silks), natural, ½ lb. Dye approximately 3 oz pale lavender (or color of your choice) for warp. Materials are sufficient for two scarves measuring 11½" × 72" each. Dye 2½ oz rose for weft of one scarf. Dye 2½ oz turquoise for weft of second scarf.
- ❑ Wind 602 ends of pale lavender silk 7 yds long.
- ❑ Sley 4 ends/dent in a 12-dent reed (48 epi); center for 12½" width.
- ❑ Thread according to the draft, beginning and ending with a floating selvedge: at right side to balance: *b* to *c*, *b* to *d*; for main repeat (3x): *a* to *d*, *a* to *c*, *b* to *d*.
- ❑ Weave as drawn in for 74" for each scarf. Expect approximately 3" of the warp tied to the apron rod to become fringe for the first scarf. Either hemstitch the beginning and end of each scarf while on the loom, or plan to secure with a twisted fringe after the pieces are removed from the loom. Leave approximately 6" unwoven space between scarves to allow for fringe. When weaving is complete, remove scarves from the loom, and cut them apart, leaving 3" fringe at each end.
- ❑ Finish by twisting a 4/4 plied fringe at the ends of each scarf. (If scarves were hemstitched during weaving, a plied fringe is optional.) Wash the scarves by hand in warm water; spin out excess water; press with warm iron while still damp.

3. Complete draft for Frost Crystals scarves

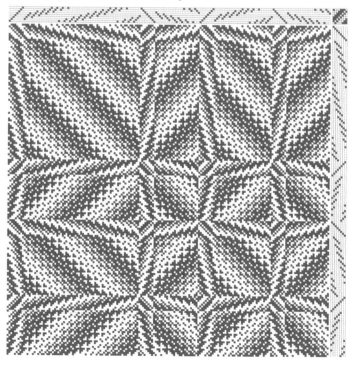

I thrills twill thrills twill thrills twill thrills twill thrills twill thrills twill thrills twill thrills twill thrills twill thrills twill thrills twill th
thrills twill thrills twill thrills twill thrills twill thrills twill thrills twill! thrills twill thrills twil
ll thrill twill thrill twill thrills twill thrills twill thrills twill thrills twill thrills twill thrills twill thrills twill thrills twill th

snowflakes and stars

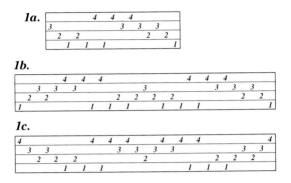

1a.

1b.

1c.

The good news is that the fancy skip twills that create snowflake and star patterns so popular with 8-shaft weavers can be designed and woven on only four shafts!

In advancing twills, a straight threading progresses for a number of shafts and then skips one or more shafts before beginning the straight progression again. The threading in *1a* shows a 3-thread progression over four shafts. Reversing the progression creates the threading in *1b*, which forms the X's in the drawdown in *2*. If that threading is inverted, as in *1c*, a different motif, an 'O,' can be woven at the same time an 'X' is produced in the first threading section and vice versa.

The twill progression can be broken at any place and repeated, reversed, or inverted to develop large and unusual threadings. Since most of the treadling orders are as-drawn-in, a long threading repeat means a long treadling repeat, usually requiring considerable concentration when weaving.

DESIGNING 4-SHAFT SKIP TWILLS

❏ Thread a straight twill for a selected number of ends. The skip can come after 3 threads, after 4, or 5, or more. The numbers of ends in each progression can also vary. Beware of too much variation; the design can become busy and indistinct.

❏ Draft the mirror image of the first progression.

❏ The first threading and its mirror image form one motif. Precede the motif with a series of 4-shaft straight or point threadings. Mirror that threading on the other side of the motif.

❏ For further variation, invert the threading you have just designed to form a second section of the draft.

❏ Treadle the draft as drawn in.

CANADIAN SNOWFLAKES

Examine the threading draft in *3*. Notice that the 'X' motif from *1* is separated from a second 'X' motif by a straight twill 4-3-2-1 on the right side and 1-2-3-4 on the left side. The center shows a 4-thread broken twill that reverses: 4-2-3-1-3-2-4. This broken twill imitates the satin threading that separates the motifs in typical 8-shaft snowflakes, see Ruth Morrison, 'Silk Snowflakes and Stars,' pp. 55–57.

The 'star' in these drafts is the large cross that fills the entire drawdown. It is less prominent in the 4-shaft version than it is in the 8-shaft version. Several point twills are threaded on both sides of the star to add a secondary motif. Use this draft for scarves or linens; see fabric examples, p. 47. ✂

2. Advancing and straight twills on four shafts

3. Advancing and broken twills on four shafts

variations on a theme

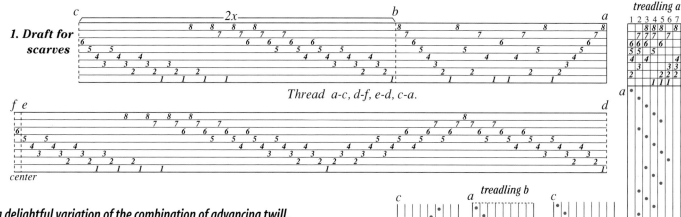

1. Draft for scarves

Thread a-c, d-f, e-d, c-a.

center

Here's a delightful variation of the combination of advancing twill, straight twill, and satin used in snowflake threading drafts. By trying a variety of different treadlings, you can thread once and then keep tying on different-colored short warps to weave a multitude of scarves on the same threading—each unique.

These two scarves use the same threading and treadling but different warps. Cut the first scarf from the loom, securing cut warp ends at the reed. Wind the second warp and tie each end of the new warp to a successive end of the old warp with an overhand knot. Secure the new warp with lease sticks while tying on, or hold the cross in your left hand and pick off each end in turn. Beam the new warp, jiggling the knots carefully through the reed and heddles.

❑ Equipment. 8-shaft loom, 10" weaving width; 10-dent reed; 1 shuttle.

❑ Materials. Warp for scarf A: 20/2 pearl cotton (8400 yds/lb, Halcyon Yarn) black 1½ oz; ½ oz total of small amounts turquoise, green, maroon, red, blue. Weft for scarf A: 20/2 rayon (8400 yds/lb, Robin and Russ Handweavers), natural, 2 oz. Warp for scarf B: 20/2 pearl cotton (8400 yds/lb), ½ oz black and 1½ oz total of yellow, yellow-gold, yellow-orange, orange, red-orange, rust, maroon, purple, red, red-violet, fuchsia, lavender, or other colors that can be gradated similarly, 2 oz total. Weft for scarf B: #6 silk cord (4650 yds/lb, The Silk Tree), black, 2 oz.

❑ Wind a warp of 399 ends 2½ yds long (includes 2 floating selvedges). For scarf A, scatter colors randomly at approx 2 for every 10 black. For scarf B, begin and end with 30 black and gradate other colors available in color-wheel order for 339 remaining ends, beginning with yellow and ending with lavender. When changing hues, alternate the new hue 1/1 with the old hue for a round or two on the warping board.

❑ Sley 4/dent in a 10-dent reed, 40 epi; center for 10".

❑ Thread following the draft in *1*, *a* to *c* (right to left), *d* to *f* (right to left), *e* to *d* (left to right), *c* to *a* (left to right).

❑ Weave *a* to *b*, *c* to *d* for 60" following treadling *a* for both scarves. Use treadling *b* if you want a scarf with an entirely different design. Allow 8" for fringe at each end of each scarf.

❑ Remove the scarf from the loom and prepare a twisted fringe: twist 4 ends in one direction; twist the next 4 ends in the same direction; twist both groups together in the opposite direction and secure with an overhand knot.

❑ Handwash in warm water with 1 tsp Ivory liquid. Squeeze out water; hang to dry. When scarf is almost dry, steam press thoroughly. ✂

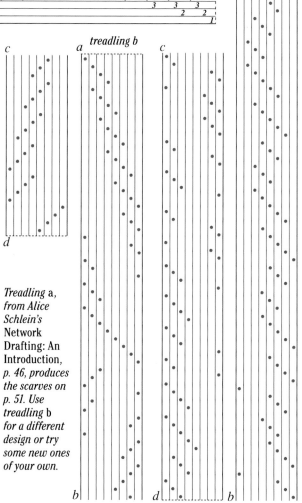

Treadling a, *from Alice Schlein's* Network Drafting: An Introduction, *p. 46, produces the scarves on p. 51. Use treadling* b *for a different design or try some new ones of your own.*

ll thrills **twill** thrills twill thrills twill **thrills** twill thrills twill **thrills** twill thrills twill thrills **twill** thrills twill thrills twill t
twill **thrills** twill thrills twill thrills twill thrills twill **thrills** twill thrills twill thrills twill thrills twill thrills twill thrills twill thrills twi
ill thrill twill thrill twill **thrills** **twill** thrills twill thrills twill thrills twill **thrills** twill thrills twill **thrills** twill thrills twill thrills twill thrills twill th

Advancing twills provide endless hours of designing delight. Select or create an advancing-twill threading, and then put on a long warp for a series of scarves, each with a different treadling (see also Diane Kelly, pages 58–60). The two scarves shown here use the same draft but a different warp and weft.

a designer's heart's desire

1. Advancing twill snowflakes

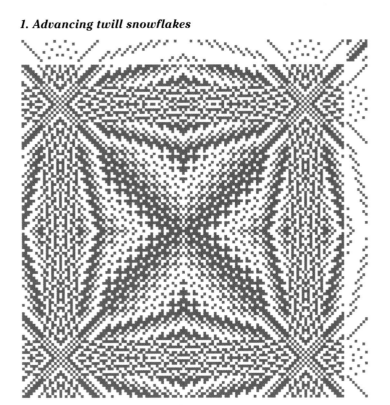

2. Advancing twill hearts

A passionate involvement with advancing twills can fulfill a weaving designer's heart's desire. Any motif which can be drafted on an ordinary 8-shaft point-twill threading can become a motif for an advancing twill. The design tool is the treadling sequence. The result is often more interesting than if it were woven in a block weave that can produce eight distinct blocks.

The advancing point-twill threading in *1* consists of 4-end runs with an advance of 1. These runs create tiny diagonals that build up to form the stronger diagonals of the X-shaped motif and give it a look of intricacy, much like finely rendered pencil lines or a delicate etching. With a computer drafting program and a mouse as the 'pencil,' weavers can freely draw beautiful images in fabric.

DEVELOPING AN IMAGE

Notice in *1* that the top half of the classic X motif or 'snowflake' looks like the bottom of a heart. Since the threading is symmetrical and the top half of a heart is also symmetrical, only the treadling need be altered to create a more accurate heart shape.

'Only the treadling' would not be encouraging words if they meant creating a new shape at the loom or doing drawdowns with pencil and paper. With a computer weaving program, however, the treadling can be altered pick by pick and the results viewed, evaluated, and accepted or rejected immediately.

To derive the heart motif with *Fiberworks PCW* or other drawdown program as the drawing tools and the draft in *1* as the starting point, first delete the bottom half of the X motif and then insert empty weft rows between the remaining V-shape and the top border. To create the curves of the heart, place harmonic runs in the empty area—notice the elongated half-heart shape in the treadling section in *2*. Can you separate visually the areas in the treadling that correspond to the bottom half of the X and top half of the heart?

To get a clear, readable image, the juxtaposition of positive and negative (black vs white) areas must be considered carefully. A 3/3/ 1/1 tie-up produces maximum contrast on eight shafts, with 3-thread floats in warp vs weft areas. The order of the ties in the tie-up also matters. 'Wrapping' the tie-up to the right one treadle at a time reveals a slightly different emphasis for the heart in each of the eight possible orders. The tie-up in *2* produces a weft-dominant background, a warp-dominant outline of the heart, and a weft-dominant center (the warp is black). Extending the bottom of the heart shape by several 4-end runs in the treadling emphasizes the heart's point. The satin border between images acts to frame the motifs.

THE PROOF IS IN THE WEAVING

A draft can only predict what the warp and weft will do. People who say that you never have to weave if you have a computer for drafting do not understand fabric. In the case of advancing twills a slight collapse occurs along the twill lines, adding depth and beauty to the finished cloth. To perfect the shape of a motif, plan to sample on the loom!

thrills **twill** thrills **twill** thrills twill thrills twill thrills **twill** thrills twill thrills twill **thrills** twill thrills twill thrills twill thrills twill **thrills** twill thrills twill t
thrills twill thrills twill thrills twill thrills twill thrills twill thrills twill thrills twill thrills twill thrills twill thrills twil! thrills twill thrills twi
thrill twill thrill twill **thrills** **twill** thrills twill thrills twill thrills twill thrills twill **thrills** twill thrills twill thrills twill thrills twill thrills twill th

Marie Bunke Kim Marie Bunke Kim Marie Bunke Kim Marie Bunke Kim Marie Bunke Kim Marie Bu

Tiny twill runs create these shimmering hearts. Follow the directions on page 54 to weave this scarf or use Kim's technique to design your own images. Start with an advancing-twill threading draft and a basic computer weaving program, and play with making changes to the treadling sequence.

will thrills twill thrills twill thrills twill thrills twill thrills twill thrills twill thrills twill thrills twill thrills twill thrills twill thrills twill thrills twill thrills twill
ills twill thrills twill thrills twill thrills twill thrills twill thrills twill thrills twill thrills twill thrills twill thrills twill thrills twill thrills twill thrills twill th
ills twill thrills twill thrills twill thrills twill thrills twill thrilss twill thrills twill thrills twill thrills twill thrills twill thrills twill thrills twill

heart-throb scarf

Kim Marie Bunke Kim Marie Bunke Kim Marie Bunke Kim Marie Bunke **Kim Marie Bunke** *Kim Marie*

1. Draft for Heart-Throb scarf

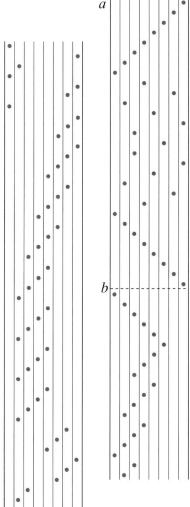

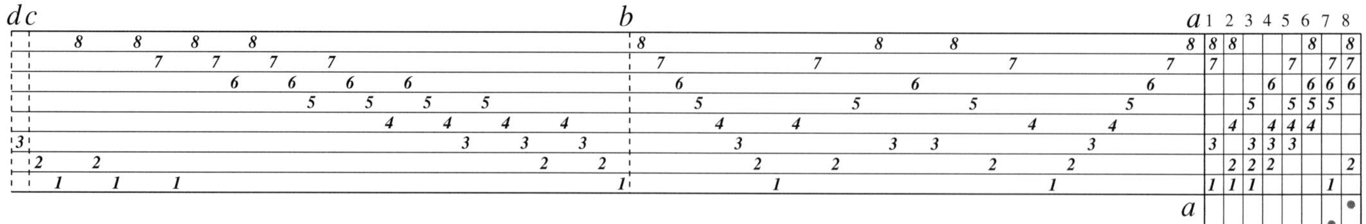

Hearts in advancing twill shimmer in this dressy scarf. Just the right beads are added as fringe, repeating the heart motif as well as lending weight and drape to the scarf. Wear it on special occasions—and display it in the loom room on its days off.

The delicacy of these shimmering hearts (see p. 53) and the elegance of the fabric are due to very fine threads in both warp and weft—both are sewing thread. If you haven't woven with sewing thread before, a narrow scarf makes a good first project. Instructions here are for a back-to-front warping method that works well with fine threads.

❑ Equipment. 8-shaft loom, 8" weaving width; 10-dent reed; 1 shuttle; ¼" raddle; beading and hand-sewing needles.

❑ Materials. Warp: 50/3 mercerized cotton sewing thread (14,000 yds/lb), black, 1400 yds. Weft: 50/3 mercerized cotton sewing thread, red, 864 yds; 42 red heart-shaped beads, 328 size 11 black opaque seed beads (about one 12" strand), beeswax.

❑ Wind a warp of 495 ends 2½ yds long with a threading cross at one end and at the other end a cross that groups together the number of threads in each ¼" raddle dent (15 threads). If you don't have a ¼" raddle, you can easily make one by hammering finishing nails ¼" apart along the center of a narrow board; stagger them on two sides of the center line to avoid splitting the board.

❑ Spread the warp in the raddle using the raddle cross, 15 ends/dent (8¼" weaving width). Attach this end of the warp to the apron rod and beam the warp with firm and even tension using only the raddle's divisions to straighten and spread the threads (do not use lease sticks). When the threading cross (at the other end of the warp) reaches a convenient threading position behind the shafts, insert lease sticks in the cross and secure them for threading. Drop the last 2 ends on each side (more threads are beamed than needed so that all raddle dents have an equal number of ends) and use 1 end on each side as a floating selvedge.

❑ Thread following the draft in *1*: [*a* to *d* (right to left), *c* to *b* (left to right)] 5x, *a* to *b* 1x.

❑ Sley 6/dent in a 10-dent reed, 60 epi; center for 8⅙".

❑ Weave following the draft in *1*. For the first half of the scarf weave *a* to *c* for about 27", ending with a complete repeat of *a* to *c*. Then weave *a* to *b* 1x, then *c* to *a* for about 27" (or whatever number of inches equals the length of the first half of the scarf). This keeps the hearts right-side up on both sides of the finished scarf during wear.

❑ Finish by removing the scarf from the loom. Fold the scarf at the reversal point and make sure you have the same number of hearts on each half. If not, trim the longer side so that both sides are equal (allowing for hem). Secure the ends with narrow machine zigzagging. Soak the fabric in warm water and mild soap; then gently wash by hand. Rinse well and squeeze dry. Press with iron while still damp. Turn ends under twice and handsew hems with tiny stitches.

❑ Prepare the beaded fringe by first coating a length of black sewing thread with beeswax to prevent tangling, and thread in a beading needle. Anchor the thread to the hem at one selvedge. Bring the needle up at the center of the first satin section on the edge. String 3 black seed beads, 1 heart bead, and 1 more black seed bead as a stop. Run the thread back up through all but the stop bead. Stitch through the fabric to anchor the fringe. Pass the needle through the hem to a point midway between the satin border and the center of the heart motif. Make another fringe strand in exactly the same way as the first except use 7 seed beads. Move to the center of the heart motif and make another fringe strand in exactly the same way as before except use 11 seed beads. Move to the next midway point, use 7 beads for a fringe; use 3 seed beads for the next fringe, and continue (the order of seed beads per fringe is: 3-7-11-7-3-7-11-7-3-7-11-7-3-7-11-7-3-7-11-7-3). Anchor the thread in the hem at the other edge of the scarf and repeat the fringe process on the other end of the scarf. ✄

Thread (a–d, c–b)5x; a–b.
Weave a–c for 27"; c–a for 27"
(include only complete repeats).

54

ll thrills twill thr lls twill thrills twill thrills twill thrills twill thrills twill thrills twill thrills twill thrills twill thrills twill thrills twill
twill thrills t ll ll thr ll s twill thr twill thrills twill thrills twill thrills twill thrills twill thrills twill
ll thrill twill thrill twill thrills twill thrills twill thrills twill thrills twill thrills twill thrills twill thrills twill

silk snowflakes and stars

You'd never think to look at it that this odd threading draft could produce such spectacular patterning. The discoveries begin with its appearance in an old Shuttle-Craft Guild Bulletin (see the Bibliography, page 45). The original draft does not show a twill progression in the threading—instead it looks almost completely random—and the connection between it and the large stars or snowflakes it produces appears quite mystifying!

A section of the original draft is shown in *1*. The structure is a simple weave (one warp and one weft) that produces a twill-like progression of floats of varying lengths along a diagonal. The fabric is woven 'tromp as writ,' or 'as drawn in'—i.e., the treadles are depressed following the threading order. (For example, treadles 1–8 are first used in sequence followed by treadles 3, 6, 1, 4, 7, etc.) Keeping track of one's position in either the threading or the treadling sequences for this draft is not easy!

1. Swedish snowflake (part of original draft)

2. Swedish snowflake (complete revised draft)

FROM SKIP SATIN TO SKIP TWILL

David Xenakis puzzled over this threading order, observing the satin-like sequence of the threads in the field and the straight-twill sequence in the border. Knowing that a threaded twill can be treadled to produce satin or vice versa, he tried reversing the positions of the almost-satin and the twill. The result is the draft in *2*. (To maintain exactly the same structure, the same exchanges must be made in the tie-up and in the order of the treadles in the tie-up, that is, every 1 becomes a 3, 2 becomes 6, 3→1, 4→4, 5→7, 6→2, 7→5, 8→8; treadle 1 becomes treadle 3; treadle 2 becomes treadle 6, etc.)

Rewriting the draft not only makes the threading and treadling sequences easier to follow, it also reveals the previously obscured source of the irregular floats that form the star-shaped motifs. The center motif is created by an advancing—or skip—twill in which each twill run consists of 4 ends. Each group of 4 begins on the next shaft up in the ascending sequence or on the next shaft down in the descending sequence (an advance of 1; see Ingrid Boesel, pp. 38–41). When treadled with a 3/1/1/3 twill tie-up, the scattered skips produce a wide variety of interlacements, from plain weave to 1:3 twill to areas with 6-thread floats (wherever the two adjacent 4-thread groups share the three shafts that are not raised, for example).

David's stars

In the draft in *3*, p. 56, David extends the advancing twill so that it includes 2-, 3-, 5-, 6-, and 7-end runs. A single repeat of all of these sequences and their miror-image reverse requires almost 400 ends! The resulting motif, when treadled as drawn in, is a very large star that melts into a twill background—a design that like the original Swedish snowflake appears much more complex than seems possible on only eight shafts. Two factors contribute to that impression: the varying nature of the interlacements and the absence of a regular and small- or medium-scale repeat.

SWEDISH SNOWFLAKE SHAWL

Ruth Morrison uses the draft in *2* to weave a fine natural-silk shawl. A bit of beading in the fringes adds a touch of luxury. The silk is heavy enough to produce drape suitable for a shawl, yet fine enough to give the snowflake design special delicacy.

❏ Equipment. 8-shaft loom, 40" weaving width; 10-dent reed; 1 shuttle.

❏ Materials. Warp and weft: 30/2 pearl silk (7850 yds/lb, Halcyon, item 142), natural, six 3½ oz skeins; about 1200 small beads such as are used for earrings (crystal and silver).

❏ Wind a warp of 1541 ends (includes 2 ends for floating selvedges) 3 yds long. This amount pro-

duces one shawl with finished measurements (including 6" fringe) of 100" x 35". (If your loom requires an unusual amount of loom waste, use a dummy warp to conserve the expensive silk: Wind, thread, and beam a 1–2 yd 20/2 cotton warp following the directions given for the silk warp. Then wind the silk warp and tie on each silk end to a cotton end using an overhand knot. Pass the knots through reed and heddles by tugging and jiggling gently, and beam the silk warp in the same way as the cotton warp.)

❏ Sley 4/dent in a 10-dent reed, 40 epi; center for 38½" weaving width.

❏ Thread following the draft in *2*: a to b 8x (border), a to d 14x, a to e 1x, c to e 8x (border).

❏ Weave as drawn in (i.e., read the threading draft as though it is the treadling draft, using the corresponding treadle number for each shaft number in the threading).

❏ Finish by preparing twisted fringe: Take 4 warp ends in each hand and twist them in the same direction until they are almost overtwisted. Then lay them beside each other and let them twist back on each other. Tie the end in an overhand knot to secure.

❏ Machine wash the shawl, gentle cycle, cool water, in Ivory liquid. Lay flat to dry. For beaded finish, see instructions for shawl, p. 56.

ill thrills twill thrills twill thrills twill thrills twill thrills twill thrills twill thrills twill thrills twill thrills twill thrills twill thrills twill thrills twill
thrills twill thrills twill thrills twill thrills twill thrills twill thrills twill thrills twill thrills twill thrills twill thrills twill thrills twill thrills twill th
lls twill thrills twill thrills twill thrills twill thrills twill thrillss twill thrills twill thrills twill thrills twill thrills twill thrills twill thrills twill thrills twill

3. The draft for David's stars

STARBURST SHAWL

- ❑ Equipment. 8-shaft loom, 38" weaving width; 12-dent reed; 1 shuttle.
- ❑ Materials. Warp and weft: 30/2 Gemstone silk (7350 yds/lb, Halcyon Yarns, item 157); for warp Garnet (color #8), three 3½ oz skeins, for weft Rose Jade (color #7), three 3½ oz skeins, about 1200 small beads (such as are used for earrings).
- ❑ Wind a warp of 1332 ends (includes 2 ends for floating selvedges) 3 yds long. This provides one shawl with finished measurements (including 7" fringe) of 103" x 35".
- ❑ Sley 3/dent in a 12-dent reed, 36 epi; center for 37".
- ❑ Thread following the draft in 3: d–g 8x, g–h 1x for border (113 ends); c–j 1x (154 ends); i–a 1x (199 ends); b–j 1x (199 ends); i–a 1x (199 ends); b–j 1x (199 ends); i–c 1x (154 ends); repeat border above (113 ends); 1330 total ends plus 2 floating selvedges. For a diamond-shaped center in the star, substitute e for i and f for j in the above instructions (the design pivots in the center of the satin sequence instead of repeating it).
- ❑ Weave as drawn in.
- ❑ Finish as for first shawl. For beading, thread a needle with matching sewing thread and run the thread along the fringed edge until reaching a point between the bouts of twisted fringe. Bring the needle out to pick up 7 beads (or preferred number), then through an 8th (silver is used for this bead on the natural silk shawl), and then back through the first seven and again into the edge of the shawl; repeat. ✄

56

The natural silk shawl, woven by Ruth Morrison, uses the Swedish snowflake draft introduced to North American weavers by Mary Meigs Atwater. David Xenakis adds twill runs of increasing and decreasing sizes to the original draft for a much larger star motif in the garnet shawl, also woven by Ruth Morrison.

ill thrills twill thrills twill thrills twill thrills twill thrills twill thrills twill thrills twill thrills twill thrills twill thrills twill thrills twill thrills twill
thrills twill thrills twill thrills twill thrills twill thrills twill thrills twill thrills twill thrills twill thrills twill thrills twill thrills twill thrills twill th
ills twill thrills twill thrills twill thrills twill thrills twill thrills twill thrills twill thrills twill thrills twill thrills twill thrills twill thrills twill thrill

no two alike

1. Draft for 8-shaft scarves

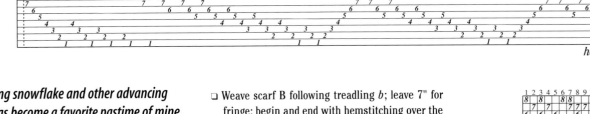

c b
a 1 2 3 4 5 6 7 8 9 10

heading a

Designing snowflake and other advancing twills has become a favorite pastime of mine. Combining advancing, point, and straight twills creates patterns that seem much more complicated than they really are. Experiment with combinations in the treadling, too, and the design options become truly amazing.

Most snowflake twills are treadled as drawn in, but there are many other possibilities (see pp. 38–57 for more about snowflake and other advancing twill variations). Even when designs are limited to only eight shafts there are seemingly endless options. Here are two treadling sequences on a single 8-shaft threading for two scarves. In these scarves, a matte merino weft against a silk warp makes the pattern shine. Follow the directions given here to weave these scarves or try other treadling options on the same threading—or draft some combinations of your own. You will find that snowflake twills become a passion for you, too!

❑ Equipment. 8-shaft loom, 9" weaving width; 7-dent reed (a 10-dent reed can be substituted); 1 shuttle.

❑ Materials. Warp: 12/2 silk (2950 yds/lb, Treenway Silks), natural, 5½ oz. The warp for these scarves is hand-dyed in subtle shades of light gray. Weft for scarf A: 18/2 merino (5040 yds/lb, JaggerSpun), Black, 1 oz. Weft for scarf B: 18/2 merino (5040 yds/lb, JaggerSpun), Shale, 1 oz.

❑ Wind a warp of 189 ends, 5 yds long (includes 2 floating selvedges and approximately 1 yd loom waste, some of which is used for fringe).

❑ Sley 3/dent in a 7-dent reed, 21 epi; center for 9". (If you are using a 10-dent reed, sley 2/dent, 20 epi; center for 9½".) Sley the floating selvedges in a separate dent on each side.

❑ Thread following the draft in *1*. Thread from *a* to *c* 1x; then reverse and thread from *b* to *a*.

❑ Weave scarf A following treadling *a*; leave 7" for fringe. Weave 10 pattern repeats. After weaving the first inch or so, hemstitch over the first 2 picks. Hemstitch again over the last 2 picks.

❑ Weave scarf B following treadling *b*; leave 7" for fringe; begin and end with hemstitching over the first and last 2 picks. Weave 20 pattern repeats.

❑ Finish by removing the scarves from the loom and securing the ends with a twisted fringe (twist two groups of 2 ends each in the same direction separately; then twist the two groups together in the opposite direction, 4 ends/fringe, and secure with an overhand knot).

❑ Soak scarves in lukewarm water in the washing machine for 10–15 minutes, using a mild soap such as Ivory liquid or Orvus Paste. Agitate on gentle cycle for 10 seconds. Remove scarves to add clean rinse water. (Make sure the rinse water is the same temperature as the wash water.) Soak again for 10–15 minutes in the rinse water and spin to remove excess water. Lay flat to dry. This process will full the merino yarn very slightly and accentuate the twill designs. The finished sizes are 7½" x 60" for scarf A and 7½" x 57" for scarf B (scarves woven with a 10-dent reed will be slightly wider).

Combining twills on 16 shafts

If you're intrigued by the design possibilities of mixing advancing, point, and straight twills on eight shafts and you are lucky enough to have a loom with more than eight, you'll want to apply these same principles to the number of shafts you have. The scarves on p. 60 are woven on 16 shafts; the threading is a simple point twill. The treadling for scarf C is a networked treadling, and the treadling for scarf D is an advancing twill.

To weave these scarves, use the same materials as for the 8-shaft scarves. Thread a 16-shaft point 6x (183 ends, includes 2 ends for floating selvedges). The networked treadling for scarf C is shown in *2*, p. 60. The treadling for scarf D is a straight advancing twill (with a run of 4 and an advance of 1, i.e., 1234, 2345, 3456, 4567, etc.) using a similar twill tie-up. Don't stop with these treadling ideas, try other advancing, M and W, and networked twills! ✄

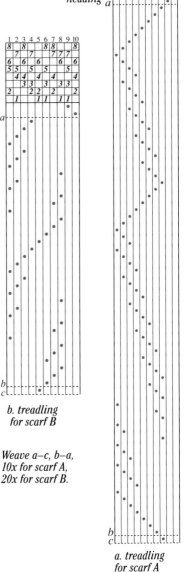

b
c

b. treadling for scarf B

Weave a–c, b–a, 10x for scarf A, 20x for scarf B.

b
c

a. treadling for scarf A

thrills twill thrills twill thrills twill thrills twill thrills twill thrills twill thrills twill thrills twill thrills twill thrills twill thrills twill thrills twill thrills twill thrills twill thrills twill t
twill thrills twill thrills twill thrills thrills twill thrills twill thrills twill thrills twill thrills twill thrills twill thrills twi
twill thrill twill thrill twill thrills twill thrills twill thrills twill thrills thrills twill thrills twill thrills twill thrills twill thrills twill thrills twill thrills twill th

These scarves both share the same threading: a mix of straight, advancing, and point twills. The two treadlings mix point and advancing twills in different ways to produce two very different designs. Use a computer drawdown program to test other treadling schemes and put on a long warp!

twill thrills twill thrills

2. Scarf C treadling

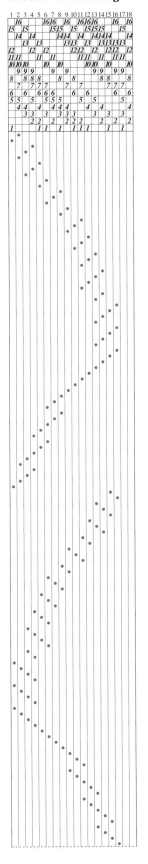

1	2	3	4	5	6	7	8	9	10	11	12	13	14	15	16	17	18
16			16	16		16		16	16	16			16		16		
15		15			15	15		15	15	15	15			15			
	14		14				14	14		14		14	14	14		14	
		13		13				13	13		13		13	13	13	13	
12			12		12			12	12		12		12	12		12	
11	11			11		11			11	11		11		11	11		
10	10	10			10		10			10	10		10		10		
	9	9	9			9		9			9	9		9	9		9
8		8	8	8			8		8			8	8			7 7	8
	7		7	7	7			7		7					7	7	7
6		6		6	6	6			6		6				6		6
5	5		5		5	5	5			5				5			5
		4	4		4	4	4		4			4		4			4
		3	3		3	3	3		3	3		3			3		
		2	2		2	2	2		2			2		2			2
1				1	1		1		1	1	1			1		1	

On sixteen shafts, the possibilities increase dramatically, even with a simple point-twill threading. The lovely feather design in scarf C is created with the networked treadling in 2, the long points in scarf D with an advancing twill treadling (a run of 4, an advance of 1).

I thrills twill thrills twill thrills twill thrills twill thrills twill thrills twill thrills twill thrills twill thrills twill thrills twill thrills twill thrills twill thrills twill thrills twill th
twill thrills twill thrills twill thrills twill thrills twill thrills twill thrills twill thrills twill thrills twill thrills twill thrills twill thrills twill thrills twill thrills twill thrills twill th
I thrill twill thrill twill thrills twill thrills twill thrills twill thrills twill thrills twill thrills twill thrills twill thrills twill thrills twill thrills twill thrills twill thrills twill th

network drafting with twills

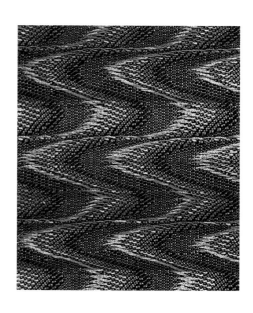

network drafting: more for less

1a. Allowed: traveler progresses from east to west

1b. Not allowed: traveler backtracks to the east

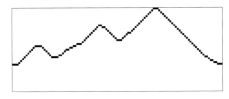

1c. Design created when pattern line is 'treadled' as drawn in

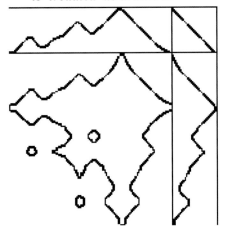

2. Flipping threadings and treadlings

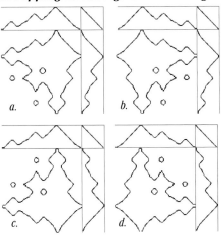

The publication in 1988 of Shaft Weaving and Graph Design, *an English translation of* Tissage à Lames et Graphisme *by French mathematicians Olivier Masson and François Roussel, introduced to English-speaking weavers a new type of patterning. This new patterning produces circles, sweeping curves, and other large-scale designs normally not possible with block weaves, yet can be woven in all of the familiar block-weave structures such as twill, satin, double weave, summer and winter, overshot, and more. Best of all, they can be woven on a conventional loom without draw devices, jacquard heads, or even pick-up sticks!*

This new design technique that American weavers call 'network drafting' is suitable for both treadle and dobby looms. A dobby provides an advantage: one quickly runs out of treadles weaving networked patterns on a conventional loom. As few as eight shafts can produce interesting designs, although the more shafts available, the greater the design potential.

A 16-shaft loom with mechanical dobby attachment is ideal for networked patterning. A computer-assisted dobby device makes the weaving process easier, but is not essential since all the drafting can be done with paper, pen, scissors, and paste.

Curiously, the table loom is useful for weaving networked samples, allowing free choice of shafts to lift if you don't mind weaving s-l-o-w-l-y!

DOWN SIDE

What *won't* network drafting do? It won't produce sharp-edged pattern blocks. The savvy weaver will use its characteristic fuzziness to advantage. Imagine the watery-looking edges of ikat designs, and you can visualize the effect.

Network drafting won't replace the jacquard loom. If you want to weave verses, railroad locomotives, or Victorian mansions, then get yourself a drawloom, a jacquard mechanism, or a pick-up stick. But if you'd like to use the multishaft loom you already own to expand the scope of your patterning opportunities, then give network drafting a try.

GAME PLAN

In order to produce a weavable draft, the following steps are necessary:

1. Draw a curve to produce a *pattern line*
2. Reduce the pattern line to the shafts available by
   a. *digitizing*, or
   b. *telescoping*
3. Decide on a weave structure and place the reduced pattern line onto a *network* to develop a threading draft
4. Devise a lifting sequence
   a. a tie-up and treadling for treadle loom, or
   b. dobby peg plan

THE PATTERN LINE

The first step is to draw the pattern line that will be used to create the threading. Imagine a traveler with a road map of Colorado, a state whose borders constitute a rectangle, planning a motor trip. This traveler wishes to travel from Colorado's eastern border to its western border, sometimes taking in the sights to the north and sometimes veering south, but *at no time backtracking to the east*; compare *1a* and *1b*.

If this 'threading' is woven as drawn in using a direct tie-up (one treadle per shaft), the resulting drawdown appears in *1c*. (Note that this is not yet a draft for weaving; it is a design, similar to the way a profile draft is a design. It must be translated into a weave structure.)

A different 'treadling' will produce a different design. Return to the example of the Colorado traveler, and start at the northern border and meander in any direction *except north* until you reach the southern border.

Any portion of this 'draft'—threading, treadling, or tie-up—can be flipped vertically or horizontally to produce different orientations of the pattern (*2*). A computer drafting program is useful for quickly visualizing the results of these metamorphoses.

A pattern line can be created in many different ways: by drawing freehand with a pencil, brush, or other drawing tool; by cutting shapes from stiff paper and tracing their curves onto the rectangle; by using a computer drawing or weaving program with a mouse. I have derived pattern lines from drawings of musical instruments, the contours of automobiles from magazine ads, and the leaves of house plants—all have yielded interesting results.

thrills twill thrills twill thrills twill thrills twill thrills twill thrills twill thrills twill thrills twill thrills twill thrills twill thrills twill t
twill thrills twill thrills twill thrills twill thrills twill thrills twill thrills twill thrills twill thrills twill thrills twill thrills twill
thrill twill thrill twill thrills twill thrills twill thrills twill thrills twill thrills twill thrills twill thrills twill thrills twill th

ce Schlein Alice Schlein Alice Schlein Alice Schlein Alice Schlein Alice Schlein Alice Schlein Alice Sc

To practice, start with a graph-paper rectangle 32 squares high and 96 squares wide, a 32-shaft 'threading' of 96 warp ends. (Few weavers have looms with 32 shafts, but a 32–shaft grid allows a large and sweeping curve. The draft can be reduced later to the number of shafts available.) Select a freehand curve representing, say, an automobile, and plot the resulting curve on graph paper to get a pattern line. Every vertical column must contain one, but only one, marked square. A drawdown resulting from an 'automobile' pattern line and a direct tie-up 'treadled' as drawn in is shown in *3*.

There are practical limits to this process, of course—the smoother the curve, the greater the number of required horizontal rows on the graph. Most looms are limited to *fewer* than 32 shafts rather than more, which leads to the next step.

THE NETWORK AND THE INITIAL

Once the pattern line is developed, it can be turned into a weavable draft by placing it on a *network* based on a weave structure.

A network is a map of *possible* positions for each warp thread. It is created by multiples of what is called the *initial*, a group of threads capable of producing a selected weave structure. For example, the 4-shaft/4-thread twill initial in *4a* is repeated twice for an 8-shaft draft, three times for a 12-shaft draft, and four times for a 16-shaft draft (*4b-4d*). The network is extended horizontally to equal the number of warp ends in the repeat, including only *complete* repeats of the initial (*4e*).

A variety of initials can be used as bases for developing threadings. *5d* shows an initial that repeats on four shafts and six ends, and *5e* shows

an initial that repeats on five shafts and five ends. (The latter can produce patterns based on 5-shaft satin.) Weavers with more than 20 shafts can select initials that use larger numbers of shafts, but the weaver with 16 or fewer shafts will be wise to stick to initials using five or fewer.

LIMITING PATTERN-LINE HEIGHT: THE SHAFT RULE

To determine the maximum height (number of horizontal rows) of a pattern line for the number of shafts available, subtract the number used in the selected initial from the number of shafts on the loom, and add 1. Using the 4-thread twill initial on a 16-shaft loom, therefore, subtract 4 from 16 = 12; add 1 = 13. To use the same initial on a 12-shaft loom: 12 – 4 + 1 = 9 is the limiting height of the pattern line. The same initial used on an 8-shaft loom yields a limiting height of 5, which is not a lot of room to develop curves, but it can be done! (See more about this restriction, which I call the shaft rule, and exceptions to it on pp. 71–77).

There are two choices for reducing the height of a pattern line, *digitizing* and *telescoping*, each with its advantages and disadvantages. To see how they work, we'll use each to reduce the 32-row pattern line in *3* to a 13-row height to place on a 16-shaft network based on a 4-end initial.

DIGITIZING AND TELESCOPING

To reduce a pattern line by digitizing, take the height of the original line (32); divide it by the height of the new line (13). The quotient, 2 *plus a remainder*, tells us how many shafts in the 32-shaft draft must be threaded as one shaft in the new draft. Since there is a remainder, we must alternate the substitution of two shafts for one with three shafts for one. Warp threads assigned to shafts 1 and 2 in the *old* draft will be assigned to shaft 1 in the *new* draft; 3, 4, and 5 in the *old* draft become 2 in the *new* draft, and so on, until 31 and 32 in the *old* draft become 13 in the *new* draft. It is helpful to set up a table of old and new shaft numbers as in *6a*, p. 64, to effect the transformation. Or, you can simply cut up the pattern line into 2- and 3-square segments and assign each segment its new shaft number.

To reduce a pattern line by telescoping, divide it into horizontal segments so that *each segment* is the same number of rows high as the new reduced height (or fewer if the division doesn't come out even). Thirty-two rows contain two segments of 13

3. 'Automobile' pattern line

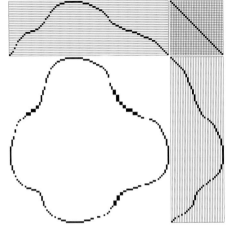

4a. 4-shaft initial

4b–4d. 4-shaft initial used for 8-, 12-, and 16 shaft networks

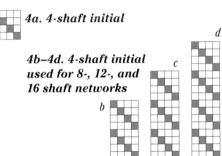

4e. 16-shaft network with 32 ends

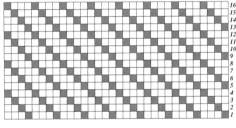

5. Some other initials

height 3
height 4
height 5
height 6
height 8

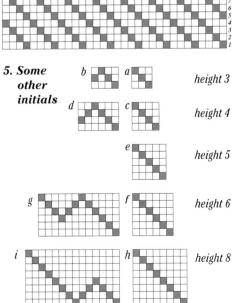

will thrills twill thrills twill thrills twill thrills twill thrills twill thrills twill thrills twill thrills twill thrills twill thrills twill thrills twill thrills twill thrills twill thrills twill thrills twill th thrills twill thrills twill thrills twill thrills twill thrills twill thrills twill thrills twill thrills twill thrills twill thrills twill thrills twill thrills twill thrills twill thrills twill thrills twill t ills twill thrills twill thrills twill thrills twill thrills twill thrillss twill thrills twill thrills twill thrills twill thrills twill thrills twill thrills twill thrills twill thri

6a. Digitizing		6b. Telescoping	
old	*new*	*old*	*new*
32	13	32	6
31	13	31	5
30	12	30	4
29	12	29	3
28	12	28	2
27	11	27	1
26	11	26	13
25	10	25	12
24	10	24	11
23	10	23	10
22	9	22	9
21	9	21	8
20	8	20	7
19	8	19	6
18	8	18	5
17	7	17	4
16	7	16	3
15	6	15	2
14	6	14	1
13	6	13	13
12	5	12	12
11	5	11	11
10	4	10	10
9	4	9	9
8	4	8	8
7	3	7	7
6	3	6	6
5	2	5	5
4	2	4	4
3	2	3	3
2	1	2	2
1	1	1	1

rows each and one segment of 6. The segments are then stacked one on top of another, or telescoped. (Imagine the original pattern line as if drawn on clear acetate with all the layers showing through in the final sandwich.) *6b* shows the table of old and new shaft numbers derived by telescoping.

Reducing a pattern line by digitizing produces a blockier-looking curve than the original but without parallel curves or 'harmonics.' Reducing a pattern line by telescoping retains the smoothness of the original curve but does produce harmonics. Blockiness and/or harmonics are neither desirable nor undesirable in themselves; the informed weaver can choose the best method for an intended effect. Compare *7a* and *7b*.

Pattern lines in the treadling can be reduced in the same way as threading pattern lines.

THE WEAVE DRAFT

It is now time to put all the pieces together and create a thread-by-thread draft to weave 'Automobile.' Using the network in *4e* and the pattern line in *7a*:
☐ Step 1. Trace the pattern line onto the 16-shaft network, restraining the pattern line to the lower 13 shafts (*8a*). For the sake of clarity, use a colored pen for the pattern line.

☐ Step 2. Wherever the pattern line falls on a network square (shaded gray in *8a*, you have a 'hit.' Fill in each 'hit' square with a heavy black mark.
☐ Step 3. For the sections of the pattern line that do *not* fall on network squares ('misses'—these will be the majority), make an x-mark on the *next available shaded square above the pattern line*. Every vertical column must have one mark, and only one mark. The resulting collection of black squares and x's is the threading draft (see *8b*).

The telescoped pattern line in *7b* can also be fitted to a network (see *9a* and *9b*) to yield the draft in *9c*. Compare *8c* and *9c*, two different drawdowns derived from the same original pattern line.

You are now almost ready to weave. The next article in this series explores ways to develop treadlings and dobby peg plans for twills and other weave structures using network drafting. But if you simply can't wait to get started, thread your loom to the draft in *8c* or *9c* (or develop your own network draft), use your favorite twill tie-up, and treadle as drawn in. You have now created your first cloth based on network drafting and have entered the exciting world of unlimited curves! ✄

7a. Digitizing

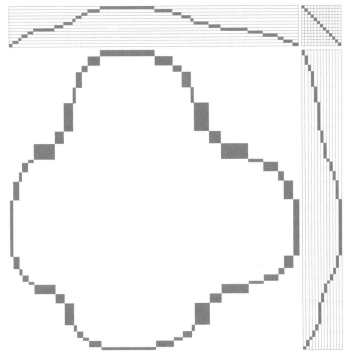

7b. Telescoping

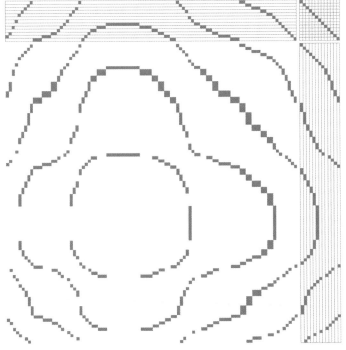

ll thrills **twill** thrills **twill** thrills twill thrills twill thrills **twill** thrills twill thrills twill thrills twill thrills twill thrills twill thrills **twill** thrills twill t
twill thrills **twill** thrills **twill** thrills twill thrills twill thrills twill thrills twill thrills twill thrills twill thrills twill thrills twill thrills twill thrills twi
ll thrill twill thrill twill **thrills** **twill** thrills twill thrills twill thrills twill **thrills** twill thrills twill **thrills** twill thrills twill thrills **twill** thrills twill th

NETWORK DRAFTING
Terms to Know

Initial: a threading group (much like a threading unit but more freely formed) that is used to build a threading grid (network) of more than one initial.

Network: a base grid containing initials repeated horizontally and vertically on which the actual threading is plotted.

Digitizing: reducing a threading profile to one that uses fewer horizontal rows (hence fewer shafts) by substituting one shaft for two (or more).

Telescoping: reducing a threading profile to one that uses fewer horizontal rows (hence fewer shafts) by returning to the first row of the draft to thread segments that extend beyond the shafts available.

Pattern line: a continuous line drawn on a threading grid that becomes the basis for a pattern drawdown.

Harmonics: parallel or incidental curves appearing in a pattern drawdown when a pattern line has been reduced by telescoping.

8a. *Pattern line overlaid on network and 'hits' marked*

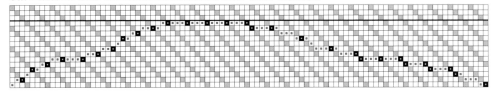

8b. *X's plotted above the pattern line on network positions*

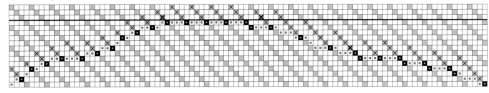

9a. *Pattern overlaid on network and 'hits' marked*

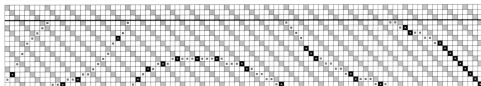

9b. *X's plotted above the pattern line on network positions*

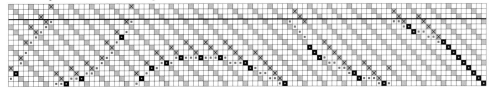

8c. *'Automobile' threading as developed in* 8a *and* 8b

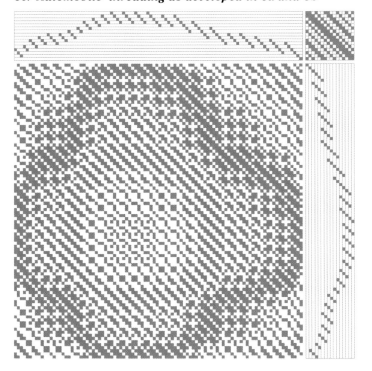

9c. *'Automobile' threading as developed in* 9a *and* 9b

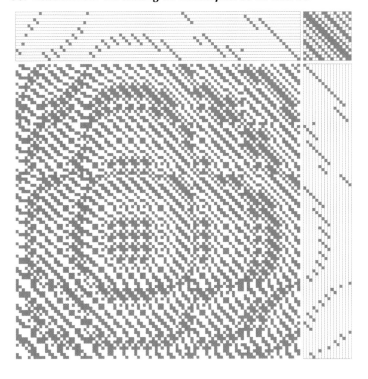

network drafting: part II

This article explores design options using network techniques to develop tie-ups and treadling sequences. We'll examine three basic methods using our familiar 'Automobile' draft from pages 62–65.

AS DRAWN IN

The weaver with a conventional treadle loom can select any favorite twill tie-up and weave networked threadings as drawn in (see *1* and *Photo a*). On a multishaft loom many twill tie-ups are available, but not all of them are useful. Eliminate tie-ups with warp or weft floats of more than four or five ends to protect fabric stability.

'Weave as drawn in' is easy to say but sometimes hard to *do* with twill threadings generated by network drafting. They usually extend well beyond 50 picks per repeat and skip around the treadles erratically. The trick to managing complex treadlings is: *divide and conquer!* Divide the treadling sequence into sections of about eight picks each and copy each section onto an index card. Suspend the deck of cards from the castle of the loom. As you finish treadling each section, flip the card to the back of the deck. (As an error-checking device, plan an even number of picks per card so the shuttle completes the sequence on the same side of the web.)

It is not necessary to use the draft that is actually threaded for the as-drawn-in treadling. You can use any threading draft based on the same initial.

Dobby weavers must derive the as-drawn-in peg plan row by row (see the peg plan in *1*)—a conversion made easy with most computer weaving programs. Computerized dobby looms have an advantage over mechanical dobbies for weaving these drafts, since most mechanical dobbies have a limited number of dobby bars.

DIVIDED TIE-UPS

A second way of weaving networked twill drafts is to divide the tie-up into sections based on the initial used to derive the threading. Each section can be filled with any structure that can be woven using that initial. With our 4-end initial from 'Automobile' (pp. 62–65), for example, plain weave, basket weave, and straight and broken 2/2, 1/3, and 3/1 twills can be woven (see *3*, p. 68). The 4 x 4 square sections can be used like building blocks and plugged into any of the positions in the tie-up. The tie-up for an

1. 'Automobile' threading, twill tie-up, treadled as drawn in; note that the peg plan rotates each treadle 90 degrees clockwise.

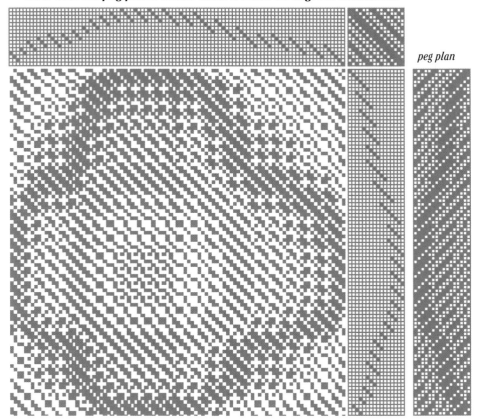

peg plan

a. Fabric woven as drawn in with a twill tie-up

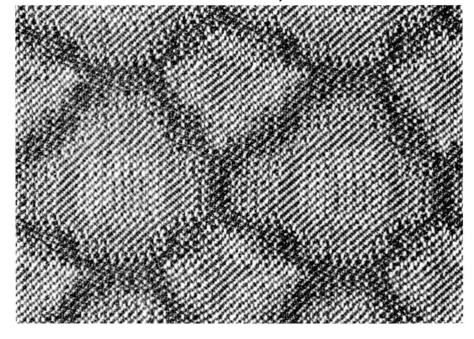

thrills twill thrill twill thrill twill thrills twill thrills twill thrills twill thrills twill thrills twill thrills twill thrills twill thrills twill thrills twill thrills twill th

Schlein Alice Schlein Alice Schlein Alice Schlein Alice Schlein Alice Schlein Alice Schlein Alice Schlein Alice Sc

Network drafting techniques for creating twill threading and treadling sequences produced this evening bag and scarf. See page 68 for the threading draft and divided tie-up used to weave the evening bag. The same threading produces the scarf. The first 32 rows of the 96-bar cut-and-paste peg plan used to weave the scarf are shown on page 69. The warp for both is 10/2 rayon, 36 epi; the weft is 2-ply silk.

will thrills twill thrills twill thrills twill thrills twill thrills twill thrills twill thrills twill thrills twill thrills twill thrills twill thrills twill thrills twill thrills twill thrills twill
thrills twill thrills twill thrills twill thrills twill thrills twill thrills twill thrills twill thrills twill thrills twill thrills twill thrills twill thrills twill thrills twill thrills twill th
thrills twill thrills twill thrills twill thrills twill thrills twill thrills twill thrills twill thrills twill thrills twill thrills twill thrills twill thrills twill thrills twill thrills twill thril
thrills twill thrills twill thrills twill thrills twill thrills twill thrillss twill thrills twill thrills twill thrills twill thrills twill thrills twill thrills twill thrills twill thrills twill thril

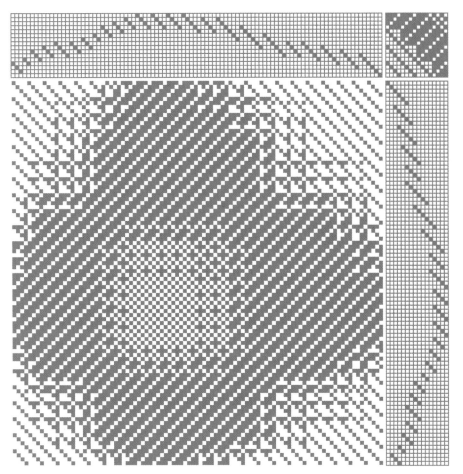

*2. 'Automobile' threading with divided tie-up containing units
of plain weave, 3/1 straight twill, and 1/3 straight twill*

8-end initial has four such positions, the tie-up for a 12-end initial nine positions, for a 16-end initial sixteen positions, etc.

Once the tie-up has been formed with its component parts, the cloth can be treadled as drawn in similarly to the example in *1*. The more shafts available, the more interesting the possible designs.

More than two structures can be combined in a tie-up. One of my favorites is a combination of 3/1 broken twill, 1/3 broken twill, and plain weave (see *2* and **Photo b**). If woven with a warp and weft of strongly contrasting colors, this tie-up yields a cloth containing very dark areas, very light areas, intermediate areas (plain weave), and lovely boundary areas where one section 'bleeds' into another.

It is entertaining to explore these many divided tie-ups treadled as drawn in with a computer drawdown program. But additional surprises are in store when the cloth is woven, since the boundary areas are actually new textures—something that is not evident on the computer screen. Sett becomes critical with divided tie-ups; cloths with more plain weave require a greater openness of sett than those with more twill.

b. Fabric woven with the draft in 2

3. Divided tie-ups

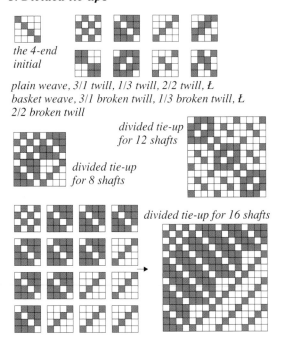

the 4-end initial

plain weave, 3/1 twill, 1/3 twill, 2/2 twill, Ł basket weave, 3/1 broken twill, 1/3 broken twill, Ł 2/2 broken twill

divided tie-up for 12 shafts

divided tie-up for 8 shafts

divided tie-up for 16 shafts

thrills twill thrills twill thrills twill thrills twill thrills twill thrills twill thrills twill thrills twill thrills twill
twill thrills twill thrills twill thrills twill thrills twill thrills twill thrills twill thrills twill thrills twill thrills tw
thrill twill thrill twill thrills twill thrills twill thrills twill thrills twill thrills twill thrills twill thrills twill th

CUT AND PASTE

A third way of deriving the treadling is to design directly in the peg plan—the row-by-row diagram of the shafts that are lifted for each weft pick. To combine structures in the peg plan, first prepare a peg-plan template for each basic weave you will be using (see the components for building peg plans for a 16-shaft loom using a 4-end initial in plain weave, basket weave, broken 1/3 twill, etc., in **4**). Each row of the template must have the same number of squares as the number of shafts available. The template can have as many rows as the number of bars that can be pegged or picks that can be programmed.

Write in the shaft numbers with a black pen on graph paper with black lines for good reproduction on copy machines. Use the same scale for all the templates so that the finished peg plans will mesh together accurately. (You can also prepare templates with computer drawing or weaving programs. Just remember to keep the same scale for all the templates.) Then use a photocopier to make many copies of each one.

Place your pattern line (at *the same scale as your templates*) on graph paper (it can be flipped horizontally or vertically as desired; see **5a–b**). It helps to glue the graphed pattern line to heavy card stock for repeated use. Cut out the section that includes the pattern line with sharp scissors following the jogs of the line as accurately as possible (**5c**).

Overlay the cutout (**5d**)—you can choose either of the two pieces you cut apart—onto one of your templates (3/1 broken twill is used in **5e**), and trace around it with a colored pen. Cut on the colored line (**5f**), and paste this cutout on top of another template, for example 1/3 broken twill in **5g**, lining up the rows and columns exactly.

You now have a new peg plan that you can use with your networked threading on either a mechanical or computerized dobby. You can also use the peg plan as a row-by-row lifting sequence for a multishaft table loom. Hand lifting can be tedious, but it is a good way to weave samples and view the exciting possibilities. The same peg plan can be used with other threadings based on the same initial.

4. Componants for building peg-plan templates for a 4-end initial

1	3	5	7	9	11	13	15		*plain*
2	4	6	8	10	12	14	16		*weave*

1 2		5 6		9 10		13 14		*basket*
1 2		5 6		9 10		13 14		*weave*
	3 4		7 8		11 12		15 16	
	3 4		7 8		11 12		15 16	

	4		8		12	16	*broken*
2		6		10		14	*1/3 twill*
	3		7		11	15	
1		5		9		13	

2 3 4	6 7 8	10 11 12	14 15 16	*broken*
1 2	4 5 6	8 9 10	12 13 14	16	*3/1 twill*
1	3 4 5	7 8 9	11 12 13	15 16	
1 2 3	5 6 7	9 10 11	13 14 15	

1	5	9	13	*straight*
2	6	10	14	*1/3 twill*
3	7	11	15	
4	8	12	16	

1 2 3	5 6 7	9 10 11	13 14 15	*straight*
1 2	4 5 6	8 9 10	12 13 14	16	*3/1 twill*
1	3 4 5	7 8 9	11 12 13	15 16	
2 3 4	6 7 8	10 11 12	14 15 16	

Use cut-and-paste techniques to blend two or more weave structures in the same fabric for great texture and design interest!

5. Create a peg plan using a pattern line

5d–g shows the steps for deriving the cut-and-paste peg plan for the top 32 rows of the pattern line in **5c**.

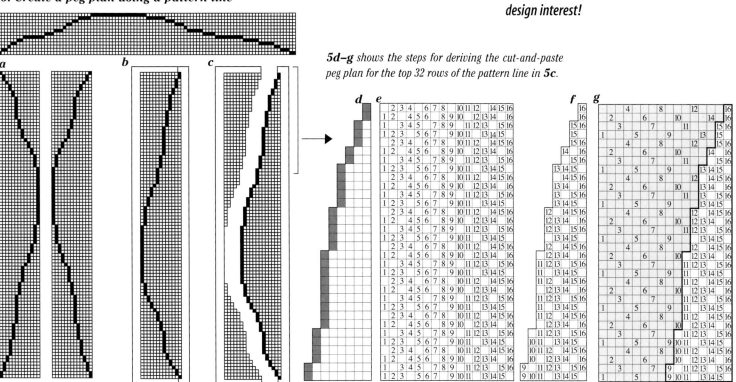

vill thrills twill th
lls twill thrills twill thrills twill thrills twill thrills twill thrillss twill thrills twill thrills twill thrills twill thrills twill thrills twill thrills twill thri

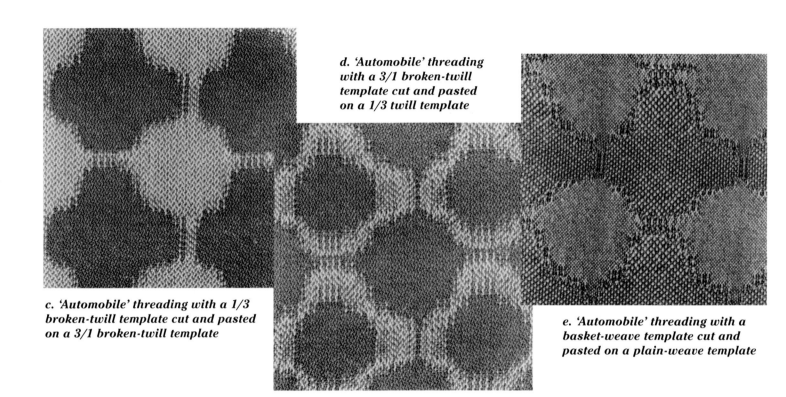

d. 'Automobile' threading with a 3/1 broken-twill template cut and pasted on a 1/3 twill template

c. 'Automobile' threading with a 1/3 broken-twill template cut and pasted on a 3/1 broken-twill template

e. 'Automobile' threading with a basket-weave template cut and pasted on a plain-weave template

FURTHER OPTIONS FOR CUT AND PASTE

The pattern line can be shifted and/or altered in the cut-and-paste operation. In *6*, the pattern line has been made into a ribbon four squares wide, cut from a 3/1 broken-twill template, and pasted onto a 1/3 broken-twill template.

Templates from more than two weaves can also be combined into a final peg plan. There is great scope for experimenting here, but be warned that the strongest effects are usually achieved through the simplest combinations. Drawdowns should always be made before committing yarn and time to the loom. Pay particular attention to the boundary areas between weaves. It is often possible to fine-tune a weave by making small changes in the peg plan where an overly long float occurs in an otherwise excellent peg plan.

Notice that in the drawdowns shown on these pages, 'twill' sometimes only loosely describes the interlacements, and the boundaries between straight twill, broken twill, and plain weave are not distinct lines. It is important to realize that an initial is much more flexible than our familiar term 'unit,' and this flexibility is an important benefit of network drafting. ✄

6. A ribbon pattern line (a) is placed on a 3/1 broken-twill template and traced. The traced section is cut out (b) and placed on a 1/3 broken-twill template (c) for a new peg plan.

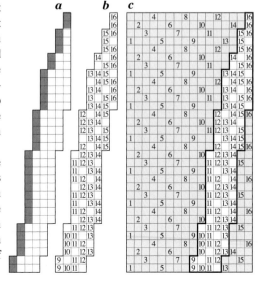

a   b   c

DESIGN STEPS AT A GLANCE

- ❑ Step 1. Draw a pattern line.
- ❑ Step 2. Telescope or digitize.
- ❑ Step 3. Build the networked threading.
- ❑ Step 4. Choose a twill or divided tie-up, or, to design in a peg plan:

  a. Prepare templates of the treadling units of the basic weaves that can be woven using the original initial. Each row in the template must have as many squares as the number of shafts on the loom. There must be as many rows as in the pattern line.

  b. Plot the pattern line on a grid with the same number of horizontal and vertical squares as the templates.

  c. Cut out the pattern line.

  d. Trace the pattern line on one of the templates and cut out the piece.

  e. Overlay the piece (in one weave) on the template of another weave.

For more design tips and information about network drafting, see Alice Schlein, *Network Drafting: An Introduction*, Greenville, South Carolina: Bridgewater Press, 1994.

Il thrills twill thrills twill thrills twill thrills twill thrills twill thrills twill thrills twill thrills twill thrills twill thrills t
twill thrills twill thrills twill thrills twill thrills twill thrills twill thrills twill thrills twill thrills twill thrills twill thrills t
twill thrills twill thrills twill thrills twill thrills twill thrills twill thrills twill thrills twill thrills twill thrills twill th

the pattern line: telescoping and digitizing

1. Examples of pattern lines

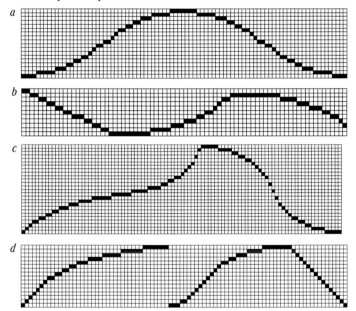

a

b

c

d

2. The 'shaft rule' limits the height of the pattern line.

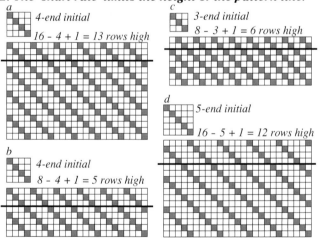

a
4-end initial
16 – 4 + 1 = 13 rows high

c
3-end initial
8 – 3 + 1 = 6 rows high

d
5-end initial
16 – 5 + 1 = 12 rows high

b
4-end initial
8 – 4 + 1 = 5 rows high

Plotting the pattern line on the network following the shaft rule results in design areas that are cleaner and more distinct.

3a. A 13-row pattern line on a 16-shaft network

3b. A 16-row pattern line on a 16-shaft network

The pattern line is the starting point for designing on a network. For successful designs, different types of pattern lines require different treatments.

The pattern line indicates the shape or general outline of a design. It is not a thread-by-thread draft, and it is not related directly to any weave structure. It is analogous to the profile in block drafting in that it can be used to derive a thread-by-thread draft in a specific weave structure.

A pattern line is a straight or curved line, or a combination of the two, which wanders over a given field in any direction vertically, but in only one direction horizontally. Think of an east-to-west journey plotted on a road map. The traveler starts at the eastern border of the map and heads generally toward the western border, meandering sometimes northward and sometimes southward, but never back to the east (review pp. 62–65).

The pattern line is represented by marked squares on graph paper, as in **1a–d**. Only one mark is allowed per vertical column. Any number of consecutive marks is allowed per horizontal row. It is easiest to draw a curve freehand and then go back and fill in the closest squares for each point on the line. Shallower curves work better than steep curves, as there are then fewer skipped squares along the line, although a skip now and then does no harm; see **1c**.

How big?

In drawing the pattern line, personal preference is the only limit to horizontal length. For smaller patterns that repeat frequently in the cloth, the pattern line should be relatively short. For a large pattern that is threaded once in the total width of the cloth, the pattern line should be long.

There is no theoretical limit to the height of the pattern line. But once it is drawn, unless it already fits within the shaft limit of the weaving technique and the loom, it must then be reduced by either digitizing or telescoping.

THE SHAFT RULE

For most design purposes, the maximum desirable height of the pattern line is the number of shafts on the loom, minus the height of the initial, plus one. For instance, for a 16-shaft draft using a 4-end initial, the maximum height is $16 – 4 + 1 = 13$, as in **2a**. The example in **2b** shows the maximum desirable height for a 4-end initial on eight shafts, in **2c** for a 3-end initial on eight shafts, and in **2d** for a 5-end initial on 16 shafts. I call this restriction the shaft rule.

Why use the shaft rule?

The shaft rule prevents unnecessary harmonics (incidental parallel lines and curves) in certain types of patterns. The shaft rule keeps motifs as self-contained as possible, limiting spillover of motifs into adjacent areas. It keeps designs clean.

When do you use the shaft rule?

Use the shaft rule if your pattern line begins and ends on the same shaft or an adjacent shaft, if it has not been reduced by telescoping, and if you want to create isolated motifs (see also pp. 74–77). A pattern line that begins and ends on shaft 1 and that is not telescoped is shown following the shaft rule in **3a**.

You need not use the shaft rule if your pattern line has been telescoped, and/or if it begins and ends at opposite corners of its bounding rectangle. When you do not use the shaft rule, you can use the full height of the threading network for your pattern line. For example, when the shaft rule is not in use, a pattern line 16 rows high

will thrills twill thrills twill thrills twill thrills twill thrills twill thrills twill thrills twill thrills twill thrills twill thrills twill thrills twill
thrill twill thrills twill thrills twill thrills twill thrills twill thrills twill thrills twill thrills twill thrills twill thrills twill thrills twill thrills twill th
ills twill thrills twill thrills twill thrills twill thrills twill thrills twill thrills twill thrills twill thrills twill thrills twill thrills twill thrills twill thrills twill thrill

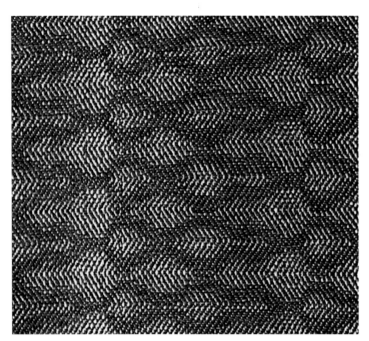

*Fabrics designed with a digitized pattern line on 16 shafts
by Hayoung Song using the shaft rule*

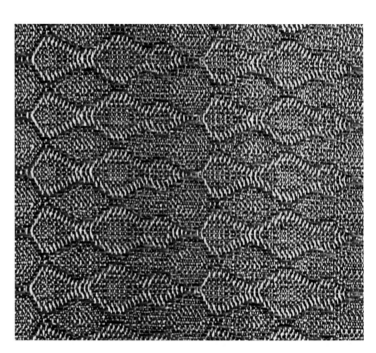

4a. 39-row pattern line...

can be used for a 16-shaft threading draft. In *3b*, a 16-row telescoped pattern line
is placed on a 16-shaft network; the shaft rule is not used. (See 'The Pattern Line:
Turtles, Snails, and Fleas,' pp. 74–77, for further discussion of the shaft rule.)

CHOICES: DIGITIZING AND TELESCOPING

There are two ways to reduce a pattern line in height: digitizing and telescoping.
Each has its own characteristics and ideal uses. Digitizing squashes the pattern
line vertically, maintaining its original form. Telescoping slices the line into horizontal segments which are then sandwiched on top of one another.

Drawdowns made from digitized lines have a blocky appearance but maintain
their essential original identity. Drawdowns made from telescoped lines have
smoother curves, but show harmonics—extra concentric images surrounding the
original lines. The choice of reduction type depends on which effect you prefer:
a blockier appearance without harmonics, or a smoother curve with harmonics.
Your choice of reduction also determines, in part, whether you observe the shaft
rule or instead use the full height of the threading draft for your pattern line.

How to digitize

To reduce a pattern line by digitizing, divide the number of rows in the original
line by the number of rows desired. *The quotient will be the number of rows you
will have to combine into one.* Draw heavy horizontal 'slicing' lines at intervals
the size of the above quotient on your original pattern line. If the desired height
of the digitized pattern line does not divide evenly into the height of the original
line, the slices will not be exactly equal in size. No matter. Distribute the slices
as evenly as possible. Whatever marks fall within each slice will be combined into
one row of your digitized line.

4a shows a 39-row pattern line. The grid is marked into sections of three
rows each; all marks appearing in one section of the original grid appear in one
row of the new grid in *5b*.

4b. ...digitized to 13 rows

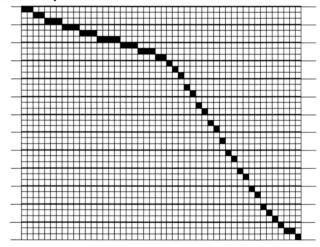

To reduce a pattern line by digitizing:
*1. Divide the number of rows in the original grid (39 in 4a) by the number of
   rows desired (13 in 4b = 3).*
*2. Mark the original graph into sections: the number of rows in a section = the
   quotient from step 1 (3).*
3. The bottom section is 1, the next section 2, etc.
*4. Mark black squares on each row of the new grid that correspond to black
   squares in each section of the original grid. Reading from right to left in the
   original grid, the first four black squares appear in section 1. Fill in the first
   four squares in row 1 of the new grid. The next three squares are in section 2
   of the original grid; mark three squares in row 2 of the new grid; continue.*

thrills twill thrills twill thrills twill thrills twill thrills twill thrills twill thrills twill thrills twill thrills twill thrills twill thrills twill thrills twill thrills twill
twill thrills twill thrills twill thrills twill thrills twill thrills twill thrills twill thrills twill thrills twill thrills twill thrills twill thrills twill
thrill twill thrill twill thrills twill thrills twill thrills twill thrills twill thrills twill thrills twill thrills twill thrills twill thrills twill thrills twill th

5a. 48-row pattern line...

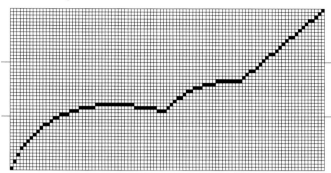

5b. ...telescoped to 16 rows

To reduce a pattern line by telescoping:
1. *Divide the original pattern line into sections, each with the number of rows equal to the desired number. (In 5a, the 48-row pattern line is divided in three 16-row sections to reduce it to 16 rows.)*
2. *Stack the sections on top of each other as though they are drawn on transparent graph paper. All marks remain in the same (vertical) columns; they merely change their (horizontal) rows. (In 5b, all marks on shafts 1–16 of the original pattern line remain in the same position. Marks on rows 17–32 are moved to rows 1–16; marks on rows 33–48 are moved to 1 through 16.)*

How to telescope

To telescope a pattern line of a given height, draw heavy horizontal 'slicing lines' on your original pattern line such that each slice is the desired height of your new pattern line. All slices must be the same height except the final one (which may be the same or smaller). There may be any number of slices. Superimpose the slices one on top of another, as if you were constructing a sandwich out of transparent slices of bread. When reducing a pattern line by telescoping, do not observe the shaft rule. The 48-row pattern line in **5a** is telescoped to 16 rows in **5b** for use on a 16-shaft network as in **3b**, p. 71.

HEIGHT OF NETWORK: DESIGN CONSIDERATIONS

The height of the initial has a strong effect on the woven designs. For any given number of shafts, a shorter initial height yields smoother curves. For instance, in 16-shaft designs a 4-end straight initial yields smoother curves than an 8-end straight initial, which is twice its height. Curves plotted on the latter network exhibit a strong sawtoothed character. This is not to be deemed a fault, but an effect to consider. Compare the thread-by-thread drafts in **6a** and **6b**. The same pattern line is used for both drafts, but a 4-end initial is used in **6a** and an 8-end initial in **6b**.

A network's height need not be an exact multiple of the initial. For example, a 16-shaft draft allows for a 5-end straight initial to be repeated three times with one shaft remaining unused. The network can simply be extended to repeat the first row of the initial, or it may be limited to 15 rows. If the full 16 shafts are used, the woven designs have slightly more curve definition and less of a sawtooth effect. Peg plan 'wrapping' options can be used only when the number of rows in the network *is* an exact multiple of the number of rows in the initial, however; see pp. 74–77. Other factors, such as pattern-line type, affect the decision of network height. ✄

6a. Pattern line in 5b used with a 4-end initial

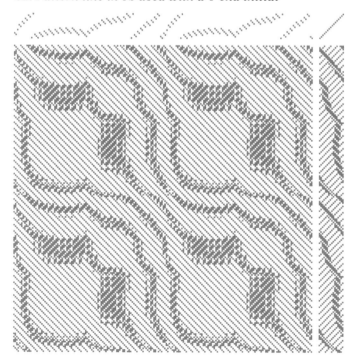

6b. Pattern line in 5b used with an 8-end initial

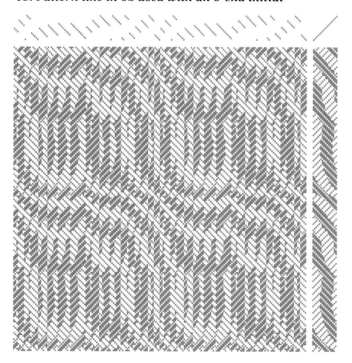

The pattern line indicates the shape or general outline of a design. It is not a thread-by-thread draft, and it is not related directly to any weave structure. It is analogous to the profile threading for block weaves in that it can be used to derive a thread-by-thread draft in a specific weave structure (review pages 62-73).

Once the pattern line has been derived it is ready to be transformed into a threading draft. It has been reduced (if necessary) by telescoping or digitizing to fit within the shaft constraints of the loom. It can be used to generate a drawdown without regard to cloth structure (see *1a–c*) just as profile threading drafts can be used to generate profile drawdowns without regard to cloth structure.

Pattern lines behave in certain ways depending on their orientation to the imaginary rectangle that bounds them. Consider the properties and behaviors of the three possible pattern-line types shown in *2a–c*:

- Turtles: continuous lines that start and end at the same height on the right and left sides of their bounding rectangles;
- Snails: continuous lines that start and end at opposite corners of the bounding rectangles;
- Fleas: discontinuous lines.

These labels are my idiosyncratic memory aids, suggesting the general shapes of the patterns produced, and are not (so far!) official weaving terms. Turtle shells resemble self-contained blobs, snails remind me of the meandering diagonal Snail's Trail coverlet patterns, and a group of fleas is (guess what) jumpy and disconnected!

Any of these pattern-line types—turtles, snails, or fleas—can be used to develop threading or treadling drafts. Any of the resulting threading drafts can be used with treadling drafts derived from other pattern-line types as long as they are plotted on compatible networks. The special properties and limitations of each type of pattern line are indicated in *2a–c*. (See pp. 62–73 for definitions and explanations of: network, initial, digitizing, telescoping, and the shaft rule.)

PUTTING IT ALL TOGETHER

The decision as to which type of pattern line to use (turtle, snail, or flea) is based on the desired look of the pattern. In general, if discrete (not connected to each other) motifs are wanted, choose a turtle-type line (a turtle pattern line was used to weave the scarf fabric in *Photo a*, p. 75). If flowing lines that connect and meander are wanted, choose snails. If jumpy, disconnected line segments are wanted, choose fleas. All of the three types of pattern lines can be digitized or telescoped.

Special characteristics of flea and snail pattern lines

If you choose flea or snail-type pattern lines, you must use a network that is an exact multiple of the initial. For example, if you choose a 4-shaft initial, the network must be 8, 12, 16 , 20, 24, etc. rows high. With all flea and snail pattern lines, peg plans can be wrapped successfully; see pp. 76-77.

Special characteristics of turtle pattern lines

Turtle pattern lines can be used both with networks that are not equal in height to exact multiples of the initial and with those that are, with some restrictions in both cases.

If they are not equal: You must use the shaft rule and pattern lines that are not telescoped. (If you do not use the shaft rule, major disruptions in the structure will occur; if you use telescoped pattern lines, the design will be disrupted.) Peg plans cannot be wrapped (wrapping will disrupt the structure).

If they are equal: You can choose to use or not use the shaft rule. If you use the shaft rule, the pattern line cannot be telescoped (telescoped lines will show disruptions in the pattern). Peg plans can be wrapped, but if they are wrapped, the shaft rule will cause designs to lose their discrete shapes.

If you do not use the shaft rule, pattern lines can either be telescoped or not telescoped. Peg plans can be wrapped successfully in both cases—the pattern will be continuous. The designs will not be discrete shapes in either case, however, because the shaft rule has not been observed.

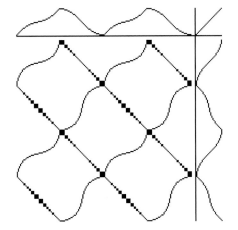

1a. 24-row pattern line

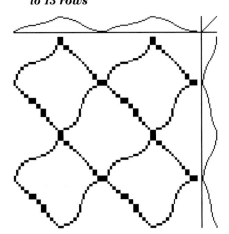

1b. 24-row pattern line digitized to 13 rows

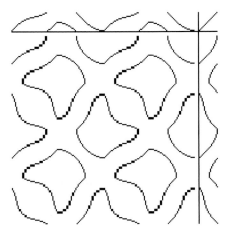

1b. 24-row pattern line telescoped to 13 rows

ll thrills **twill** thrills **twill** thrills twill thrills **twill** thrills twill thrills twill **thrills** twill thrills **twill** thrills twill thrills twill thrills twill **thrills** twill thrills twill

twill **thrills** twill thrills twill thrills twill thrills twill **thrills** twill thrills twill thrills twill thrills twill thrills twill thrills twill thrills twill

ll thrill twill thrill twill **thrills** **twill** thrills twill thrills twill thrills twill **thrills** twill thrills twill **thrills** twill thrills twill thrills twill **thrills** twill thrills twill

ce Schlein Alice Schlein Alice Schlein Alice Schlein Alice Schlein Alice Schlein Alice Schlein Alice Sc

2. Three types of pattern lines

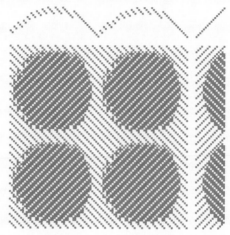

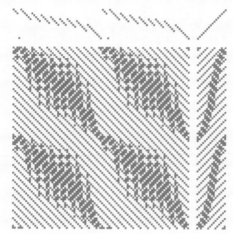

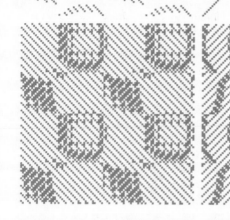

a. Turtle

Starts and ends at same height on side borders

b. Snail

Starts and ends at opposite corners

c. Flea

Starts and ends at any height; can have vertical breaks

Continuous line

Network height does not have to be an exact multiple of initial height (use shaft rule and a non-telescoped line). Peg plans cannot be wrapped.

If network height is equal to exact multiple of initial height, you can use or not use the shaft rule. Peg plans can be wrapped.

For discrete shapes, use non-telescoped pattern lines and the shaft rule.

Continuous line

Network height must be an exact multiple of initial height.

Peg plans can be wrapped.

Do not use the shaft rule.

Discontinuous lines

Network height must be an exact multiple of initial height.

Peg plans can be wrapped.

Do not use the shaft rule.

Shaft rule: To derive the height of the pattern line subtract the height of the initial from the total number of shafts in use and add 1.

DESIGNING THE TREADLING

The pattern line is plotted on the network (after reduction by digitizing or telescoping if necessary) to derive the actual threading draft (see pp. 62-65 for step-by-step directions for deriving networked threadings). The same pattern line can also be used to derive the treadling sequence, either as a peg plan or as a treadling order to be used with a tie-up.

The quarter turn

The pattern line is oriented horizontally when it is used to develop a threading draft. One method for deriving the treadling is simply to rotate the pattern line a quarter turn as shown in *3*. It can then form the basis for a networked treadling order or it can be used with cut-and-paste techniques to create peg plans (pp. 69-70).

3. A treadling pattern line designed by rotating the threading pattern line

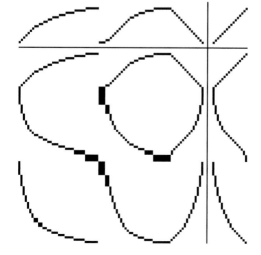

a. Scarf fabric designed from a non-telescoped turtle pattern line

will thrills twill thrill

4a. The pattern line from 3 is placed on a network to derive the threading.

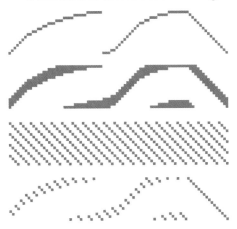

A 32-row pattern line is telescoped to fit a 16-shaft network composed of a 4-end straight initial. (The shaft rule is not observed.) The pattern line is expanded to a 4-row ribbon and plotted on the network. Black squares in the network covered by the ribbon become the threading.

The same pattern line is rotated to derive the peg plan. The pattern line is expanded to become a 6-row ribbon that is used as a template on a 3/1 twill peg plan, cut, and pasted on a 1/3 twill peg plan to produce the drawdown in **4c**. The peg plan is wrapped to produce the drawdown in **4d**.

4b. The pattern line is rotated and expanded to create a 1/3 vs 3/1 twill peg plan.

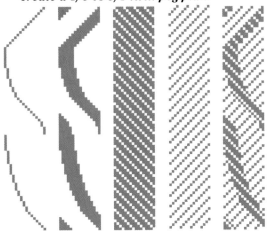

Wrapping

Computer jargon has added the term 'wrapping' to our drafting vocabulary. Wrapping means chopping information off one side of a rectangle and reattaching it at the opposite side. It is as if the dropped information passes behind the viewing screen and then jumps back into sight in its new position. Imagine a picket fence composed of 16 pickets. Remove the four right-hand pickets (numbers 13–16), and reattach them at the left side of the fence. They are now in positions 1–4, and the other 12 pickets have all moved four places to the right in the count. You have just 'wrapped' your picket fence four places to the right.

If a 16-shaft peg plan is wrapped four places to the right, it is as if the squares for shafts 13–16 were lopped off the peg plan and reattached on the left-hand side to become the new shafts 1–4. The old shaft 1 is the new shaft 5, the old 2 is the new 6, etc. Although threadings and tie-ups can also be wrapped, I find it prudent to restrict the wrapping to the treadling alone for sanity's sake. In practical terms, once the loom is threaded, you can't wrap the actual threading without rethreading the heddles; but it is an easy matter to wrap a computerized peg plan—even to repeg a short dobby chain—or to change the order in the treadling.

4c. The cut-and-paste peg plan from 4b is used with the threading in 4a.

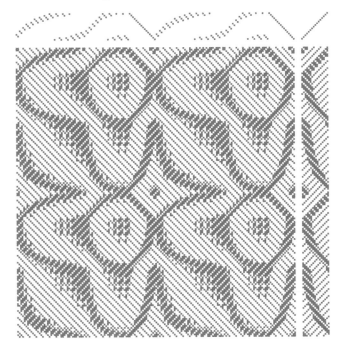

4d. The peg plan in 4b is wrapped and used with the same threading to produce a new effect.

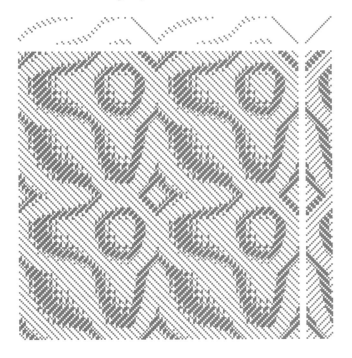

ll thrills twill thrills twill thrills twill thrills twill thrills twill thrills twill thrills twill thrills twill thrills twill thrills twill thrills twill thrills twill t
twill thrills twill thrills twill thrills twill thrills twill thrills twill thrills twill thrills twill thrills twill thrills twill thrills twill thrills twill thrills twill thrills tw
ll thrill twill thrill twill thrills twill thrills twill thrills twill thrills twill thrills twill thrills twill thrills twill thrills twill thrills twill thrills th

5a. 8-shaft network, 3-end twill initial

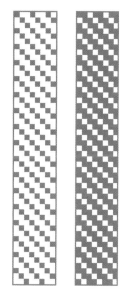

These threading and peg-plan networks are made up of two 3-end initials and two rows of a third (3 + 3 + 2 = 8) to produce a well-defined curve. Wrapping will not produce a weavable draft if partial initials are used in the threading.

The principles of wrapping

In network drafting, if the pattern line for the peg plan is based on a snail or flea pattern line, then the peg plan can be wrapped if desired (note that to maintain structural stability, the network for these two types of pattern lines must always be made of exact repeats of the height of the initial). The peg plan can be wrapped with a turtle pattern line only if the shaft rule is not in use (as is the case in *4a*). (Remember that if the network is not composed of full repeats of the initial, only a non-telescoped turtle-type pattern line can be used, the shaft rule must be followed, and the peg plan cannot be wrapped.)

Wrapped peg plans will work just as well as the original peg plan does; compare *4c* and *4d*. If wrapping is allowed, the peg plan can be wrapped as many steps as there are shafts, minus one. An 8-shaft peg plan can be wrapped one, two, three, four, five, six, or seven positions to the right; add to these seven the original plan, and you have eight options for an 8-shaft loom. Wraps to the left mimic their complementary wraps to the right and do not provide any additional design options.

To wrap or not to wrap

Why wrap? Try it and see. There can be subtle or dramatic differences in the various drawdowns, depending on the amount of wrapping. A wrap equal to half the number of shafts/treadles produces the greatest change; if the wrap is greater than half, the peg plan approaches the original again. But a wrap of only one can sometimes produce exactly the effect you are looking for. Wrapping is a very powerful tool for fine-tuning a networked draft. It is so powerful, in fact, that it is a good reason to use only networks that are an exact repeat of the initial.

On the other hand, using a network that is not an exact repeat of the initial allows one to eke out a little extra pattern definition from some structures if the number of shafts on the loom is limited. A 3-end twill networked on eight shafts is a good example. A network composed of two repeats of the initial gives only six shafts on which to design a curve, and three repeats

5b. An 8-shaft networked threading is used with 1/2 vs 2/1 twill peg plans; the peg plan cannot be wrapped.

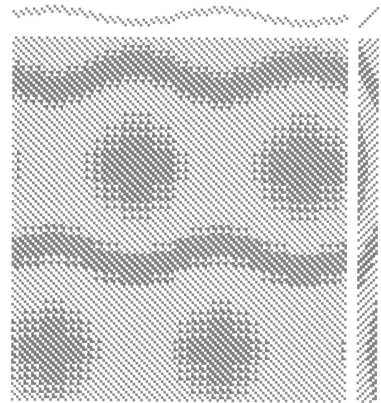

(nine shafts) are too many for the loom. But 2⅔ repeats permit the use of all eight shafts, and some nice curves can be designed this way; see *5a–b*. The trade-off is that the peg plans cannot be wrapped.

BIBLIOGRAPHY

Schlein, Alice. *Network Drafting: An Introduction.* Greenville, South Carolina: Bridgewater Press, 1994. Includes a complete discussion of network drafting for a wide range of weave structures and loom types. ✂

DESIGN STEPS

Begin your experiments in network designing by drawing a pattern line. Take into consideration all of the following factors:

- ❏ the weave structure and its initial,
- ❏ the number of shafts on the available loom,
- ❏ the style of the pattern line (turtle, snail, or flea),
- ❏ the type of pattern line reduction (digitizing, telescoping, or none),
- ❏ whether or not the network height is an exact multiple of the height of the initial, and
- ❏ whether or not peg plans will be wrapped.

network drafting for eight

*Alice Schlein Alice Schlein Alice Schlein Alice Schlein Alice Schlein **Alice Schlein** Alice Schlein Alice*

1. An 8-shaft network based on a 4-row initial

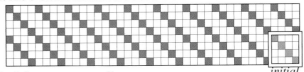

initial

2. A 5-row pattern line

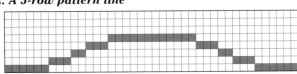

3a. Draw the pattern line on the network.

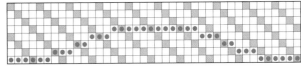

3b. Mark the 'hits' (white dots).

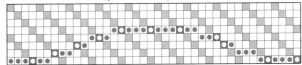

3c. Mark the next square above the pattern line.

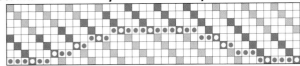

3d. The hits and marked squares are the threading.

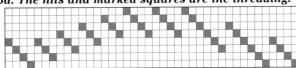

4a. Expand the pattern line to a 4-row ribbon.

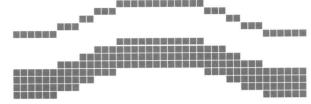

4b. Lay the ribbon on the network.

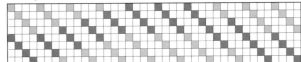

4c. The squares under the ribbon are the threading.

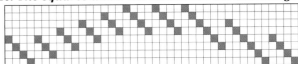

Two common misconceptions are that (1) network drafting is not worth doing on fewer than 16 shafts, and (2) network drafting requires a dobby loom. While it is true that 16 or more shafts offer the most scope for fancy curved designs in network drafting (encouraging the spread of that vile illness, 'harness envy') there is still much the 8-shaft weaver can do with the technique. The notion that a dobby loom is necessary in this mode of designing is not true, either.

Let's outline the development of an 8-shaft networked twill threading that can be woven on a conventional, unmodified jack loom. Next we'll explore some of the many ways it can be varied, amplified, and combined with other drafts to produce interesting designs that look as though they require a lot more shafts.

DERIVE AN 8-SHAFT THREADING

To generate a threading, begin with a pattern line. The formula (using the shaft rule; see p. 71) to calculate the number of rows to use for the pattern line is: [number of shafts available] minus [height of the initial] plus 1. The 8-shaft network in *1* is based on an initial 4 rows high, so the height of the pattern line is $8 - 4 + 1 = 5$ (see *2*). The pattern line is then plotted on the network (*3a*). Wherever the pattern line falls on a shaded square, mark that square (white dots in *3b*); these are 'hits.' For non-hits, mark the next shaded network square directly above the pattern line (*3c*). The marked squares become the networked threading (*3d*).

Another way of developing the same threading is to imagine the pattern line expanded into a ribbon four squares high (the number of rows in the initial), see *4a*. This ribbon is laid over the network *4b*, and every shaded network square that the ribbon covers now constitutes the threading, *4c*.

EXPERIMENT WITH TWILL TIE-UPS

Use any favorite 8-shaft twill tie-up (see the four tie-ups in *5*, p. 80) for your new draft and treadle as drawn in. Experiment with slanting the tie-up to the right or left; see *6a-b*. (Note that twill is not the only structure that is suitable for network drafting. Especially when 16 or more shafts are available, good networked patterns can be developed in satins, double weaves, and other structures.)

If the treadling unit is not too long, you can easily weave your draft without a dobby. Write the treadling in big numbers and tack it on the loom castle. Take the phone off the hook and put the cat out. Concentrate! If you must stop weaving, try to pause at the end of a sequence. Insert a temporary contrasting-color sewing thread in the shed at the conclusion of every treadling repeat as a place to count from in case you get lost. These treadlings are easily memorized and after a few inches you will be weaving them with no trouble.

THE FUN BEGINS: THEME AND VARIATIONS

Of course you can repeat your new threading as desired for the width of your warp and treadle as drawn in. New designs can be created, however, by changes to both threading and treadling orders. One exciting way to enhance the pattern, especially for the limited capacity of an 8-shaft loom, is to mirror sections of the threading and combine the result with other twills. A section of the threading draft in *6* is reversed and repeated in *7*. Remember not to double the ends at reversing points.

thrills twill thrills twill thrills twill thrills twill thrills twill thrills twill thrills twill thrills twill thrills twill thrills twill thrills twill th

thrills twill thrills twill thrills twill thrills twill thrills twill thrills twill thrills twill thrills twill thrills twill thrills twill thrills twill tw

thrill twill thrill twill thrills twill thrills twill thrills twill thrills twill thrills twill thrills twill thrills twill thrills twill thrills twill thr

Use network drafting to weave the curves and waves in Alice's 8-shaft placemats. Try different treadling orders for a variety of unique patterns; every placemat can be different!

Draft for placemats

ALICE'S PLACEMATS

❑ Equipment. 8-shaft loom, 18" weaving width; 10-dent reed; 1 shuttle. No dobby required!

❑ Materials. Warp: Perlé Cotton (2000 yds/lb, Henry's Attic), black, 1 lb (although this strong and glossy cotton yarn is advertised at 2000 yds/lb, I have found that the yardage is closer to 1900 yds/lb). Weft: Linen & Cotton (1500 yds/lb, Henry's Attic), natural, 1 lb. (Yarns for this project donated courtesy of Henry's Attic). A small amount unmercerized 10/2 cotton, natural, for hems. Sewing thread for handsewing hems.

❑ Wind a warp of 353 ends Perlé 5¼ yds long for five mats, finished size 14" x 19¾" with 1 yd loom waste. If you can manage less waste, you might be able to eke out six mats. If you must have six mats for sure, wind a 6-yd warp (1¼ lbs of Perlé).

❑ Spread warp in raddle at 20 epi, 17⅔" wide, and beam. Thread following draft: *a* to *b* 5x; *b* to *d* 4x, *c* to *b* 1x; *b* to *a* 5x.

❑ Sley 2/dent in a 10-dent reed.

❑ Weave a plain-weave hem (treadles 1 and 2) with 10/2 cotton for 30 rows. With Linen & Cotton weave as drawn in *a* to *b* 5x, *b* to *d* 6 x, *c* to *b* 1x, *b* to *a* 5x. End with 30 rows plain weave in 10/2 cotton. Weave four more mats as above, separating them with a colored marker thread.

❑ Finish by removing mats from loom; secure ends with zigzag machine stitching or serging; machine wash and dry, warm water. Cut mats apart at marker threads. Choose black spots on white or white on black as the right side, and fold plain-weave ends under twice to wrong side and hem by hand.

will thrills twill thrills twill thrills twill thrills twill thrills twill thrills twill thrills twill thrills twill thrills twill thrills twill thrills twill thrills twill thrills twill
ll thrills twill thrills twill thrills twill thrills twill thrills twill thrills twill thrills twill thrills twill thrills twill thrills twill thrills twill thrills twill thrills twill th
ills twill thrills twill thrills twill thrills twill thrills twill thrillss twill thrills twill thrills twill thrills twill thrills twill thrills twill thrills twill thrills twill thrills

5. 8-shaft twill tie ups

7a-d. Expanded threading with different twill tie-ups

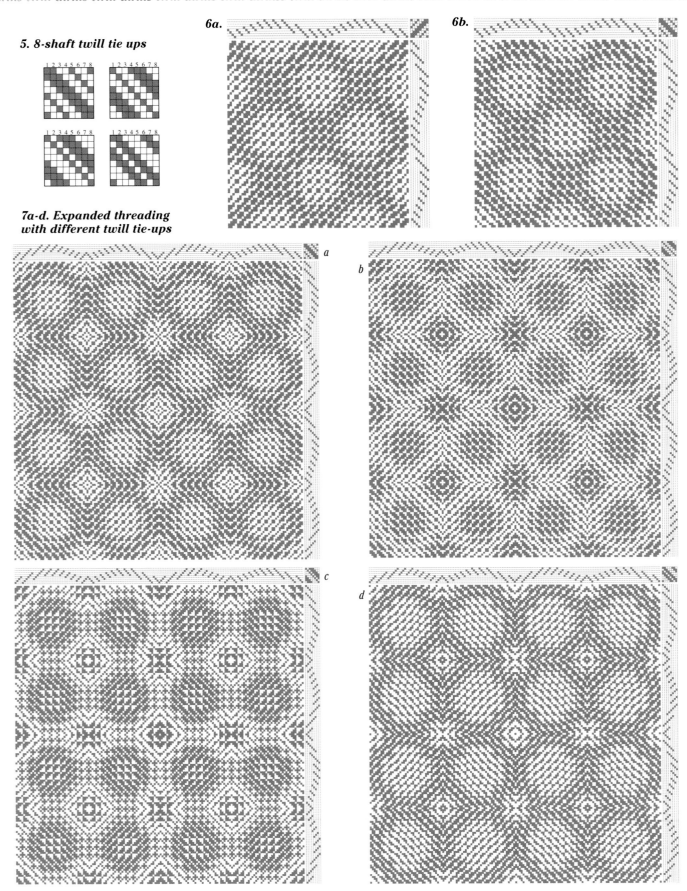

6a.

6b.

a

b

c

d

I thrills twill thrill twill thrill twill thrills twill thrills twill thrills twill thrills twill thrills twill thrills twill thrills twill thrills twill thrills twill thrills twill thrills twill thrills twill thrills twill thrills twill thrills twill thrills twill thrills twill thrills twill thri

8. Extended-point, point, and straight-twill treading orders

In *7a–d* the expanded threading is woven with the four tie-ups shown in *5*. Since as-drawn-in treadlings for lengthy skip twills require so much concentration, you might experiment with the effects produced by simpler treadling orders. In *8a* the draft is woven with an extended point-twill treadling order, in *8b* a point-twill order, and in *8c* a straight-twill order. In these versions the foot need only 'remember' to move from treadle to treadle. The straight order in *8c* is the easiest to treadle and produces an attractive fabric with deeply indented, curved ridges.

Sections of a basic networked threading can be combined with straight twill, as in *9a*, and/or separated by sections of extended point twill, as in *9b*. A border of straight twill can be combined with a fabric of networked twill, as in *10a* (p. 82), or a networked twill border can be combined with a fabric of straight twill, as in *10b* (p. 82). All of these effects can be treadled as drawn in with the twill tie-up of your choice.

Truly spectacular effects can be developed by combining sections of a networked threading with sections of point twill. This fabric is surprisingly easy to treadle, as the sections of point twill in the treadling go quickly. The same threading creates slightly different fabrics in *11a* and *11b* (p. 82) because of the two different ways of 'wrapping' the 3/2/1/2 tie-up. (Note: 'wrapping' a tie-up means arranging the treadles in a different order in the tie-up, i.e., beginning the tie-up with a different treadle in the sequence; see pp. 74–77). There are six *more* ways of wrapping this same tie-up. If you change the direction of the tie-up from a right diagonal to a left diagonal, there are yet *eight more* versions of just this one tie-up. The differences in the resulting fabrics are subtle, but interesting and worth exploring.

Try swapping networked drafts in your 8-shaft study group. Have each weaver develop a networked twill draft on the same network. Then exchange drafts so that each of the drafts is treadled with each of the treadling orders from the other participants. Eight weavers = 64 designs! ✂

9b. Extended point twill added to threading

9a. Straight twill added to threading

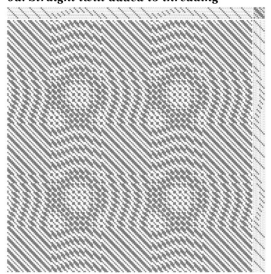

will thrills twill thrills twill thrills twill thrills twill thrills twill thrills twill thrills twill thrills twill thrills twill thrills twill thrills twill thrills twill thrills twill thrills twill thrills twill th
thrills twill thrills twill thrills twill thrills twill thrills twill thrills twill thrills twill thrills twill thrills twill thrills twill thrills twill thrills twill thrills twill thrills twill th
rills twill thrills twill thrills twill thrills twill thrills twill thrills twill thrillss twill thrills twill thrills twill thrills twill thrills twill thrills twill thrills twill

10a. Networked threading, twill border

10b. Twill border, networked threading

11a. Point-twill and networked threading: tie-up 1

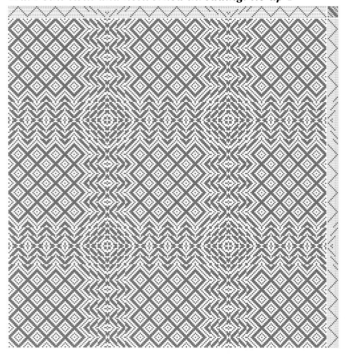

11b. Point-twill and networked threading: tie-up 2

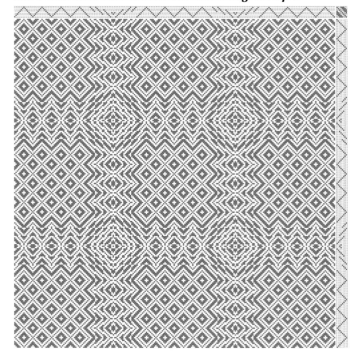

McConnell Jane Bird and Marjorie McConnell Jane Bird and Marjorie McConnell Jane Bird and M

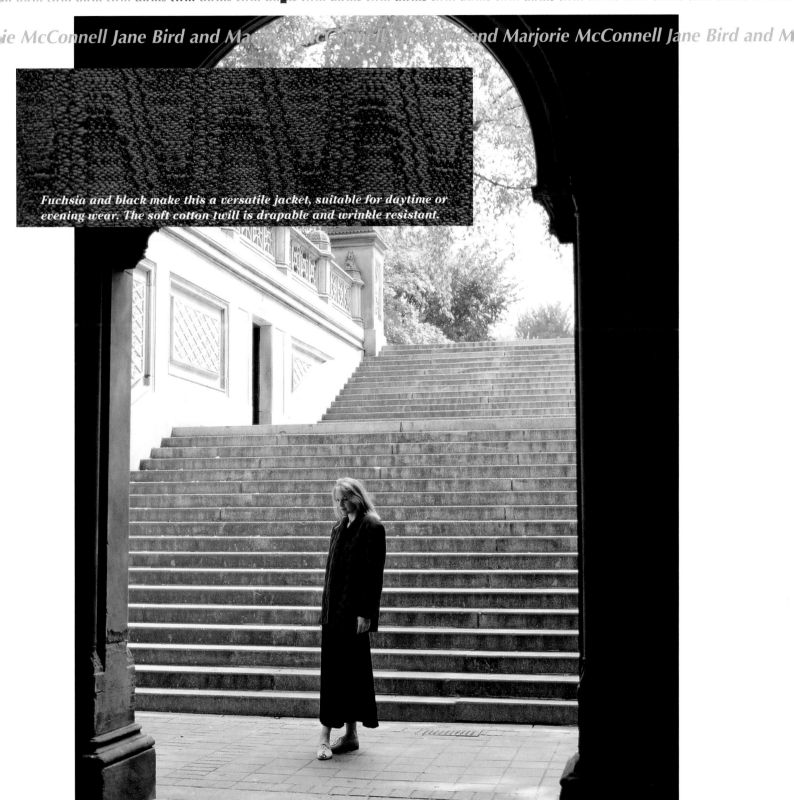

Fuchsia and black make this a versatile jacket, suitable for daytime or evening wear. The soft cotton twill is drapable and wrinkle resistant.

A combination of 8-shaft networked and advancing twills provides the movement in these wavy fabrics. Use black in either the warp or weft direction to intensify the other colors for a dramatic effect. A variegated rayon novelty adds gleam to Jane's vest fabric (page 85). Marjorie's advancing point-twill treadling echoes and emphasizes the networked zigzag design (see instructions on page 84).

will thrills twill

1. Draft for Marjorie's jacket fabric

The mainframe in a weaver's network is the workshop system. Marjorie McConnell and Jane Bird are inspired by samples from a workshop in network drafting and advancing twills—Making Waves. Selecting from their samples, they choose drafts that mix networked threadings with advancing-twill treadlings. Jane's fabric evokes sea-green waves and Marjorie's suggests sunset mountains and valleys. Both make ideal garment fabrics.

MARJORIE'S MAKING WAVES JACKET

❑ Equipment. 8-shaft loom, 36" weaving width, 12-dent reed, 1 boat shuttle.

❑ Materials. Warp: 10/2 pearl cotton, (4280 yds/lb) black, 1⅛ lb. Weft: 10/2 pearl cotton, magenta, 14½ oz; commercial jacket pattern (Kwik Sew #2089 is adapted for this jacket), lightweight iron-on interfacing, sewing notions required by the pattern.

❑ Wind a warp of 762 ends black, 5½ yds long, 32" wide. This length allows 36" loom waste.

❑ Sley 2/dent in a 12-dent reed; center for 32". Add 1 end each side for floating selvedges.

❑ Thread following the draft in *1*: *a* to *c* 9x, *a* to *b* 1x.

❑ Weave with magenta weft following the treadling sequence in *1*.

❑ Finish by machine zigzagging ends.

❑ Machine wash in warm water, normal cycle; machine dry, warm. Remove promptly when dry to avoid wrinkling the fabric.

❑ Cut, assemble, and sew following pattern directions. The pattern selected for this jacket avoids seaming, darts, cuffs, collars, or extra detail in order not to disturb the design in the fabric. The back seam in the Kwik Sew pattern is eliminated by placing the cutting line for the back piece on the fold of the fabric. An iron-on interfacing provides stability and maintains fabric flexibility.

ll thrills **twill** thrills **twill** thrills twill thrills **twill** thrills **twill** thrills twill thrills twill **thrills** twill thrills **twill** thrills twill **thrills** twill thrills twill t
twill **thrills twill thrills** twill thrills twill thrills twill thrills twill thrills twill **thrills** twill thrills twill **thrills** twill thrills twill **thrills** twill thrills tw
ill thrill twill thrill twill **thrills** **twill** thrills twill thrills twill thrills twill **thrills** twill thrills twill **thrills** twill thrills twill thrills **twill thrills** twill th

2. Draft for Jane's vest fabric

b — denting and color order

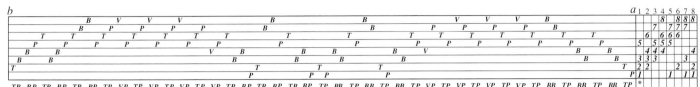

(threading draft showing rows of letters B, V, P, T with right-side shaft numbering *a* 1 2 3 4 5 6 7 8:)

```
                B  V  V  V        B        B          V  V  V  B                        8 | 8 8 8
             B  P  P  P  P  P        B        B     P  P  P  P  P  B                  7 |    7 7 7
          T  T  T  T  T  T  T     T        T     T  T  T  T  T  T  T  T            6 |    6 6 6
       P  P  P  P  P  P  P     P        P     P  P  P  P  P  P  P  P  P          5 |    5 5 5
       B  B              V        B     B        B  V              B  B            4 4 4 |        4
    B  B                    T              T                    B  B              3 3 3 |        3
 T                    T     T     T                          T                T    2 2 |     2 2
                      P        P  P     P                                P          P 1 |     1 1 1
```

denting order:
TB BP TB BP TB BP TP VP TP VP TP VP TP VP TB BP TB BP TB BP TP BB TP BB TP BB TP VP TP VP TP VP TP VP TP BB TP BB TP BB TP

JANE'S MAKING WAVES VEST

- Equipment. 8-shaft loom, 30" weaving width; 12-dent reed; 1 shuttle.
- Materials. Warp: 18/2 wool/silk (5040 yds/lb, Zephyr, JaggerSpun), Peacock (P), 3 oz; Sable (B), 2½ oz; 8/2 wool (2240 yds/lb, Maine Line, JaggerSpun), Teal (T), 5 oz; rayon novelty (1000 yds/lb, Robin and Russ Handweavers) variegated turquoise, black, brown (V), 4¼ oz. Weft: 18/2 wool/silk, Ebony, 10 oz; Butterick vest pattern #4307, view D (without slits), 3 buttons, lining.
- Wind a warp of 656 total ends 4 yds long holding 1 end each of two different yarns together in the following order: 120 pairs (240 total working ends) Peacock and Teal (PT); 64 pairs (128 total ends) Peacock and variegated rayon (PV); 48 pairs (96 total ends) Peacock and Sable (PB), 48 pairs (96 ends) Sable and Teal (BT), and 48 pairs (96 ends) Sable and Sable (BB).
- Sley 2/dent in a 12-dent reed, 24 epi; center for 27½"; add 1 end Peacock each side for floating selvedges. Follow the chart in *2* for denting order; i.e., sley PT pairs skipping dents for the other colors, then sley BB pairs, then sley PV pairs, etc. Repeat the denting order 8x.
- Thread following *2*: *a-b* 8x.
- Weave with Ebony for app 110" as in *2*.
- Finish by removing the fabric from the loom and securing ends. Soak 10 minutes in washing machine in cold water and small amount gentle detergent or synthrapol. Spin out excess water. Rinse and soak for 10 more minutes in cold water; spin out excess. Hang to dry. Finished fabric is 24" x 102". Cut and sew vest following pattern directions. ✄

vill thrills twill thrills twill thrills twill thrills twill thrills twill thrills twill thrills twill thrills twill thrills twill thrills twill thrills twill thrills twill thrills twill thrills twill
thrills twill thrills twill thrills twill thrills twill thrills twill thrills twill thrills twill thrills twill thrills twill thrills twill thrills twill thrills twill thrills th
lls twill thrills twill thrills twill thrills twill thrills twill thrills twill thrills twill thrills twill thrills twill thrills twill thrills twill thrills twill thrills twill thrills twill th

a mix of twills

1. 16-shaft draft for scarf

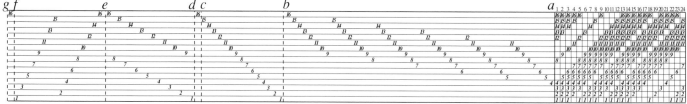

2. 8-shaft draft for scarf

MIXED-TWILL SCARF

❑ Equipment. 8-shaft loom or 16-shaft loom, raddle, 12-dent reed.

❑ Materials. Warp: 16/1 silk bourette (8400 yds/lb), 2 oz. Warp and weft: 40/2 silk (11,000 yds/lb) natural, 2 oz. (Can substitute 20/2 cotton, 8400 yds/lb, white; or 30/2 Boil-Off silk, 7500 yds/lb, Robin and Russ Handweavers, natural.)

❑ Wind a warp holding one end 2-ply silk and 1 end silk bourette of 383 ends 3 yds long. If using color plan in project scarf, wind 193 ends in colorway A and 190 ends in colorway B. (For this scarf, the warp threads are painted with thickened Procion MX dyes. Paint the entire warp so that colors flow into the fringes. Colorway A is variegated lavender blending to gold/orange; color way B is variegated aqua blending to coral/pink.)

❑ Arrange warp in raddle at 36 epi, centering for 10.6", in color order: A 48 ends, B 95 ends, A 97 ends, B 95 ends, A 48 ends; beam.

❑ Thread following 16-shaft or 8-shaft draft (for 8-shaft draft thread section 2x if marked with *; for 16-shaft draft ignore *): colorway A: *a* to *b*; colorway B: *b* to *d*, *d* to *e**, *f* to *e*, *b* to *d*, *c* to *b*, *e* to *f*; colorway A: *e* to *d**, *d* to *b*, *e* to *g*, *f* to *e*, *b* to *d*, *d* to *e**; colorway B: *f* to *e*, *b* to *d*, *c* to *b*, *e* to *f*, *e* to *d**, *d* to *b*; colorway A: *b* to *a*.

❑ Sley 3/dent in a 12-dent reed, 36 epi.

❑ Weave using an advancing twill treadling order (1-2-3-4; 2-3-4-5; 3-4-5-6; etc.) with 8-shaft or 16-shaft tie-up at 32 ppi with 2-ply silk for 62". For 16-shaft treadle looms without 24 treadles, substitute any 16-shaft twill tie-up. Tie-ups allowing for 5- or 6-thread floats show the most pattern. Allow 3–6" for fringe at each end.

❑ To finish, tie fringe in bouts of 12 ends each; handwash in warm water, neutral soap. Roll in towel and line dry. Press with a steam iron and trim fringe. Finished scarf length is 60"; width is 9½". ✂

'Night Rain'

'The Storm'

ll thrills **twill** thrills **twill** thrills twill thrills twill **thrills** twill thrills twill **thrills** twill thrills twill thrills twill thrills twill **thrills** twill thrills twill t
b twill **thrills** twill thrills twill thrills twill thrills twill thrills twill thrills twill thrills twill thrills twill thrills twill thrills twill thrills twill twill twill thrills **twill** thrills twill thrills twill thrills twill **thrills** twill thrills twill **thrills** twill thrills twill thrills twill **thrills** twill th

Combine a mix of twills with warp painting to weave this scarf on eight or 16 shafts. 'The Storm' and 'Night Rain' (page 88) are woven on the same networked and extended twill threading but use different pattern lines for their networked treadling sequences.

thrills twill thrills twill thrills twill thrills twill thrills twill thrills twill thrills twill thrills twill thrills twill thrills twill
thrills twill thrills twill thrills twill thrills twill thrills twill thrills twill thrills twill thrills twill thrills twill
thrills twill thrills twill thrills twill thrills twill thrills twill thrills twill thrills twill thrills twill thrills twill

slim, silk, saddle-shoulder sheath

1. Layout for dress

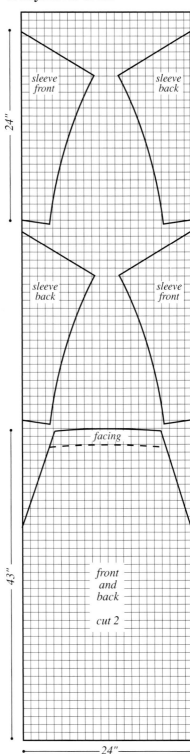

Here is a basic black dress that is perfect for both business and dressy occasions! It is comfortable to wear, virtually wrinkle-free, and easy to make. Worn belted or loose-fitting, the sheath can be accessorized with jewelry and stiletto heels. The focus is on the fabric design without the distraction of busy tailoring.

The dress fabric is charcoal cotton and black silk, subtly tone-on-tone. It can be woven either in a 16-shaft advancing twill with a shimmering moiré effect (see photo, p. 89) or a 4-shaft undulating twill (not shown) that curves symmetrically from the center to each side and includes a small basket weave to accentuate verticality.

Saddle-shoulder raglan sleeves give the slim sheath real panache. They incorporate narrow contrasting panels inset between the two lower parts of the sleeve and extending from each side of the neckline to the wrist. These panels can contrast with the dress fabric in color, weave structure, or texture. In this dress, the panels are woven in a different twill from the dress fabric, and a cream silk warp with a black silk weft provide contrasting color.

For looms with eight, ten, or twelve shafts, you can very successfully substitute any advancing or networked twills for the dress body and sleeve insert fabrics—pick from among the many that appear in this volume!

THE DRESS FABRIC

- Equipment. 4-shaft or 16-shaft loom (with dobby interface for the dress fabric), 25" weaving width; 12-dent reed; 1 shuttle.
- Materials. Warp: 10/2 pearl cotton (4200 yds/lb, Yarn Barn), charcoal, 12 oz. Weft: 30/2/2 English spun silk, (5400 yd/lb, Robin and Russ Handweavers), black, 8 oz; 2 packages Flexi-lace Seam Binding, black or color-coordinated to the colors in your fabric; sewing thread, black. Amounts allow 28" loom waste and 12% draw-in and shrinkage.
- Wind a warp of 600 ends 10/2 cotton 4½ yds long for 16-shaft draft in *2a*, p. 90, or wind 593 ends 10/2 cotton 4½ yds long for 4-shaft draft in *4*.
- Sley 2/dent in a 12-dent reed, 24 epi; center for 25".
- Weave following the peg plan in *2b* (or use any networked or advancing twill treadling draft if you have a 16-shaft treadle loom) or follow the treadling sequence in *4* on four shafts. Hemstitch both ends of front and back dress pieces.

SLEEVE PANEL INSERTS

- Equipment. 4-shaft or 16-shaft loom, 6" weaving width; 15-dent reed; 1 shuttle.
- Materials. Warp: #6 2-ply fine silk cord (4650 yd/lb, The Silk Tree), natural, 2 oz (or substitute 10/2 beige cotton, 4200 yds/lb). Weft: 30/2/2 English spun silk, (5400 yd/lb, Robin and Russ Handweavers), black, 2 oz. Amounts allow 21" loom waste, 15% draw-in and shrinkage.
- Wind a warp of 180 ends silk 2¼ yds long for 16-shaft draft in *3*, p. 90, or 172 ends 2¼ yds long for 4-shaft draft in *5*.
- Sley 2/dent in a 15-dent reed, 30 epi; center for 6".
- Weave two 30" sleeve inserts using the tie-up in *3* (treadled as drawn in) or following the treadling sequence in *5*; hemstitch at beginning and end of each.
- Finish sleeve insert and dress fabrics by handwashing in tepid water with Ivory flakes or hair shampoo; line dry until slightly damp; press.

SEWING THE DRESS

- On brown grid paper with 1" squares, enlarge the layout in *1* to full scale, using the squares as a guide. Cut pattern pieces out of brown paper and lay them out on the fabric so that the twill direction is the same for all pieces. Notice that the side edges are deliberately placed on the selvedges to avoid cutting. Pin all pieces in place and trace around all of them with disappearing-ink marking pen or with tailor's chalk or by basting around all pieces with contrasting thread. Before cutting, reinforce all edges to be cut with two rows of machine straight stitching to prevent raveling except where hemstitched, and then cut out pieces. A couturier touch is to bind/enclose all cut edges with black Flexi-lace seam binding (or use a color that is coordinated with your fabric).
- To assemble, fold under 2" at top edge of dress front and back as facing. With warm iron, fuse an interfacing strip 1½" wide and 14" across between inner (wrong) sides of facing and dress. Attach each sleeve back to dress back and each sleeve front to dress front with ⅝" seam allowances. Press seams toward sleeves.
- Check to ensure that the direction of the twill is the same on both sleeve insert panels. Turn under 2" facings at each (top) shoulder edge. Overlap the panel selvedges a scant ¼" over the selvedge edges of each dress sleeve front and back, aligning so that the head opening is 5" deep (over the shoul-

ll thrills **twill** thrills **twill** thrills twill thrills **twill** thrills twill thrills twill **thrills** twill thrills twill thrills twill thrills twill **thrills** twill thrills twill
thrills **thrills** twill thrills twill thrills twill thrills **twill** thrills twill thrills twill thrills twill thrills twill thrills twill **thrills** twill thrills twi
ll thrill twill thrill twill **thrills** **twill** thrills twill thrills twill thrills twill **thrills** twill thrills twill thrills twill **thrills** twill thrills twill thrills **twill** **thrills** twill th

Use this dress style with any drapable handwoven fabric. Twills are especially suitable, providing a soft flowing line that complements the smooth lines of the sheath. A networked twill creates the moiré effect of this fabric, but 4-shaft undulating twills or any skip or advancing twills are all appropriate.

2a. 16-shaft draft for dress fabric

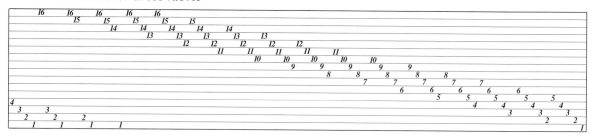

3. 16-shaft draft for sleeve inserts

b   *Thread a-b, c-d 1½ x*   *a* 1 2 3 4 5 6 7 8 9 10 11 12 13 14 15 16

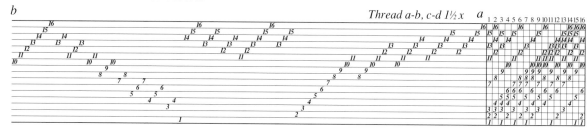

d   *c*

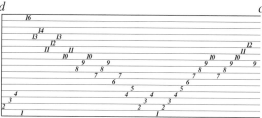

4. 4-shaft draft for dress fabric

d c   2x   2x   *ba* 1 2 3 4

Thread a-d, c-b 16x.

2lx   2lx   1 2 3 4

5. 4-shaft draft for sleeve inserts

2b. Peg plan for dress fabric (with 2a)

ders) and 6" across (front and back). Baste, and then with black sewing thread topstitch in place close to the selvedge edge, from neckline to wrist. Stitch front and back sides together with ⅝" seam allowances in one continuous seam from wrist to hemline on each side, stopping 8" from each lower edge to allow 6" side vent after the hem is sewn. Press seams open.

❑ Sew the dress hem with Flexi-lace seam binding: Overlap the lace ¼" in from (and parallel to) the raw edge on the right side of the fabric and machine stitch. Then turn the fabric to the inside for a 2" hem and sew lace binding to the fabric by hand. (This avoids the bulk created by turning the handwoven fabric twice and makes a neater hem.) Face and hem the wrist edges in the same way, adjusting hem measurement to fit. ✂

twill thrills twill th

twill blocks and beyond

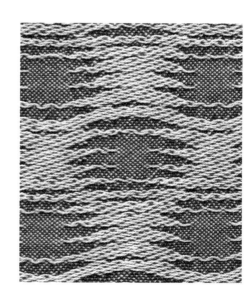

twill thrills twill thrills twill thrills twill thrills twill thrills twill thrills twill thrills twill thrills twill thrills twill thrills twill thrills twill thrills twill
thrills twill thrills twill thrills twill thrills twill thrills twill thrills twill thrills twill thrills twill thrills twill thrills twill thrills twill th
ills twill thrills twill thrills twill thrills twill thrills twill thrills twill thrills twill thrills twill thrills twill thrills twill thrills twill th

glacier scarf

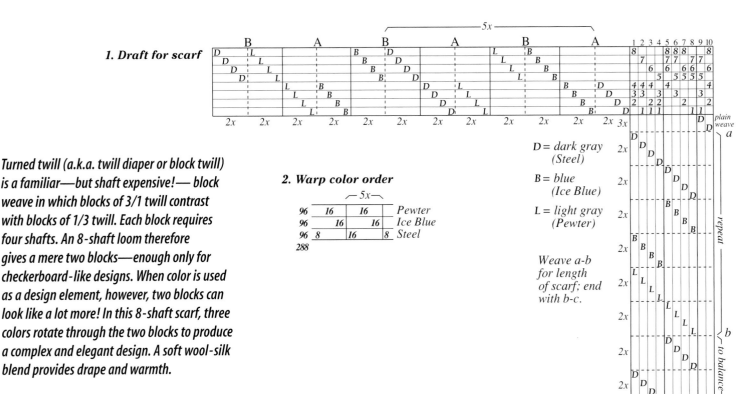

1. Draft for scarf

2. Warp color order

D = dark gray (Steel)

B = blue (Ice Blue)

L = light gray (Pewter)

Weave a-b for length of scarf; end with b-c.

Turned twill (a.k.a. twill diaper or block twill) is a familiar—but shaft expensive!— block weave in which blocks of 3/1 twill contrast with blocks of 1/3 twill. Each block requires four shafts. An 8-shaft loom therefore gives a mere two blocks—enough only for checkerboard-like designs. When color is used as a design element, however, two blocks can look like a lot more! In this 8-shaft scarf, three colors rotate through the two blocks to produce a complex and elegant design. A soft wool-silk blend provides drape and warmth.

Since the Glacier scarf is designed as a man's scarf, the colors are subtle: dark gray, light gray, and a medium light blue. Blocks A and B produce 3/1 vs 1/3 twill alternately throughout. The colors are threaded and treadled in sequence (Steel, Ice Blue, Pewter), but color changes occur halfway through each block in both warp and weft rather than at block changes. This technique, introduced to me by Sharon Alderman, creates many more color and design variations than when color changes coincide with block changes.

Finished scarf measurements are 11" x 61" plus fringe. The fringe can be 2–6" in length, depending on personal preference.

- ❏ Equipment. 8-shaft loom, 12" weaving width; 12-dent reed; 1 boat or end-feed shuttle with 3 bobbins or pirns; temple for 12" width (optional but recommended).
- ❏ Materials. Warp and weft: 18/2 wool/silk (5040 yds/lb, Zephyr, JaggerSpun), Steel 1¾ oz (D), Ice Blue 1½ oz (B), Pewter 1½ oz (L).
- ❏ Wind a warp of 288 ends 3 yds long. (For faster winding, 2 ends of each color can be warped together.) Wind in the following color order (see also 2): 8D, [16B, 16L, 16D]x5, 16B, 16L, 8D.
- ❏ Sley 2/dent in a 12-dent reed, 24 epi; center for 12". Add 1 floating selvedge (in Steel) to each side.

- ❏ Thread following the draft in 1. The floating selvedges are not threaded through a heddle and are weighted separately. Before weaving, decide if fringe will be knotted or twisted or if you prefer to hemstitch the ends. If hemstitching is preferred, hemstitch on the loom over the first and last 2–3 picks. Allow 2–3 more than desired fringe length if you plan a twisted fringe.
- ❏ Weave a plain-weave header with scrap yarn. Allowing the amount desired for fringe, begin with 6 picks of plain weave and then weave the scarf following 1 (a–b) for about 65" or desired length. This yarn is easy to overbeat, so be very gentle; establish a 45° angle in the twill line to assure the correct beat and measure the picks per inch (they should equal ends per inch, i.e., 24). End with b-c using Steel weft (D) and finally 6 picks plain weave.

Since the weft color changes every 16 picks, alternate sides (right vs left) when beginning each new yarn so that the selvedges build up equally. (End a weft by bringing the shuttle around the floating selvedge back into the same shed 1–2" and trim. Enter the next weft in a new shed on the opposite side, leaving a tail to bring around the floating selvedge into the same shed 1–2".) Use a temple if available for straight sel-

vedges and to minimize draw-in, repositioning the temple at least every ¾".
- ❏ Finish by removing the scarf from the loom. Tie overhand knots in groups of 4 ends each (or prepare twisted fringe of two sets of 4) if the ends are not hemstitched. If there is extra warp length at fringes, cut fringe 2–3" longer than the desired finished length and knot the cut ends in large groups to minimize tangling during washing. Machine wash or wash by hand. To machine wash: Dissolve about a tablespoon of Orvus Paste in a small washer load of warm water, soak the scarf for 1 hour, agitate for 2 minutes, spin out water. Remove the scarf from the machine; add warm rinse water; put the scarf back in and hand swirl until soap is removed; spin out water. Hang to dry, cut temporary knots off fringe ends (if you did not prepare a twisted fringe), and untangle ends gently. When almost dry, hard press with hot steam iron. This will raise the sheen of the silk and create a fabric with a beautiful hand. Trim fringe: Lay scarf flat on cutting board, comb out fringe, and trim with rotary cutter using a straight edge. ✄

I thrills twill thrills twill thrills twill thrills twill thrills twill thrills twill thrills twill thrills twill thrills twill thrills twill thrills twill thrills twill thrills twill thrills twill t
twill thrills twill thrills twill thrills twill thrills twill thrills twill thrills twill thrills twill thrills twill thrills twill thrills twill thrills twill thrills twill thrills twill thrills twill
ll thrill twill thrill twill thrills twill thrills twill thrills twill thrills twill thrills twill thrills twill thrills twill thrills twill thrills twill thrills twill th

Smetko Lynn Smetko Lynn Smetko Lynn Smetko Lynn Smetko Lynn Smetko Lynn Smetko Lynn Smetko Lynn Smetko

Three subtle colors rotate in sequence throughout Lynn's scarf. Use this 2-block draft with different colors or experiment with more than three. When color changes occur halfway through the blocks, secondary motifs can be the unexpected result. Sets of pinwheels appear along the diagonal in this scarf.

will thrills twill thrills twill thrills twill thrills twill thrills twill thrills twill thrills twill thrills twill thrills twill thrills twill thrills twill
thrills twill thrills twill thrills twill thrills twill thrills twill thrills twill thrills twill thrills twill thrills twill thrills twill thrills twill thrills th
ills twill thrills twill thrills twill thrills twill thrillss twill thrills twill thrills twill thrills twill thrills twill thrills twill thrills twill thri

pinwheel top

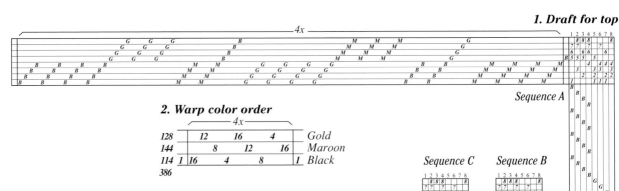

1. Draft for top

Sequence A

2. Warp color order

		4x			
128		12	16	4	Gold
144		8	12	16	Maroon
114	1	16	4	8	1 Black
386					

Sequence C *Sequence B*

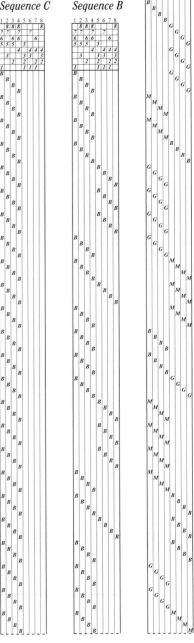

German weaver Hildburg Langen, inspired by an Anita Luvera Mayer design for a pinwheel top, turns two silk shawls into a top of her own. The drape of the silk, the variation in the turned broken-twill treadling sequences, and the clever pinwheel shape all seem to have been selected with each other in mind! The complexity of the turned-twill design in Hildburg's fabrics is a result of varying block width and length. Compare this design idea with Lynn Smetko's color rotation using the same two twill blocks (pages 92–93).

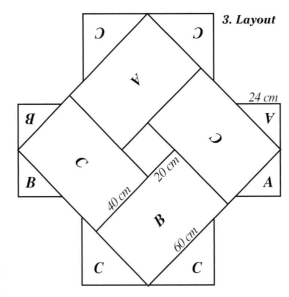

3. Layout

The two shawls are woven in 8-shaft 'false' damask (4-end broken twill; see *1*). Shawl 1 uses treadling sequence A for the first half and sequence B for the second half, and shawl 2 uses treadling sequence B for the first half and sequence C for the second half. (The half-and-half divisions in these shawls are a result of running out of maroon and gold weft!)

As I was enjoying my shawls, Issue 16 of *Weaver's* arrived. I was fascinated by Anita Mayer's 'Pinwheel Top,' pp. 40–41—but no knitting for me! I tried to make a paper model before realizing that I needed to know more about the ratios of widths and lengths. I looked, and there it all was in the text!

I realized that the basic width of 40 cm (about 15¾") is the same width as my shawls. Why not use my two already-finished shawls instead of weaving new fabric for a pinwheel top?

The half-and-half treadling sequences in the two silk shawls are especially suitable for the pinwheel design. I worked to find the most pleasing way to arrange the shawls in the pinwheel form, then cut and sewed the garment using selvedges as finished edges wherever I could.

❏ Equipment. 8-shaft loom, 16" weaving width; 12-dent reed; 3 shuttles.

❏ Materials. Warp and weft: 2-ply tussah silk (yarns for this top are available in Germany from Zürcher; substitute 2-ply tussah silk from The Silk Tree), 6680 yds/lb; Black, 8 oz; Gold, 2 oz; Maroon, 2 oz.

❏ Wind a warp of 386 ends 5 yds long in the color order in *2*.

❏ Sley 2/dent in a 12-dent reed, 24 epi; center for 16" (1 black end on each side is a floating selvedge).

❏ Thread following the draft in *1*.

❏ Weave 38" using treadling sequence A, 38" treadling sequence B, and 72" treadling sequence C.

❏ Assemble by machine stitching twice along each side of the cutting lines for the eight rectangles. Stitch selvedge edges over cut edges to join large rectangles. Stitch large rectangles over small rectangles. Fold right sides together; sew side seams; hem. ✂

ll thrills **twill** thrills **twill** thrills twill thrills twill **thrills** twill thrills twill **thrills** twill thrills twill thrills twill thrills twill **thrills** twill thrills twill t
twill **thrills** twill thrills twill thrills twill thrills twill **thrills** twill thrills twill thrills twill thrills twill thrills twill thrills twil
twill thrills twill thrills twill thrills twill thrills twill thrills twill thrills twill thrills twill thrills twill thrills twill thrills twi
ill thrill twill thrill twill **thrills twill** thrills twill thrills twill thrills twill **thrills** twill thrills twill **thrills** twill thrills twill thrills twill th

rg Langen **Hildburg** *Langen* **Hildburg** *Langen* **Hildburg** *Langen* **Hildburg** *Langen* Hildburg *Langen* **Hildburg** *Langen* Hild

This top is constructed from two fabric lengths, both woven on the same warp. A different treadling sequence is used for each half of the two fabrics. The clever pinwheel pattern, designed by Anita Luvera Mayer, and the placement and colors of the twill blocks are a perfect match.

ill thrills twill thrills twill thrills twill thrills twill thrills twill thrills twill thrills twill thrills twill thrills twill thrills twill thrills twill thrills twill thrills twill thrills twill
thrills twill thrills twill thrills twill thrills twill thrills twill thrills twill thrills twill thrills twill thrills twill thrills twill thrills twill thrills twill thrills twill thrills twill
ills twill thrills twill thrills twill thrills twill thrills twill thrills twill thrillss twill thrills twill thrills twill thrills twill thrills twill thrills twill thrills twill thrills twill thr

twill illusions with two and four blocks

Holst Pellekaan Freya van Holst Pellekaan Freya van Holst Pellekaan **Freya van Holst Pellekaan** *Freya*

1a. Two blocks

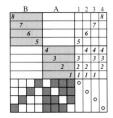

1b. Thread-by-thread draft for part of 2a

1c. Thread-by-thread draft for part of 2b

Grace your holiday table with a runner in turned twill. Wrap hot rolls in a turned-twill bread cloth—or, do both! These pieces are quick and easy to weave with one shuttle, and the optical curves created by the simple two-block pattern are magnetizing. You'll find it hard, in fact, to tear yourself away from watching circle after circle grow on the loom.

In turned twill (also called twill damask, twill blocks, and twill diaper!), blocks of pattern are produced by 4-thread units of warp-emphasis 3/1 twill against a background of weft-emphasis 1/3 twill (or vice versa). Each block requires four shafts.

TWO BLOCKS ON EIGHT SHAFTS

The draft in *1a* shows one unit of Block A weaving 3/1 twill and one unit of Block B weaving 1/3 twill. To thread turned twill following a 2-block profile draft such as in *2a*, substitute one 4-thread unit of Block A for each black square on the A row of the profile threading draft and one 4-thread unit of Block B for each black square on the B row. The draft in *1b*

shows the thread-by-thread draft for the first seven squares of the profile threading draft in *2a*.

FOUR BLOCKS ON 16 SHAFTS

If sixteen shafts are available, four blocks can be woven. For each square on the C row, thread 9-10-11-12; for each square on the D row, thread 13-14-15-16. The thread-by-thread draft for the bracketed squares in *2b* is shown in *1c*.

TIE-UP AND TREADLING

To weave 3/1 twill in any block, the four shafts of that block must be raised in the same order as the Block A shafts in *1a*. To weave 1/3 twill they must be raised in the same order as the Block B shafts. *3a* (see p. 98) shows the order in which any four shafts must be raised to produce 3/1 twill and *3b* shows the order in which any four shafts must be raised to produce 1/3 twill. *3a* and *3b* are templates that can be used to derive the tie-up for any profile draft.

For example, to derive the turned-twill tie-up for a specific profile draft, first choose whether pattern is to be 3/1 or 1/3 twill. If pattern is 3/1 twill, substitute the template in *3a* for every black square in the selected profile tie-up. Substitute the template in *3b*

2a. Two-block profile draft
see 1b

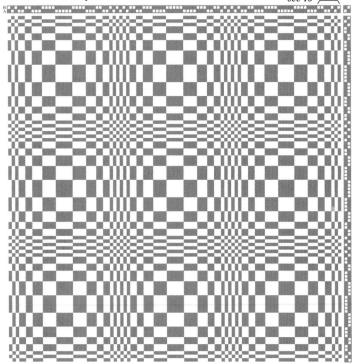

2b. Four-block profile draft
see 1c

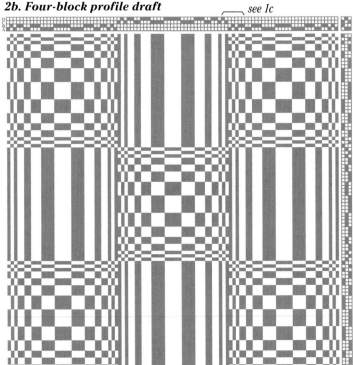

96

thrills twill thrills twill thrills twill thrills twill thrills twill thrills twill thrills twill thrills twill thrills twill thrills twill thrills twill thrills twill thrills twill t twill thrills twill thrills twill thrills twill thrills twill thrills twill thrills twill thrills twill thrills twill thrills twill thrills twill thrills twill thrills twill thrills twi twill thrills twill thrills twill thrills twill thrills twill thrills twill thrills twill thrills twill thrills twill thrills twill thrills twill thrills twill thrills twill th

It is hard to believe that the complex, circular design in this runner is created with only two blocks. Weave this runner on only eight shafts, or place the circles in four corners on sixteeen. The damask-like texture of turned twill makes these fabrics especially appropriate for table linens.

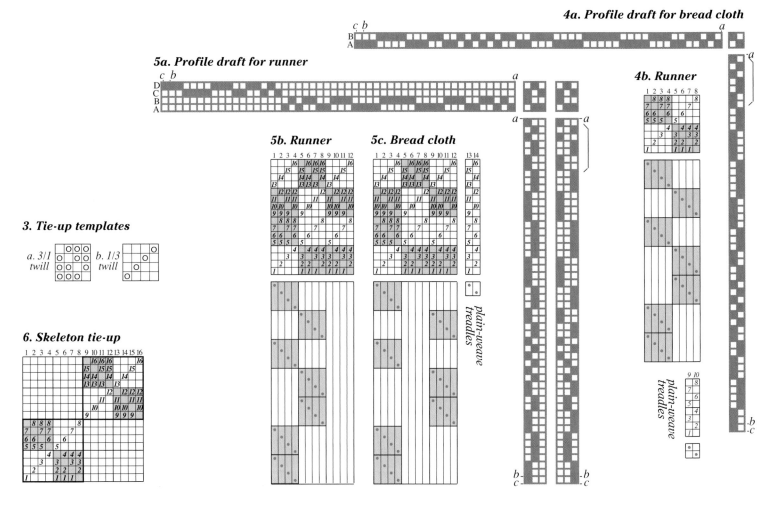

4a. Profile draft for bread cloth

5a. Profile draft for runner

5b. Runner **5c. Bread cloth**

4b. Runner

3. Tie-up templates

a. 3/1 twill *b. 1/3 twill*

6. Skeleton tie-up

plain-weave treadles

for every blank square. Compare the profile tie-ups in *4a* and *5a* with the actual tie-ups for turned twill in *4b* and *5b-c*.

To derive the treadling order, substitute the 4-pick sequence from *1a* for each black square in the profile treadling draft, as shown in *4b*, *5b–c*.

Skeleton tie-up as a design tool

The 16-shaft design in the bread cloth is a result of playing with a skeleton tie-up (a skeleton tie-up is one in which more than one treadle is depressed at the same time). Instead of thinking of the profile in *2b* as a 4-block design, think of it as two independent 2-block designs. With the tie-up in *6*, use one foot for treadles 1–8 (the A/B design) and the other for treadles 9–12 the (C/D design). Using both feet together, treadle each of the two designs as desired. In the first section of *2b*, the A/B pair weaves circles, and the C/D pair weaves stripes; in the next section, the C/D pair weaves circles and the A/B pair weaves stripes.

FREYA'S TABLE RUNNER AND BREAD CLOTH

❏ Equipment. 8-shaft loom for table runner (see *4a–b*), 16-shaft loom for bread cloth and table runner (see *5a–c*), 12-dent reed, 1 shuttle.
❏ Materials. Warp 10/2 cotton (4200 yds/lb), natural, ½ lb. Weft: 16/2 linen (2750 yds/lb, Nordic Studio); light brown for table runner, ½ lb; gray blue for bread cloth, 3 oz.
❏ Wind a warp of 398 ends 10/2 cotton, 4 yds long for 1 runner, 1 bread cloth, and sampling. For other amounts, estimate 2 yds for each runner and ¾ yd for each bread cloth. Add 1 end on each side for floating selvedges.
❏ Sley 2/dent in a 12-dent reed, 24 epi; center for 16⅝".
❏ Thread substituting 4-thread units (A = 1-2-3-4; B = 5-6-7-8; C = 9-10-11-12; D = 13-14-15-16) for squares in the profile threading draft in *4a* or *5a*: a-c; b-a.
❏ Weave the table runner on eight shafts substituting a 4-pick treadling unit for each square in the

profile treadling draft in *4a* (a-c; b-a). Weave the table runner and bread cloth on 16 shafts substituting a 4-pick treadling unit for each square in the profile treadling draft in *5a* (a-c; b-a).

Begin by inserting sticks or cardboard in plain-weave sheds to provide 2½" fringe. Weave 2 picks of plain weave with weft yarn. Weave pattern for length of piece (11 sets of circles for runner, 3 sets for bread cover). Weave 2 picks of plain weave. Insert sticks or paper between pieces to provide approximately 2½" fringe at both ends of each piece, 5" between projects. Begin and end each piece with 2 picks of plain weave.
❏ Finish by removing cloth from loom and fringe sticks from cloth. Cut pieces apart and make a twisted fringe: twist two bouts of 6 ends each in one direction and then twist both groups together in the opposite direction; secure with an overhand knot. Wash in hot water; rinse and press (as for linen) with hot iron before dry. Starch lightly if desired. Expect 15-20% shrinkage. ✳

homage to Escher: networked imagery

Create Escher-like images with network drafting—on only eight shafts—without a dobby! Play at the loom for two one-shuttle yards and turn the result into a dramatic and unique silk scarf.

will thrills twill thrills twill thrills twill thrills twill thrills twill thrills twill thrills twill thrills twill thrills twill thrills twill thrills twill thrills twill thrills twill
thrills twill thrills twill thrills twill thrills twill thrills twill thrills twill thrills twill thrills twill thrills twill thrills twill thrills twill thrills twill thrills twill th
ills twill thrills twill thrills twill thrills twill thrills twill thrills twill thrillss twill thrills twill thrills twill thrills twill thrills twill thrills twill thrills twill thrills twill thr

Virginia West Virginia West Virginia West Virginia West Virginia West Virginia West Virginia West Vi

For years the drawings of graphic artist Maurits Escher have intrigued me. I love the way his geese appear to fly to the right and then to the left as they move across the surface of a drawing. I've never planned such imagery in weaving, but one day, in a few hours of treadling spontaneity, a fish motif emerged that seemed to change direction as it moved.

Neither a computer nor a dobby loom is required!—only eight shafts, a 28-end networked threading draft, eight treadles, and one shuttle. This project began as a sampler and was transformed into a scarf; see p. 99. Use the threading in Step *1e* or design your own—the only rule is to let yourself go.

MIX AND MATCH

The fabric in *Photo a* uses a 1/3/3/1 twill tie-up with the treadling in *4f*; see also *3a*. The fabric in *Photo b* uses the same tie-up treadled as drawn in; see also *3b*. To weave your sampler (a.k.a. scarf!) mix and match tie-ups and treadling orders from *3* and *4* or try some of your own. A computer is handy for recording your ideas and cutting and pasting tie-ups and treadling orders from other projects.

SILK SCARF OR SAMPLER

❏ Equipment. 8-shaft loom, 15-dent reed, 1 shuttle.
❏ Materials. Warp: 2-ply tussah silk (6680 yds/lb, The Silk Tree), natural, 2 oz. Weft: 20/2 silk (5000 yds/lb, Treenway Silks) or 10/2 pearl cotton (4200 yds/lb) black, 2 oz.
❏ Wind a warp of 252 ends, 3 yds long. This allows a generous 2-yd scarf. You may get carried away with your discoveries and need a longer warp, however; add to warp and weft amounts accordingly.
❏ Sley 2 ends/dent in a 15-dent reed, 30 epi; center for 8½".
❏ Thread following the draft in Step 1e 9x for this scarf (see p. 99).
❏ Weave selecting from tie-ups *2a–2d* and from treadling sequences *4a–4f* or use any 8-shaft twill tie-up and treadling sequence. When you find a sequence you particularly like, make a record! Hemstitch beginning and end of scarf.
❏ Wash in lukewarm water with Ivory liquid or hair shampoo (good for silk). Squeeze out water in a dry towel. Lay flat to dry, but steam press while still slightly damp. ✄

STEPS FOR DESIGNING NETWORKED TWILLS ON EIGHT SHAFTS

1a. Draw a curve or shape 5 rows high.

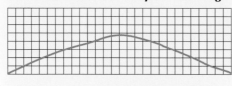

1b. Place the curve on a grid 8 rows high; fill in squares crossed by the curve (one in each vertical column).

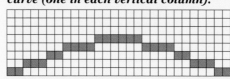

1c. Copy the squares using 'x's on a network made of 4-shaft, 4-end initials.

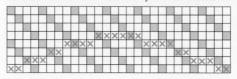

1d. Blacken all gray squares that have x's on them (see * below); these are 'hits.' Blacken one network (gray) square directly above every 'x' that is not a hit (x's on a blank square). The black squares are the new networked threading.

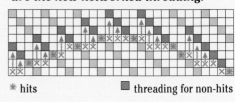

* hits   ■ threading for non-hits

1e. Rewrite the threading, and repeat it or reverse it as desired.

2. Twill tie-ups

a. Fabric from draft in 3a

b. Fabric from draft in 3b

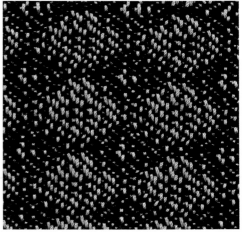

thrills twill thrills twill thrills twill thrills twill thrills twill thrills twill thrills twill thrills twill thrills twill thrills twill thrills twill
thrills twill thrills twill thrills twill thrills twill thrills twill thrills twill thrills twill thrills twill thrills twill thrills
thrills twill thrills twill thrills twill thrills twill thrills twill thrills twill thrills twill thrills twill thrills twill thrills twill
thrill twill thrills twill thrills twill thrills twill thrills twill thrills twill thrills twill thrills twill thrills twill thrills twill thrills twill th

Virginia West Virginia West Virginia West Virginia West Virginia West Virginia West Virginia West

3a. Networked draft: 1/3/3/1 twill tie-up, advancing point-twill treadling

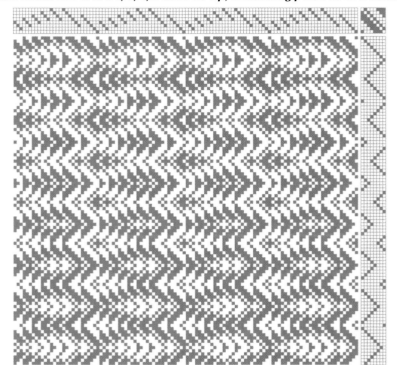

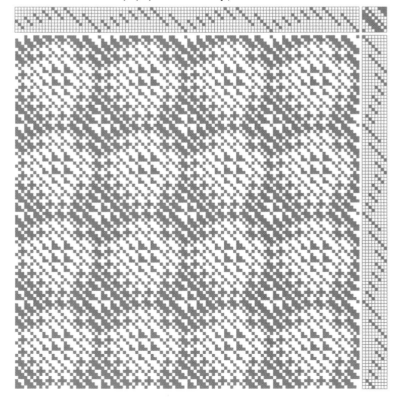

3b. Networked draft: 1/3/3/1 twill tie-up, treadled as drawn in

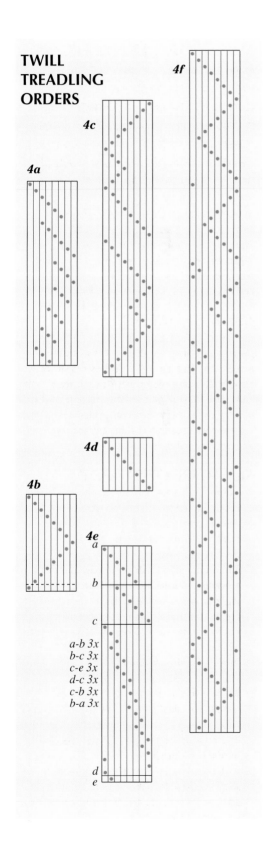

**TWILL
TREADLING
ORDERS**

4f

4c

4a

4d

4b

4e

a

b

c

a-b 3x
b-c 3x
c-e 3x
d-c 3x
c-b 3x
b-a 3x

d
e

fancy twill extravaganza on only four shafts

Bonnie Inouye Bonnie Inouye Bonnie Inouye Bonnie Inouye Bonnie Inouye Bonnie Inouye **Bonnie Inouye** Bonnie Inc

1. Two blocks of 2/1 vs 1/2 twill

2. Four blocks of 2/1 vs 1/2 twill

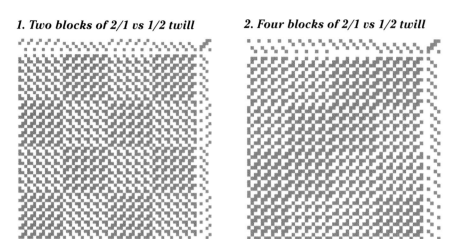

3. Four blocks of 2/1 vs 1/2 twill framed with sections of straight twill

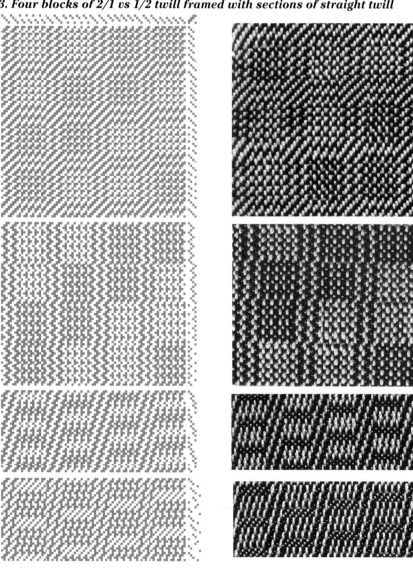

If you're a 4-shaft weaver who loves a very contemporary look, you might feel left out of the current twill revolution with its optical networked and advancing twills. Even if you prefer a more traditional look, you probably wish you could weave the turned-twill block designs that require at least eight shafts. It might surprise you to learn that with an adaptation here and a bit of mixing there, you can weave them all—and some unusual new hybrids—on your 4-shaft loom!

Here are several new ways to design twills on four shafts. Once you understand the drafting principles, you can create an even greater variety of patterns by mixing treadling sequences from one system with threading sequences from another.

TWILL BLOCKS ON FOUR SHAFTS

In 8-shaft turned twill, blocks of warp-dominant (3/1) twill alternate with blocks of weft-dominant (1/3) twill (review pp. 6–7 and pp. 92–98). A 3-thread 'jeans' twill (2/1 vs 1/2 twill) can provide a similar effect on four shafts even though blocks share shafts. In *1*, Block A = 1-2-3; Block B = 1-4-3. Contrast between the blocks is not as strong as on eight shafts, but the blocks show reversed twill directions, they can be threaded following any 2-block profile draft, and they can be mixed successfully with other twill threadings and treadlings.

Moreover, the threading in *1* can be extended to produce *four* blocks on four shafts: A = 1-2-3, B = 2-3-4, C = 3-4-1, and D = 4-1-2. Two blocks must always weave pattern together; see the drawdown in *2*.

In order to make the blocks more distinctive and the pattern more unusual, a 4-thread twill can be inserted as a frame for each block. The resulting draft maintains all the advantages of twill—good drape, diagonal movement, one-shuttle weaving—and is successful with a variety of twill-based treadlings; see *3* and the accompanying samples, woven by Lauren Jensen McNitt.

MERGING: ADVANCING TWILL MEETS OVERSHOT

In advancing twill threadings, straight (or point) twill runs are arranged in succession. Each run begins on one or more shafts above the previous run (1-2-3-4-5, 2-3-4-5-6, 3-4-5-6-7, etc.) and the runs continue through the number of shafts available (see Ingrid Boesel, 'Advancing Twills,' pp. 38–41). Most advancing twills are woven on six or more shafts.

...ll thrills **twill** thrills **twill** thrills twill thrills twill **thrills** twill thrills twill **thrills** twill thrills twill thrills twill thrills twill thrills twill thrills twill **thrills** twill thrills twill t
twill **thrills twill** thrills twill thrills twill thrills twill thrills twill thrills twill thrills twill thrills twill thrills twil! thrills twill thrills twi
ill thrill twill thrill twill **thrills twill** thrills twill thrills twill thrills twill **thrills** twill thrills twill **thrills** twill thrills twill thrills twill **thrills** twill th

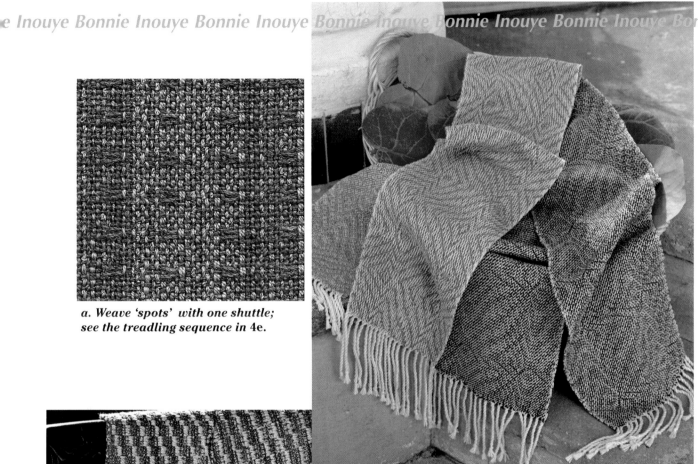

a. Weave 'spots' with one shuttle; see the treadling sequence in 4e.

c. The patterns in these 4-shaft networked fabrics are more effective when viewed from a distance than at close range.

b. This scarf uses an overshot Blooming Leaf treadling. Many other twill and overshot sequences can be used with the same threading.

vill thrills twill thrills twill thrills twill thrills twill thrills twill thrills twill thrills twill thrills twill thrills twill thrills twill thrills twill thrills twill thrills twill
thrills twill thrills twill thrills twill thrills twill thrills twill thrills twill thrills twill thrills twill thrills twill thrills twill thrills twill thrills twill thrills twill th
ills twill thrills twill thrills twill thrills twill thrills twill thrillss twill thrills twill thrills twill thrills twill thrills twill thrills twill thrills twill

4. Advancing twill and overshot

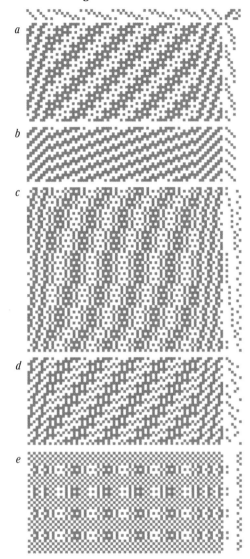

a

b

c

d

e

5. Sample networks

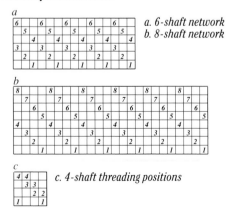

a. 6-shaft network
b. 8-shaft network

c. 4-shaft threading positions

A 4-shaft advancing twill threading with three threads in each run (1-2-3; 2-3-4; 3-4-1; 4-1-2, as in *4*) looks a lot like a threading draft for overshot. With this threading, advancing twills and overshot seem to merge, much like a corporate merger. One management—the threading—oversees all the operations of *two* companies: overshot treadlings work with this threading, twill treadlings still produce the diagonal lines expected of twills, and some new hybrid treadlings emerge as well.

Because these threadings are not symmetrical and generally develop along the diagonal, when they are woven as overshot (with separate pattern and tabby wefts) the results have a more contemporary look than traditional symmetrical overshot patterns. The scarf in *Photo b* uses an overshot treadling that produces a Blooming Leaf type of design, in which the number of times a block is treadled increases and decreases in a variety of different arrangements (one of them is shown in sequence *4c*).

This threading can be woven as drawn in, in straight order, or with any other twill treadling sequence. Especially interesting effects come from combining twill and overshot treadling systems. In *4d*, for example, only one shuttle is used (as for twill) and the treadling sequence is as-drawn-in except every fourth pick is made in alternate tabby sheds. The final sequence in *4e* produces the spot-weave variation shown in the fabric in *Photo a*.

NETWORK DRAFTING—ALMOST!

A true networked twill needs at least six shafts (review Alice Schlein, 'Network Drafting: More for Less,' pp. 62–65). Why bother trying to weave networked twills on four shafts? Networked twills have advantages: there are no long floats, they can provide as many pattern 'blocks' as there are shafts on the loom, and they allow designing freedom with diagonal lines and smooth curves (though the more shafts available, the smoother the curves). There is great flexibility in the scale of a networked design, with no minimum or maximum block size.

Deriving a 4-shaft 'networked' threading

Before you begin drafting, first determine the yarn to be used, the appropriate sett, and the desired scale of the design. For a small scale, the threading might repeat every inch or two. For a larger scale, the repeats can be much longer. The draft for the 8"-wide scarves in *Photo c* contains two threading repeats of 84 ends each.

Next, determine the general outline of the pattern: one broad curve, or one broad and one steep, or

a curve and a diagonal line. Will the curve continue in one direction or turn back? The general segments of the pattern can then be placed within the scale: if the repeat is to be 4" and there is to be one steep and one broad curve, allow about 1" for the first curve and 3" for the second. At 20 epi, for example, 20 ends would form the first curve and 60 ends the second.

Sample networks for six and eight shafts are shown in *5a–b*. The 6-shaft network uses a 3-thread initial repeated twice vertically, and the 8-shaft network uses a 4-thread initial repeated twice vertically. The first thread in the actual threading must be one of the two numbers in the first column, the next thread must come from one of the two numbers in the second column, etc. (see Alice Schlein, p. 65).

A 4-shaft network, however, cannot be more than one initial high, giving no threading choices except one in each column, i.e., straight twill. Instead, use the chart in *5c*. Begin with either shaft 1 or 2 in the first column—let's say 1. Move to the left to select from the next column, in this case either a 2 or a 3. Pick 2 or 3. Then notice that both 2 and 3 appear in two adjacent columns. For the next thread, choose from the column to the left of both. If you picked 2, for example, your next thread will be either a 3 or 4; if you picked 3, your next thread will be either a 4 or 1. Continue in this way—you will never pick the same number twice in succession. For the first four threads, beginning with shaft 1, here are some possible choices: 1-2-3-4 or 1-3-4-1 or 1-2-4-1 or 1-2-3-1. (Note that true tabby cannot be woven with these drafts.) The steepest twills occur when moving from column to column (1-2-3-4); a shallower curve occurs when columns are skipped (1-2-3-2-3-4).

Once a threading draft is plotted, it can be reversed to produce symmetrical curved designs. If it is to be repeated, make sure that no two adjacent ends are threaded on the same shaft.

Tie-up and treadling sequences

For any networked draft, the tie-up must be appropriate for the network used. For this 4-shaft network to produce a viable fabric, all treadles must be tied so that two shafts are up and two are down for each pick.

Networked drafts are always successful when woven as drawn in as in *6*, but also consider: advancing twill, M and W, broken point, and countless other treadling orders (see *7–8*). Some interesting designs occur when treadles raising shafts 1-3 and 2-4 are added to the sequences. A sequence using three picks of a twill treadling, for example, then 1-3, then three more twill picks, then 2-4, is especially

thrills twill thrills twill thrills twill thrills twill thrills twill thrills twill thrills twill thrills twill thrills twill thrills twill thrills twill t
twill thrills twill thrills twill thrills twill thrills twill thrills twill thrills twill thrills twill thrills twill thrills twill thrills twill thrills tw
ill thrill twill thrill twill thrills twill thrills twill thrills twill thrills twill thrills twill thrills twill thrills twill thrills twill thrills twill th

effective. Such a treadling emphasizes the twill lines; see **7** and the blue scarf in **Photo c**.

The pattern can be difficult to see during weaving unless very fine threads are used. (Using fine threads has the same effect as viewing the piece from a distance.) Make a complete drawdown to see the pattern. If adjustments need to be made, refer to the network and pick a different shaft from the same column. Try a curve, repeat and reverse it, and enjoy the results! ✂

6. A 4-shaft networked draft treadled as drawn in

7. 1-3 and 2-4 are used alternately for every fourth pick in the treadling sequence

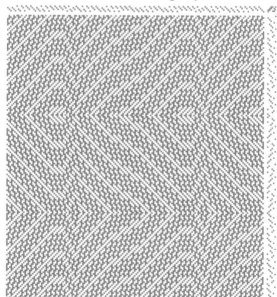

8. A mix of treadling orders with a 4-shaft networked draft

a

b

c

d

e

f

g

a. broken point twill
b. reversing point twill
c. advancing twill
d. twill and tabby
e. twill and tabby
f. extended point twill
g. expanded advancing twill
h. point twill

will thrills twill thrills twill thrills twill thrills twill thrills twill thrills twill thrills twill thrills twill thrills twill thrills twill thrills twill thrills twill thrills twill
thrills twill thrills twill thrills twill thrills twill thrills twill thrills twill thrills twill thrills twill thrills twill thrills twill thrills twill thrills twill thrills twill th
ills twill thrills twill thrills twill thrills twill thrills twill thrills twill thrills twill thrills twill thrills twill thrills twill thrills twill thrills twill thrills

imagery in advancing twills

1a. Polka dots on a straight draw

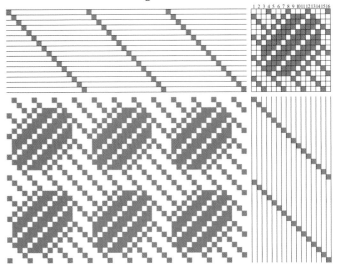

Small-scale images can be designed on a straight-draw threading by placing them directly in the tie-up. When treadled as drawn in, the images appear in the drawdown. For point threading and treadling orders, draw one quarter of the image in the tie-up.

1b. Polka dots on an advancing twill threading

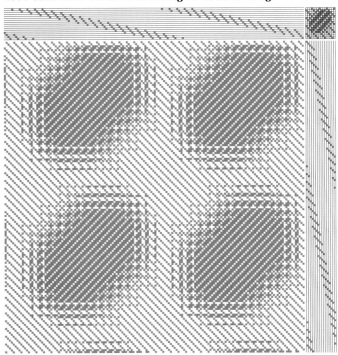

*When the same image in the tie-up is used with advancing twill threading and treadling orders, the same image is created in the drawdown as in **1a**. It is much larger, however, and is surrounded by concentric lines that are created by the transition between the shafts weaving warp-emphasis twill and the shafts weaving weft-emphasis twill. Both the size of the image and the degree of shading can be increased by expanding the advancing twill.*

I like to draw pictures in my weavings, but tapestry and inlay have always seemed too slow for me. I prefer using the shafts of my loom to create imagery through structure. A block weave is an obvious choice, providing clear contrast between image and background. Summer and winter, for example, can produce a number of blocks equal to the number of shafts on the loom minus two for the tie-down shafts. On an 8-shaft loom, summer and winter allows six blocks for imagery. But what if I want more, or if I want shadings? I now use advancing twills for these images.

In advancing twills, each small section of straight twill can be thought of as a block. In the 16-shaft draft in *1b*, in which each section of twill begins on a shaft above the preceding section, there are 16 blocks! The edges of the images created by using advancing twills this way are soft and blurred, which makes the images especially effective with hand-dyed multicolored warps. When woven with a single-colored warp, they look intricate, delicate, and complex. They can be designed to imitate weft ikat. Compare the image woven with a straight-draw threading and treadling order in *1a* with the same image woven with an advancing twill threading and treadling order in *1b*.

Drafting images in advancing twills and expanded advancing twills is best done on a computer. The long threading and treadling sequences make drawdowns on graph paper tedious and time-consuming. Although small-scale images are possible with advancing twills, especially in very fine threads, advancing twills are normally used to generate larger-scale designs than other twill types—they can even produce a single image across a wide fabric.

STRUCTURAL CHARACTERISTICS

Advancing twill drafts allow many structural interlacements to occur in the same cloth, such as warp-emphasis twills, weft-emphasis twills, balanced twills, other twill variations, and plain weave. A 5-end advancing twill threading (1-2-3-4-5; 2-3-4-5-6; 3-4-5-6-7, etc.), for example, can be used to produce 1/3, 2/2, and 3/1 twills; plain weave; basket weave; and even double weave. The different twills can be designed to progress in the same or opposing directions.

Since more interlacement takes place in plain weave than in twill, care must be taken when they are combined. The undulation of weft rows due to take-up differences between plain-weave and twill areas can be an effective design enhancement, however. Note that not all advancing twills allow plain weave to be woven throughout the cloth. If this is desired, transition threads can be added to advancing twill threadings so that odd and even shafts always alternate (see 'Advancing Twills,' by Ingrid Boesel, pp. 38–41). A 4-end advancing twill 1-2-3-4; 2-3-4-5; 3-4-5-6, etc.) does not produce plain weave, for example, but the expanded advancing twill threading in *4a* does (1-2-3-4; 1-2-3-4-5; 2-3-4-5; 2-3-4-5-6; 3-4-5-6; 3-4-5-6-7, etc.).

The most interesting images and shadings occur when a number of different interlacements are used with a single threading. Long repeats in the threading are needed if you want to weave a large design. Some simple rules must be followed when designing tie-ups. For 5-end advancing twills such as in *1b*, for example, tie-ups should produce no floats longer than three threads.

ill thrills **twill** thrills **twill** thrills twill thrills twill **thrills** twill thrills twill **thrills** twill thrills **twill** thrills twill thrills twill **thrills** twill thrills twill **thrills** twill thrills **twill** thrills twill thrills twill **thrills** twill thrills twill **thrills** twill thrills **twill** thrills **twill** thrills **twill** thrills **twill** thrills twill thrills twill **thrills** twill thrills twill **thrills** twill thrills twill thrills twill **thrills** twill thrills twill **thrills** twill thrills twill thrills **twill thrills** th

ie *Inouye* Bonnie *Inouye* Bonnie *Inouye* Bonnie *Inouye* Bonnie *Inouye* Bonnie *Inouye* Bonnie *Inouye* Bonnie *Inouye*

2a. A curved image on a straight draw

DESIGN STEPS

One way to design images for an advancing twill threading is to start with a straight twill threading on the same number of shafts.

❏ Write the straight twill threading for the number of shafts on your loom, as in *1a* and *2a*.

❏ If you have a treadle loom, draw an image directly in the tie-up. Write the treadling order to correspond with the threading order, i.e., 'as drawn in.' Place 3/1 twill inside the image and 1/3 twill outside the image. Then examine the relationship between the tie-up image and the drawdown, as in *1a*.

❏ If you have a dobby loom, prepare a peg plan grid with a sufficient number of rows to accommodate your image. Outline the image directly in the peg plan grid. Place 3/1 twill inside the image and 1/3 twill outside. Then examine the relationship between the peg plan and the image in the drawdown, as in *2a*.

❏ For a treadle loom, substitute an advancing twill threading and treadling for the straight twill threading and treadling, as in *1b*. For a dobby loom, use the peg plan you designed with an advancing twill threading, as in *2b*.

Threading and treadling variations

Experiment with threading variations. Compare the advancing twill threading in *2b* with the expanded advancing twill in *2c* (for a discussion of advancing and expanded advancing twill threadings, see Ingrid Boesel, 'Advancing Twills,' pp. 38–41). If the image becomes stretched too much horizontally, it can also be extended vertically by adding rows to the treadling. In the case of tie-ups and peg plans that use 1/3 vs 31 twills, this will mean adding multiples of four picks to maintain structural integrity.

2b. A curved image on an advancing twill threading

Shading images

It can be very interesting to use this technique on images that are not typically associated with fuzzy edges—take a dollar sign, for example. The dollar sign can be woven as a very small image using a straight twill; see *3a*, p. 108. With an advancing twill threading, the edges of the image vibrate; see *3b*. When the advancing twill is expanded, even more side effects result; see *3c*.

2c. A curved image on an expanded advancing twill threading

Note that the shadings are produced by areas of different twills, with a darker-appearing twill adjacent to a lighter one (i.e., warp-emphasis twill next to a weft-emphasis twill). The effect is quite different from the regular, all-over half-tone effect associated with block weaves like summer and winter.

When I am drawing an image on paper, I often start with a line drawing and then add small, thinner lines around the image to indicate shading. In advancing twill structures, some of these lines will occur automatically. Additional shading lines can be added in a dobby peg plan.

vill thrills twill thrills twill thrills twill thrills twill thrills twill thrills twill thrills twill thrills twill thrills twill thrills twill thrills twill thrills twill thrills twill
thrills twill thrills twill thrills twill thrills twill thrills twill thrills twill thrills twill thrills twill thrills twill thrills twill thrills twill thrills twill thrills twill th
lls twill thrills twill thrills twill thrills twill thrills twill thrillss twill thrills twill thrills twill thrills twill thrills twill thrills twill thrills twill thrills twill thrills

3a. Motif on a straight draw

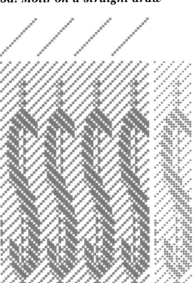

3b. Advancing twill

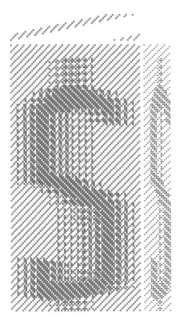

3c. Expanded advancing twill

To design advancing and expanded advancing twills, start with a straight-draw threading. Design an image in the tie-up or peg plan; adjust as necessary for the desired effect (3a). Next substitute an advancing twill threading and treadling (add rows to the peg plan; 3b). For further horizontal stretch and more shading, expand the advancing twill (3c).

4a. Plaited twill used as a pattern motif

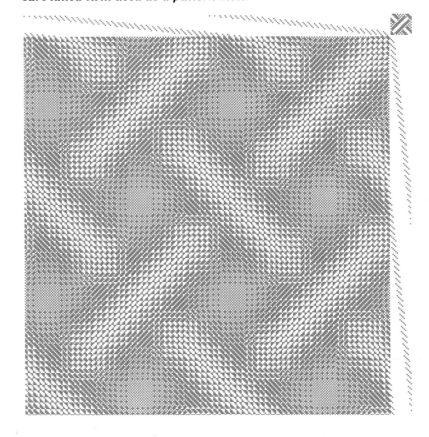

Use a twill pattern as a motif for advancing twills

An interlacement can be used as the image itself. In *4a*, for example, a plaited twill is placed in the tie-up and used with expanded advancing twill threading and treadling orders. In fact, place any 16-shaft twill in the tie-up to produce a design that is an image of that twill: see the embellished diagonal line in *5a* that results from using a straight-twill in the tie-up.

Create curvy lines

When an expanded advancing twill with equal-sized blocks is treadled as drawn in, the diagonals are straight. But straight

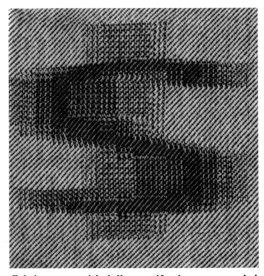

Fabric woven with dollar motif using an expanded advancing twill draft

ll thrills **twill** thrills **twill** thrills twill thrills twill **thrills** twill thrills twill **thrills** twill thrills **twill** thrills twill thrills twill **thrills** twill thrills twill t
twill **thrills** twill thrills twill thrills twill thrills twill thrillstwill **thrills** twill thrills twill thrills twill thrills twill thrills twill thrills twill! thrills twill thrills twi
ll **thrill** twill thrill twill **thrills** **twill** thrills twill thrills twill thrills twill **thrills** twill thrills twill **thrills** twill thrills twill thrills **twill thrills** twill th

5a. *Twill tie-up: blocks are equal size*

5b. *Twill tie-up: blocks increase in size in the treadling*

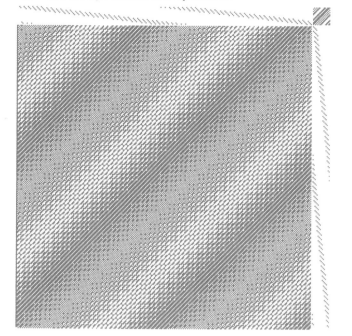

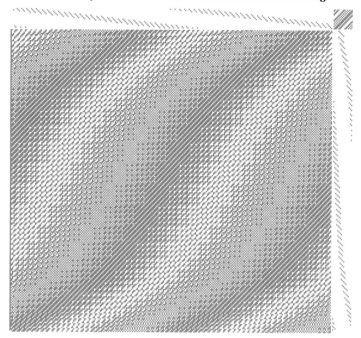

lines are not always desirable; curvy or undulating lines can create a welcome sense of movement in a fabric. As a source for curvy lines, think of the Blooming Leaf patterns from overshot structures. In these designs, curves result from repeating one block of a pattern an increasing number of times. To duplicate this effect in an advancing twill, begin with the 5-end advancing twill threading: 1-2-3-4-5; 2-3-4-5-6; 3-4-5-6-7; 4-5-6-7-8. Then expand by adding four ends to the next blocks: 5-6-7-8-5-6-7-8-9; 6-7-8-9-6-7-8-9-10. Next add still another repeat: 7-8-9-10-7-8-9-10-7-8-9-10-11, etc.; see *4b* and *5b*. Experiment with varying the number of repetitions.

The same principle can be applied to the treadling. Undulating twills can be used as profile drafts for advancing twill threading and treadling drafts. The blocks (threading and/or treadling) can also be used in discontinuous twill sequences, like dornik or broken twills. Remember that advancing twills are not unit weaves, however—since blocks share shafts, there will never be a clear distinction between pattern and background areas. To be sure that no lengthy floats occur, make and examine drawdowns before warping the loom, particularly since threading repeats are so lengthy.

What an exciting adventure advancing twills can provide! Designing images and threading the loom take some time, but weaving is quick with one shuttle. Even though the treadling repeats are long (if you are using a treadle loom), they follow a logical order. For the weaver with a computer-assisted dobby loom, advancing twills are a delight to design *and* to weave.

4b. *Plaited twill pattern motif: blocks increase in size in the threading and treadling*

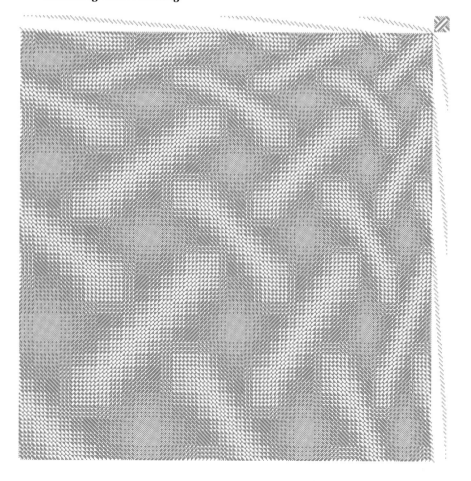

BIBLIOGRAPHY

Inouye, Bonnie. *Exploring Multishaft Design.* Hyattsville, Maryland: Weavingdance Press, 2000. Includes a complete discussion of designing and weaving advancing twills.

broken windows: networked satin and

PATTERNING WITH TWO ASPECTS OF THE SAME WEAVE

1. 1/3 and 3/1 twill

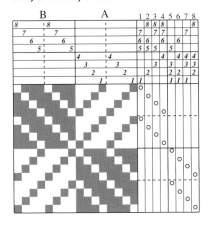

2. 1/3 and 3/1 broken twill

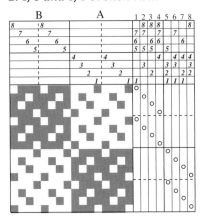

3. 1/4 and 4/1 satin

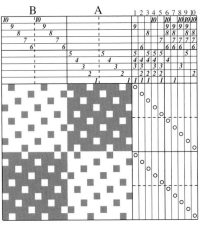

4. 1/7 and 7/1 satin

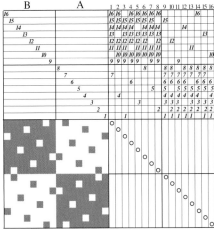

PATTERNING WITH TWO DIFFERENT WEAVES

5. Satin and plain weave on eight shafts

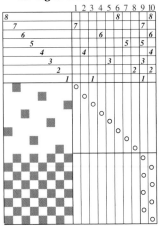

6. Satin and plain weave on 16 shafts

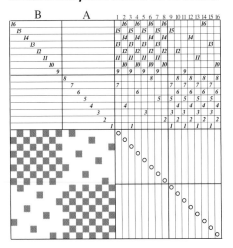

Imagine a window after a rock or a baseball has gone through it, and you might recognize the jagged outline of the motif in the Broken Windows shawl; see photo, p. 111. You might not recognize, however, the term 'damassé.'

In *The Primary Structures of Fabrics*, Irene Emery explores the many possible meanings of the term damassé and indicates that this French word, literally 'damasked' in English, refers sometimes to structure and sometimes to materials (see the Bibliography, p. 112). But Emery further suggests that ". . . the greatest usefulness of [the term] damassé would seem to lie in distinguishing the area-patterning effected by two different weaves from that effected by the two aspects of the same weave."

DAMASK

We are all familiar with patterning created with two aspects of the same weave, such as is produced by twills and satins. The block weave in *1* produces a 1/3 straight twill and its 'reverse side,' or opposite aspect, a 3/1 straight twill. In *2*, a 1/3 broken twill contrasts with its opposite aspect, a 3/1 broken twill. These patternings are often referred to as 'reverse twill' or 'turned-twill' blocks, and in Scandinavia they are sometimes called 'twill damask.'

In *3*, 1/4 satin contrasts with its opposite aspect, 4/1 satin. In *4*, 1/7 satin is shown with its opposite, 7/1 satin. These fabrics are called 'damask,' sometimes 'satin damask.' (For more information about satin and damask, see Madelyn van der Hoogt in the Bibliography.)

DAMASSÉ

One example of "area-patterning effected by two different weaves"—i.e., damassé—is a combination of 1/7 satin and plain weave. They are not two aspects of the same weave, yet they can both be woven on the same threading system (a straight draw); see *5*. On eight shafts we can weave only one of these weaves at a time and so can combine the two interlacements only in horizontal bands across the cloth. On 16 shafts, two blocks can be produced, as in *6*. On a 16-shaft dobby loom, networked damassé produces dramatically jagged, curving shapes.

The satin/plain weave challenge

The damassé combination of 7/1 satin and plain weave presents interesting challenges. These two

Weave this shawl in satin and plain-weave damassé. The jagged edges of the circles are produced by network drafting. A dramatic textural difference occurs when these two interlacements are used in a single cloth: the satin areas pop up and the plain-weave areas recede.

will thrills twill thrills twill thrills twill thrills twill thrills twill thrills twill thrills twill thrills twill thrills twill thrills twill thrills twill thrills twill thrills twill thrills twill thrills twill
thrills twill thrills twill thrills twill thrills twill thrills twill thrills twill thrills twill thrills twill thrills twill thrills twill thrills twill thrills twill thrills twill thrills twill thrills twill th
ills twill thrills twill thrills twill thrills twill thrills twill thrills twill thrillss twill thrills twill thrills twill thrills twill thrills twill thrills twill thrills twill thrills twill thrill

7. Deriving a networked damassé threading

8. Deriving a networked damassé peg plan

BIBLIOGRAPHY

Emery, Irene. *The Primary Structures of Fabrics*. Washington, D.C.: The Textile Museum, 1980.
Masson, Olivier, and François Roussel. *Shaft Weaving and Graph Design*. Montreal: Editions 'En Bref,' 1988.
Schlein, Alice. *Network Drafting: An Introduction*. Greenville, South Carolina: Bridgewater Press, 1994.
van der Hoogt, Madelyn. *The Complete Book of Drafting for Handweavers*. Petaluma, California: Shuttle-Craft Books, 1993.

structures require radically different warp and weft setts. For any given yarn, satin is sett much closer than plain weave, as there are far fewer interlacement points for the same number of ends and picks. Therefore a compromise is in order, with a damassé sett roughly halfway between the optimum sett for the selected satin and plain weave. This means that the satin areas will be quite loose, and the plain-weave areas unusually firm. In designing the cloth, care must be taken to distribute satin and plain-weave areas equally throughout the cloth, so that inequities in take-up do not occur and ruin the tension. Utmost vigilance is required in maintaining a consistent beat when weaving damassé.

The satin/plain weave benefits

Fascinating surface effects occur in satin-and-plain damassé. Small areas of satin in a larger plain-weave background will pop up in high relief. Small areas of plain weave in a larger satin background can have the appearance of deep holes or windows. Since the plain-weave areas are more densely interlaced, they tend to expand aggressively into the satin areas, causing deflected warps and wefts in the places where the two structures meet.

Most of these effects do not appear until the cloth is removed from the loom and washed. For weavers who regard the washing machine as an important item in their creative toolbox, satin-and-plain damassé is a real winner!

NETWORKED DAMASSÉ

The 16-shaft threading network for the Broken Windows shawl is based on an 8-end straight initial; see *7c*. A pattern line 80 squares long (*7a*) is expanded to an 8-row ribbon (*7b*) and placed on the network (*7d*). The shaded squares covered by the ribbon become the threading draft (*7e*).

The same pattern line is rotated 90° (*8a*) and expanded to an 8-square width (*8b*) to form a cut-and-paste template. The template is placed on a 1/7 satin peg plan (*8c*) to make a cut-out ribbon (*8d*) that is pasted onto the plain-weave peg plan (*8e*) to form the final peg plan in *8f*. The cloth for the Broken Windows shawl is woven wrong side up since fewer shafts are raised that way (the jagged high-and-low effect is more pronounced on the bottom side; compare the photos of the face and back of the cloth, p. 113). In network drafting, the larger the initial, the greater the amount of chaos or jaggedness between the weave structures.

I thrills twill thrills twill thrills twill thrills twill thrills twill thrills twill thrills twill thrills twill thrills twill thrills twill t
twill thrills twill thrills twill thrills twill thrills twill thrills twill thrills twill thrills twill thrills twill thrills twill thrills twill thrills twi
ll thrill twill thrill twill thrills twill thrills twill thrills twill thrills twill thrills twill thrills twill thrills twill thrills twill thrills twill th

BROKEN WINDOWS SHAWL

Networked damassé in plain weave and satin creates jagged designs and a dimensional texture caused by slight deflections of warp and weft threads at design edges—and it's easy to weave with one shuttle!

The finished measurements of the Broken Windows shawl are 96" long and 25" wide plus fringe.

- ❑ Equipment. 16-shaft dobby loom, 32" weaving width; 12-dent reed; 1 shuttle.
- ❑ Materials. Warp: 10/2 unmercerized cotton (4200 yds/lb), natural, 1 lb. Weft: 10/2 unmercerized cotton, cocoa, ¾ lb. This allows for 1 yd loom waste, 8" at each end for fringe, and some sampling.
- ❑ Wind a warp of 760 ends, 5 yds long. Spread warp to 31.6" in raddle, beam.
- ❑ Thread according to draft in *9* (read draft from right to left) 9½ times. No special selvedge treatment is required.
- ❑ Sley 2/dent in a 12-dent reed, 24 epi; center for 31.6" weaving width.
- ❑ Weave plain weave with waste yarn for approximately 1" (alternately raise odd and even shafts) at 24 ppi. Then loosely weave plain weave (approximately 2 or 3 ppi) for 8" to allow for later twisted fringe treatment.
- ❑ Weave 4 picks plain weave at 24 ppi with cocoa weft yarn. Then weave 3 yds at 24 ppi following peg plan in *8f.* End with 4 picks plain weave.
- ❑ Weave loose plain weave with waste yarn for 8"; then weave 1" at 24 ppi. Cut fabric from loom.
- ❑ To finish, with sewing machine or serger, secure the 1" of firmly woven waste yarn at either end (this will temporarily protect the fringe area), and machine wash and dry the fabric in hot water and detergent at normal cycle. Approximate take-up and shrinkage is 20%. Cut off the machine-sewn areas, remove waste yarn from the loosely woven 8" at either end, and prepare a twisted fringe with groups of 4/4 ends. ✂

Face (underside during weaving)

Back (top side during weaving)

9. Broken Windows threading draft

network drafting: some new approaches

*Dini Cameron Dini Cameron Dini Cameron Dini Cameron Dini Cameron **Dini Cameron** Dini Camero*

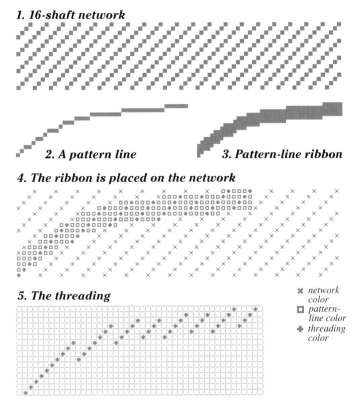

1. 16-shaft network

2. A pattern line   **3. Pattern-line ribbon**

4. The ribbon is placed on the network

5. The threading

✕ network color
▢ pattern-line color
✦ threading color

6. Deriving a peg plan from the pattern ribbon

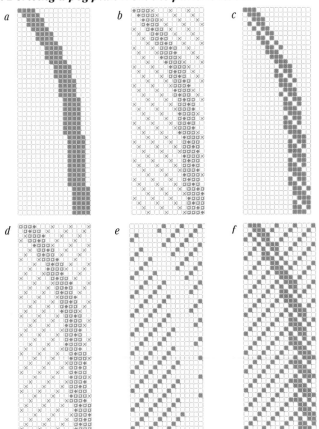

a   *b*   *c*

d   *e*   *f*

You don't have to have a computer to design a networked draft. All you need are some sheets of plastic film (such as the sheets that are used with overhead projectors), some fine graph paper, and colored marking pens that can write on plastic.

The steps for deriving a networked threading draft are: first, to prepare the network; second, to trace the pattern line on the network; and third, to plot the actual threading. If the network is drawn on durable plastic film, it can be used as a template over and over again with other pattern lines.

FROM PATTERN LINE TO THREADING

Place a sheet of graph paper (8 or 10 sq/in) sideways before you. Position a sheet of plastic film over the graph paper. With a black marker draw a frame along the long side of the plastic as wide as the graph paper and as many squares high as the number of shafts available to you; 16 are used in this demonstration.

With a marker, color in squares inside the frame as in *1*. (In these examples, the templates and threadings are read from left to right; you can work in either direction.) This is your permanent template for a 16-shaft network based on a 4-end straight initial. Templates for other initials can be made in the same way.

Next, draw a pattern line on the same size graph paper that you used to make the template; see *2*. Use a different-colored marker from the color you used for the template. Reproduce the pattern line three more times below the original line to form a ribbon four squares high, as in *3*.

Lay the network template over the pattern-line ribbon, aligning the two bottom left-hand corners, as in *4*. The squares of the network that cover squares in the ribbon will change color (✦ in *4*); these form the new networked threading. Copy them on graph paper, as in *5*.

FROM PATTERN LINE TO LIFT PLAN

The network threading template in *1* can also be used as a lift plan template. (A lift plan designates the shafts to raise on a table loom; it also acts as the peg plan for a dobby loom. For treadle looms, try twill tie-ups and treadle as drawn in.)

In this example, we'll designate 3/1 twill as pattern and 1/3 twill as background. First, draw the pattern line vertically on graph paper in the same color that you used for the pattern line in the threading. Reproduce the line three more times to the right. (To use the same pattern line in the lift plan that you used for the threading, rotate the threading pattern ribbon 90°, as in *6a*.) Position the template over the pattern ribbon, lining up the squares in the upper left-hand corner; see *6b*. The pattern-line color shows where pattern-line squares are *not* covered by network squares (three squares of every four); a new color shows where pattern line squares *are* covered by network squares.

On a separate sheet of graph paper, copy the squares of the pattern section that are *un*changed in color. These produce 3/1 twill in the pattern area; see *6c*. To prepare the lift plan for a 1/3 twill background in which the twill line runs in the opposite direction, turn the template over to reverse the twill direction and lay the template over the pattern, matching upper left-hand corners, as in *6d*. The squares that fall outside the pattern line remain unchanged in color (see *6e*). On the same grid as you used in *6c*, copy these squares to form the complete lift plan in *6f*.

Templates can be made in the same way for most networks. Some lift plans require two templates: one for pattern and one for background.

ll thrills **twill** thrills **twill** thrills twill thrills twill **thrills** twill thrills twill thrills twill thrills twill thrills twill thrills twill **thrills** twill thrills twill t
twill thrills twill thrills twill thrills twill **thrills** twill thrills twill thrills twill thrills twill thrills twill
ill thrill twill thrill twill **thrills** **twill** thrills twill thrills twill thrills twill **thrills** twill thrills twill **thrills** twill thrills twill thrills twill thrills twill th

meron Dini Cameron Dini Cameron Dini Cameron Dini Cameron Dini Cameron Dini Cameron Dini

*There are literally hundreds of motifs that can be networked on a point threading of the blocks. The
candle image, lower right, can be woven on eight shafts; another four are required for the plain
background. The other miniatures are woven on sixteen shafts.*

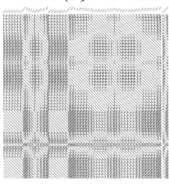

7a. 5-block Angstadt profile   7b. Profile (7a) in turned twill

8a. 5-block profile   8b. Profile is expanded in width

8c. Profile is expanded in height

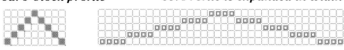

□ pattern-
line
color

8d. Network template is placed over pattern ribbon

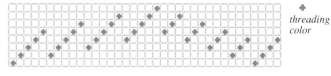

✗ network
color

8e. 8-shaft networked threading

✦ threading
color

9a. The candle   9b.   9c.

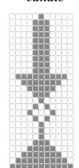
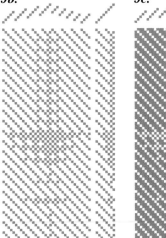
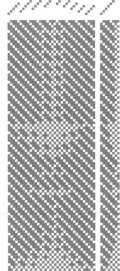

*The candle motif
is just one of
the symmetrical
images possible
on this threading.*

ALTERNATIVES TO THE PATTERN LINE

Profile drafts can be used very successfully to derive networked drafts. The reproduced manuscripts of Jacob Angstadt and John Landes (see the Bibliography) provide rich collections of profile drafts that when networked require a fraction of the usual number of shafts and give most interesting results! Jacob Angstadt's 5-block profile draft no. 38, Figure 139, (see *7a*) requires 20 shafts woven in a conventional turned twill. With networking, it can be woven on only *eight*. A subtle shading is a byproduct that adds depth and interest to the design; see *7b*.

Networking a profile draft

To 'network' a 5-block profile such as the one in *8a*, for example, first copy it on graph paper with a colored marker, expanding the width of each original square to four squares (to correspond to a 'unit' of four threads); see *8b*. Next, expand it in height by filling in three more squares *below* each of the squares in *8b* to form a ribbon; see *8c*. For an 8-row pattern 'ribbon,' an 8-row network is required. Use a different color marker from the ribbon color to prepare an 8-row template based on a 4-end twill initial (as in *1*, p. 114). Place the template over the new profile so that the bottom left corners meet, see *8d*. Three colors now appear: the network color, the ribbon color, and a new color where the network squares cover ribbon squares. This third color becomes the threading; rewrite on graph paper, as in *8e*. (Notice in *8d* that four threads appear in every 4 x 4-square 'block.')

Designing images

This point threading of five blocks is ideally suited for weaving small symmetrical images such as the candle in *9a*. The image is designed in the lift plan (to use with table or dobby looms); one interlacement is designated as the pattern interlacement and another as the background interlacement. On a 4-end straight initial, either plain weave or twill can be woven. For this candle, plain weave is selected for the image and 1/3 twill for the background; *9b* shows the face of the resulting cloth; *9c* shows the back.

Just as each block in the threading profile represents four threads, each block in the treadling profile represents four picks. Since the blocks are arranged in a point, we need only design one-half of the candle in the lift plan. Redraw half of the candle on a sheet of graph paper in color, marking four squares lengthwise for every one square in the graphed design. Draw a frame around this image eight squares wide, leaving some empty spaces above and below the candle. Make sure that the center of the candle is at one side of the frame to take advantage of the point in the threading; see *10a*.

Prepare a plain-weave template on a plastic sheet in a different color from the candle (*10b*). Position the template over the frame with the candle as in (*10c*). The colored squares of the network that fall on the squares of the candle motif will become a new color. On a clean sheet of graph paper, copy these squares; they indicate the shafts that are raised to weave the candle(*10d*).

Now position the 1/3 twill template (*10e*) over the candle (*10f*). The squares of the template which fall outside the candle form the background (*10g*). Mark these squares in the same frame of the graph paper where you marked the plain-weave squares for the candle (*10h*) to complete the lift plan.

BIBLIOGRAPHY

Atwater, Mary Meigs. *A Book of Patterns for Hand-Weaving by John Landes.* Hollywood, California: Southern California Handweavers' Guild, 1992.

Holroyd, Ruth, and Ulrike Beck. *Jacob Angstadt Designs Drawn from His Weavers Patron Book.* Pittsford, New York: Ruth Holroyd, 1976.

twill thrills twill thrills twill thrills twill thrills twill thrills twill thrills twill thrills twill thrills twill thrills twill thrills twill thrills twill
twill thrills twill thrills twill thrills twill thrills twill thrills twill thrills twill thrills twill thrills twill thrills twill thrills twill
twill thrill twill thrill twill thrills twill thrills twill thrills twill thrills twill thrills twill thrills twill thrills twill thrills twill th

10. Plain weave and 1/3 twill templates are placed on the 'candle' profile to derive the lift plan

a candle motif

b plain-weave template

c plain-weave template covers candle motif

d plain-weave lift plan for candle

e 1/3 twill template

f twill template covers candle motif

g lift plan for background

h complete lift plan

twill thrills twill thrills twill thrills twill thrills twill thrills twill thrills twill thrills twill thrills twill thrills twill thrills twill thrills twill thrills twill thrills twill thrills twill thrills twill
thrills twill thrills twill thrills twill thrills twill thrills twill thrills twill thrills twill thrills twill thrills twill thrills twill thrills twill thrills twill thrills twill
ills twill thrills twill thrills twill thrills twill thrills twill thrills twill thrills twill thrills twill thrills twill thrills twill

what's black and white and gray all over?

Alice Schlein Alice Schlein Alice Schlein Alice Schlein Alice Schlein **Alice Schlein** Alice Schlein Alice S

1a. 8-shaft twill: one tonal value

1b. Turned twill: two tonal values

2. Derive a networked threading from a pattern line

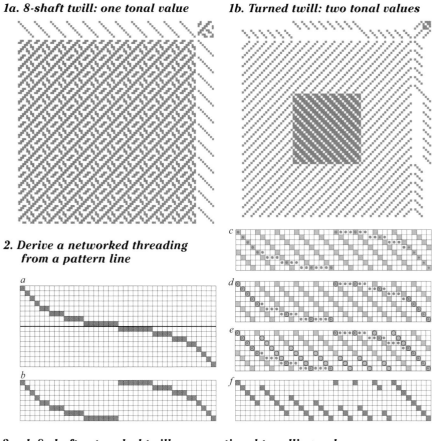

3a–d. 8-shaft networked twills: conventional treadling orders

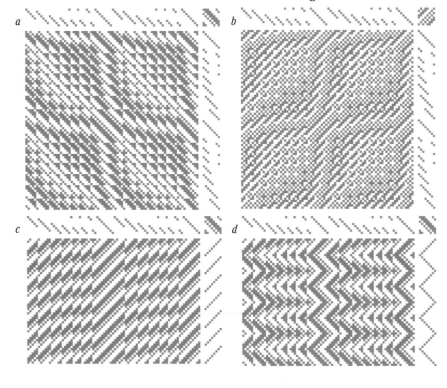

The tonal value of most twills—no matter how many shafts are used—is consistent throughout the cloth, with an equal mix of warp color and weft color or a predominance of one or the other; see a typical twill draft in 1a. Turned twills—or twill blocks— usually show two contrasting values: warp color predominates in one area, i.e., the pattern area, and weft color in the other, i.e., the background area, as in 1b. Networked drafts can be designed to produce a rich variety of tonal values, especially when a dobby loom is available.

When woven with a dark warp and a light weft, these threadings can produce very light areas, very dark areas, and midtone areas in the same cloth—using as few as eight shafts. Let's examine the development of an 8-shaft networked twill draft as an example. For a review of the steps for deriving networked twills, see pp. 62–82.

DERIVE A NETWORKED THREADING

Begin with a pattern line of any height and length. The pattern line in *2a* is 16 squares high x 40 squares long. To fit an 8-shaft network, it is telescoped to eight squares high in *2b* (a snail pattern line; the shaft rule is not used; see p. 75). It is plotted on the 8-shaft twill network in *2c* as a series of dots. The 'hits,' or places where a dot falls on a gray square, are circled in *2d*. The non-hits are circled on the next available gray square above the pattern line in *2e*. If no gray square is available *above* the dot, 'wrap' around to place the circles in the gray squares in the same column at the bottom of the threading draft. The circles become the networked threading in *2f*.

DERIVE THE TREADLING

On a conventional 8-shaft treadle loom, you can use any twill tie-up with conventional treadling sequences: as drawn in, for example, in *3a-b*; in straight twill order, as in *3c*; in point twill order, as in *3d*. You can also experiment with other networked treadling orders, as in *3e*, or advancing twill orders, as in *3f*; see p. 120.

DERIVE A PEG PLAN

If you have a dobby loom (or a table loom), the cut-and-paste method can be used to derive peg plans (lifting orders) for twills with three tonal values. Draw heavy lines to divide sections of a graph paper rectangle eight squares wide and any number of squares tall that is a multiple of four (48 squares in this example). These sections form the cutting templates; see *4a*.

thrills twill thrills twill thrills twill thrills twill thrills twill thrills twill thrills twill thrills twill thrills twill thrills twill thrills twill thrills twill
twill thrills twill thrills twill thrills twill thrills twill thrills twill thrills twill thrills twill thrills twill thrills twill thrills twi
ill thrill twill thrill twill thrills twill thrills twill thrills twill thrills twill thrills twill thrills twill thrills twill thrills twill th

Alice's Mitchell Mouse tablecloth is designed from a networked draft that produces three values: dark, light, and midtone. The networked design appears much more complex than traditional 16-shaft twill block patterns. Tilt your head to the right to see the shape of Mitchell Mouse's head and ears.

ill thrills twill thrills twill thrills twill thrills twill thrills twill thrills twill thrills twill thrills twill thrills twill thrills twill thrills twill thrills twill thrills twill thrills twill
thrills twill thrills twill thrills twill thrills twill thrills twill thrills twill thrills twill thrills twill thrills twill thrills twill thrills twill thrills twill thrills twill thrills twill th
lls twill thrills twill thrills twill thrills twill thrills twill thrillss twill thrills twill thrills twill thrills twill thrills twill thrills twill thrills twill

3e. Networked treadling order

3f. Advancing twill treadling order

4. Cut and paste from three different peg plans

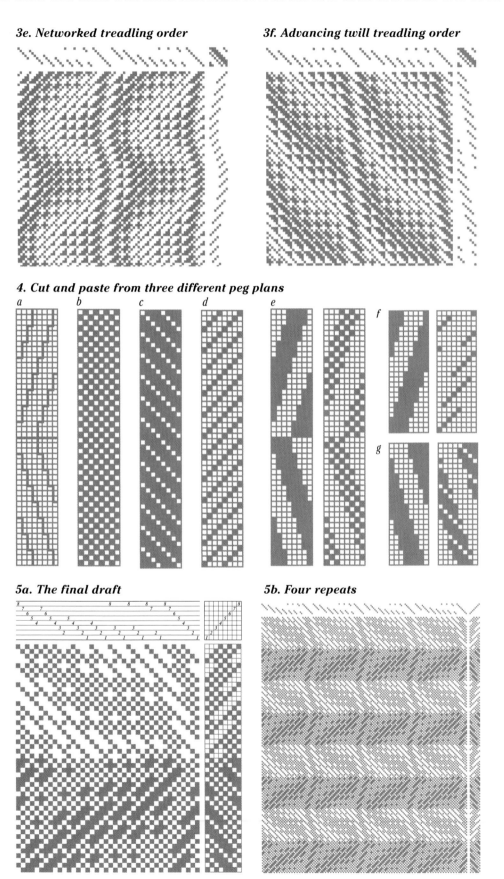

a   b   c   d   e   f   g

5a. The final draft

5b. Four repeats

Cut and paste: three tonal values on eight shafts

Select several different peg plans that can be used with a twill network: in this example plain weave as in *4b*, 1/3 straight twill as in *4c*, and 3/1 straight twill as in *4d*. With a dark warp and light weft, 3/1 twill produces a dark cloth, 1/3 twill a light cloth, and plain weave a midtone. Trace template sections (*4a*) on the peg plans and cut: the black sections are traced on the plain-weave peg plan (see *4e*), the upper-half white sections on the 1/3 twill peg plan in *4f*, the lower-half white sections on the 3/1 twill peg plan in *4g*. The peg-plan pieces are then assembled to compose the final peg plan and resulting drawdown in *5a*. Four repeats of the threading and peg plan are shown at a smaller scale in *5b*. Notice how the three tonal values enhance this design, which appears to be accordion-pleated! Weave this cloth on an 8-shaft dobby or table loom.

Cut and paste: more shafts

If 16 shafts are available, the cut-and-paste sections can be much larger. This allows greater design flexibility for producing large, smooth curves or other shapes and greater control of shading with midtone values. No matter what the number of shafts, the principles of cutting and pasting remain the same. The raw material for a cut-and-paste peg plan is any structure that is weavable on the network from which the threading was developed. Sections that are cut and pasted must maintain their original orientation with regard to horizontal and vertical position (shaft number and pick number).

Mitchell Mouse tablecloth project

In the tablecloth project, p. 121, a 16-shaft threading is derived from a 4-end twill network. The final peg plan is cut and pasted with sections of plain weave, 3/1 twill, and 1/3 twill to yield the three distinct tonal values: dark, light, and medium. These three tonal values show up only when warp and weft contrast strongly. In the places where dark warp crosses dark weft or light warp crosses light weft, we are conscious only of texture; but where dark warp crosses light weft or light warp crosses dark weft, the three tonal values pop out strongly. I call this the Restaurant Tablecloth Effect!

ill thrills twill thrills twill thrills twill thrills twill thrills twill thrills twill thrills twill thrills twill thrills twill thrills twill thrills twill thrills twill thrills twill t
s twill thrills twill thrills twill thrills twill thrills twill thrills twill thrills twill thrills twill thrills twill thrills twill thrills twill thrills twill thrills twill thrills tw
will thrill twill thrill twill thrills twill thrills twill thrills twill thrills twill thrills twill thrills twill thrills twill thrills twill thrills twill thrills twill thrills twill th

1. Threading draft for Mitchell Mouse tablecloth

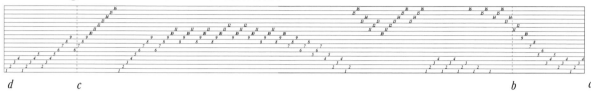

d   c   b   a

2. Peg plan

a

b

c

d

A NETWORKED TABLECLOTH

Mitchell Mouse, the world's first networked critter, dines out. Tip your head to the right when you view the drawdown, and you will see Mitchell. He's missing eyes and mouth, but he's definitely got ears. Big blue and white checks give this tablecloth a restaurant flavor.

3. The complete draft for Mitchell Mouse tablecloth

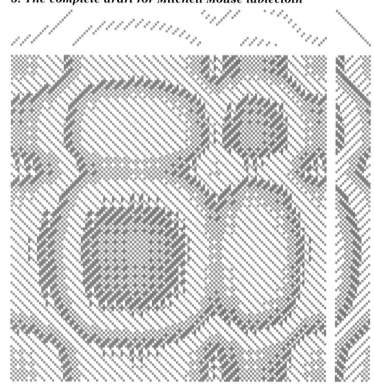

❑ Equipment. 16-shaft dobby loom, 45" weaving width, with 144 dobby bars or computer-assisted interface; 12-dent reed; 1 shuttle.

❑ Materials. Warp and weft: 20/2 pearl cotton (8400 yds/lb), 1 lb each of white and blue for finished tablecloth 40" x 62"; sewing thread for hems. Test yarn for colorfastness.

❑ Wind a warp of 1620 total ends 4 yds long in the following order: 18 white, (144 blue, 144 white) 5x, 144 blue, 18 white. This allows for 1 yd loom waste and a little sampling.

❑ Spread the warp in a raddle at 36 epi, centered for 45" weaving width, and beam under firm and even tension.

❑ Thread the loom following the draft in *1* from right to left as follows: *c* to *d* white, (*a* to *d* blue, *a* to *d* white) 5x, *a* to *d* blue, *a* to *b* white.

❑ Sley 3 ends per dent in a 12-dent reed, 36 epi, centered for 45" weaving width.

❑ Weave according to the peg plan as follows: *c* to *d* white, (*a* to *d* blue, *a* to *d* white) 6x, *a* to *d* blue, *a* to *b* white. Maintain an even beat of 36 ppi. The selvedges will be messy; if this annoys you, use a floating selvedge. Since all four sides are hemmed in my tablecloth, I ignored the selvedges.

❑ Cut the fabric from the loom and secure cut ends with machine zigzag or serging. Machine wash, warm water, and machine dry. Take-up and shrinkage are approximately 10%. Neatly hem all four sides of the tablecloth by hand, along the edges of the blue blocks. Press with a hot iron and lots of steam.

❑ Pass the spaghetti sauce! ✂

yarn and suppliers' lists

YARNS

Yarns are listed with the yards per pound and a range of appropriate setts: wide (as for laces), medium (as for plain weaves), close (as for twills).

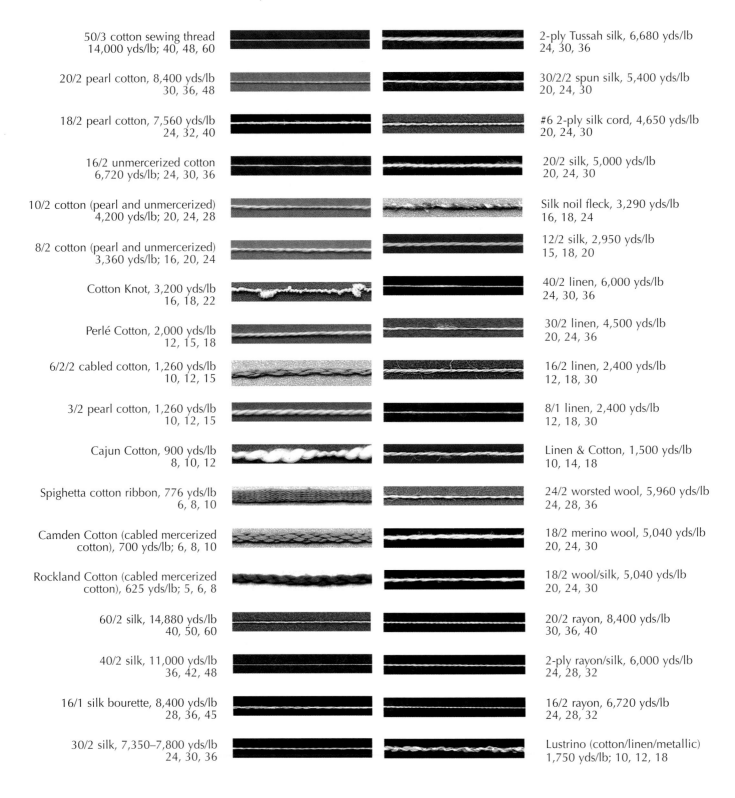

50/3 cotton sewing thread 14,000 yds/lb; 40, 48, 60	2-ply Tussah silk, 6,680 yds/lb 24, 30, 36
20/2 pearl cotton, 8,400 yds/lb 30, 36, 48	30/2/2 spun silk, 5,400 yds/lb 20, 24, 30
18/2 pearl cotton, 7,560 yds/lb 24, 32, 40	#6 2-ply silk cord, 4,650 yds/lb 20, 24, 30
16/2 unmercerized cotton 6,720 yds/lb; 24, 30, 36	20/2 silk, 5,000 yds/lb 20, 24, 30
10/2 cotton (pearl and unmercerized) 4,200 yds/lb; 20, 24, 28	Silk noil fleck, 3,290 yds/lb 16, 18, 24
8/2 cotton (pearl and unmercerized) 3,360 yds/lb; 16, 20, 24	12/2 silk, 2,950 yds/lb 15, 18, 20
Cotton Knot, 3,200 yds/lb 16, 18, 22	40/2 linen, 6,000 yds/lb 24, 30, 36
Perlé Cotton, 2,000 yds/lb 12, 15, 18	30/2 linen, 4,500 yds/lb 20, 24, 36
6/2/2 cabled cotton, 1,260 yds/lb 10, 12, 15	16/2 linen, 2,400 yds/lb 12, 18, 30
3/2 pearl cotton, 1,260 yds/lb 10, 12, 15	8/1 linen, 2,400 yds/lb 12, 18, 30
Cajun Cotton, 900 yds/lb 8, 10, 12	Linen & Cotton, 1,500 yds/lb 10, 14, 18
Spighetta cotton ribbon, 776 yds/lb 6, 8, 10	24/2 worsted wool, 5,960 yds/lb 24, 28, 36
Camden Cotton (cabled mercerized cotton), 700 yds/lb; 6, 8, 10	18/2 merino wool, 5,040 yds/lb 20, 24, 30
Rockland Cotton (cabled mercerized cotton), 625 yds/lb; 5, 6, 8	18/2 wool/silk, 5,040 yds/lb 20, 24, 30
60/2 silk, 14,880 yds/lb 40, 50, 60	20/2 rayon, 8,400 yds/lb 30, 36, 40
40/2 silk, 11,000 yds/lb 36, 42, 48	2-ply rayon/silk, 6,000 yds/lb 24, 28, 32
16/1 silk bourette, 8,400 yds/lb 28, 36, 45	16/2 rayon, 6,720 yds/lb 24, 28, 32
30/2 silk, 7,350–7,800 yds/lb 24, 30, 36	Lustrino (cotton/linen/metallic) 1,750 yds/lb; 10, 12, 18

SUPPLIERS

Cotton Clouds
5176 S. 14th Ave., Safford, AZ 85546-9252.
  800-322-7888, www.cottonclouds.com.

Halcyon Yarn
12 School St., Bath, ME 04530.
  800-341-0282, www.halcyonyarn.com.

Harrisville Designs
Center Village, Harrisville, NH 03450.
  Orders: 800-338-9415, info: 603-827-3333,
  www.harrisville.com.

Henry's Attic
5 Mercury Ave., Monroe, NY 10950.
  854-783-3930.

JaggerSpun
Water St., Springvale, ME 04083.
  207-324-4455, 800-225-8023.

Lunatic Fringe
15009 Cromartie Rd. , Tallahassee, FL 32309.
  800-483-8749, lunatic@talstar.com.

Nordic Studio
RR2, Lunenburg, ON Canada K0C 1R0.
  613-346-2373,
  www.cyberus.ca/~nordicstudio/.

Robin and Russ Handweavers
533 N. Adams St. McMinnville,OR 97128.
  800-932-8391, www.robinandruss.com.

The Silk Tree
12359-270 A St., Maple Ridge,
  BC Canada V2W 1C2. 877-891-2880,
  www.silkyarn.com.

Talisman Fibre
3747 Dezell Dr., Prince George,
  BC Canada V2L 3P1. 250-564-5244,
  morrow@bcgroup.net.

Textura Trading Company
116 Pleasant St., East Hampton, MA 01027.
  877-839-8872, www.texturatrading.com.

Treenway Silks
501 Musgrave Rd., Salt Spring Island, BC Canada
  V8K 1V5. 250-653-2345, 888-383-7455,
  www.treenwaysilks.com.

UKI Supreme Corporation
PO Box 848, Hickory, NC 28603.
  888-604-6975.

Webs
PO Box 147, Service Center Rd.,
  Northampton, MA 01061-0147.
  800-367-9327, 413-584-2225,
  webs@yarn.com, www.yarn.com.

Yarn Barn
930 Massachusetts, Lawrence, KS 66044.
  800-468-0035, info@yarnbarn-ks.com,
  www.yarnbarn-ks.com.